LOCATIONS OF THE SACRED

Essays on Religion, Literature, and Canadian Culture

WILLIAM CLOSSON JAMES

Wilfrid Laurier University Press

This book has been published with the help of a grant from the Humanities and Social Sciences Federation of Canada, using funds provided by the Social Sciences and Humanities Research Council of Canada.

We acknowledge the financial support of the Government of Canada through the Book Publishing Industry Development Program for our publishing activities.

CANADIAN CATALOGUING IN PUBLICATION DATA

James, William Closson, 1943-
    Locations of the sacred : essays on religion, literature and Canadian culture

Includes bibliographical references and index.
ISBN 0-88920-293-1

1. Canadian literature (English) – History and criticism.
2. Spirituality in literature.   3. Religion in literature.
4. Religion and culture – Canada.   I. Title.

PS8101.R4J3 1998   C810.9′382   C97-932473-4
PR9185.5.R4J3 1998

PR
9185.5
.R4
J35
1998

Copyright © 1998
WILFRID LAURIER UNIVERSITY PRESS
Waterloo, Ontario, Canada N2L 3C5

Cover design by Lisa Prentice and Leslie Macredie
Cover photograph and photograph of the author by Carolyn Kirkup

Printed in Canada

For my dear wife,
Carolyn

Contents

PREFACE

Does the title, "Locations of the Sacred," mean literally the geographical whereabouts of sacrality, the kind of specificity of site found in photographic books about sacred places or in studies of the relationship between spirituality and landscape? Not exactly. Neither religious "topophilia" (the title of a 1974 book by geographer Yi-Fu Tuan meaning "love of place") nor sacred cartography is the subject here. Rather, as Melville put it in *Moby Dick*, "It is not down in any map; true places never are." While Canadian landscape may be revelatory or a locus of meaning (and, indeed, some of the essays collected here do consider nature understood in that way), often the "locations of the sacred" are discovered in various other, perhaps metaphoric, "places." For example, the sacred may reside above the earth, within the self, in human relationships and community, in the domain of history, or in the encounter with death.

The avoidance of identifying specific and named geographic "locations" and the use of a concept like "the sacred" would have given Ernest Hemingway double grounds to condemn my approach. In *A Farewell to Arms* a list of discomfiting pious abstractions includes one of the terms of my title: "I was always embarrassed by the words sacred, glorious, and sacrifice and the expression in vain." At the same time Hemingway's soldier stakes his preference for the particulars of specified locations: "There were many words that you could not stand to hear and finally only the names of places had dignity" (see O'Reilley 1993, 60). Among the native peoples of Canada, we must remember, the sacred often has a definite and denominated spatial location. Anthropologist Hugh Brody describes how the Beaver Indians of northern British Columbia gather each summer to sing, dance, play games, engage in sports, and meet one another at a place called "Where Happiness Dwells." This affinity between a people and a sacred site is an aspect, Brody says, of "the Indians' sense of absolute and eternal belonging to particular places" (1983, 15). The Beaver Indians also have dream maps showing where heaven is and the trails to get

there, indicating a continuity of the sacred between the terrestrial
and celestial spheres.

In Judaism and Christianity such locations of the sacred cannot be readily mapped or easily designated. In monotheistic traditions, where God is beyond time and space, there is general
antagonism towards efforts to appoint any geographical site as
sacred space, especially if that place is somehow accounted as the
dwelling place of God. The abode of the divine, if situated anywhere, is considered to be within the human heart or in an eternity
beyond the earth. But in a sense the essays in this book attempt
such a locative strategy, if not exactly for God or the divine, then at
least for the sacred (usually understood as the numinous or as transcendence). Where, in Canadian culture and literature, does one
find some of these "locations of the sacred"? What are some of the
typical situations where the numinous has been experienced?

At first it seems, to judge from recent Canadian novels, the
answer is: "Not where it used to be." In the 1990s a new pluralistic
and international outlook has enlarged the scope of the religious in
Canadian fiction written in English, for some readers and critics
previously typified and dominated by the voice of small-town
Protestantism. Nino Ricci's *Lives of the Saints*, Rohinton Mistry's
Such a Long Journey, Michael Ondaatje's *The English Patient*, and
the fiction of Thomas King all illustrate an expansion of the
boundaries of our fictional terrain, an extension of the literary
domains of the sacred. The waning of the so-called moralistic puritan tradition in the fiction of English Canada, in progress for a generation or more, has now more or less reached its conclusion.
However accurate such a characterization might once have been,
the fictional rendering of the religious in Canada can no longer be
epitomized disparagingly by such traits as the stern obligations of
Jewish or Christian monotheism, the dogged pursuit of hard work
and individual effort, the introspective though guilty conscience,
and the persistent fear of sex and the body with the concomitant
avoidance of any pleasures entertained for their own sake.

Whether religion as portrayed in Canadian literature (or, even
more, the religious imagination as operative within Canadian literature) could ever be so narrowly confined or inexactly summed up
is, as we shall see, debatable. Even in supposedly classic exemplars
speaking in that small-town Canadian Protestant voice other
nuances and yearnings are detectable. In the works of some authors

so identified religious symbols provide a possible mode of imaginative escape from the confines of beliefs, creeds, and precepts. The sacred experienced as otherness, as mystery, or as the numinous is thereby potentially liberating from the binding and restrictive codes of doctrine. Moreover, supernatural theism's traditional view of eternity can be reconceived in everyday experience as transcendence.

Yet, even as fiction relocates the sacred from its older abode beyond the earth to some place or other within ordinary experience, so the broader cultural scene provides evidence that the sacred may be found at the boundaries and margins rather than at the centre, at points of crisis and limit rather than in the continuities of the conventional. New domains of sacrality emerge in the following essays: in the experience of such leisure activities as the canoe trip (and not only in the world of business, work, and the marketplace); in the encounter with the natural world (and not exclusively in the civilized domesticities of the human habitat); and, in the struggles of ethnic minorities (and not solely amid representatives of the mainstream who assume the superiority of their own ways of living and being). As Jonathan Z. Smith says, "there is nothing that is inherently sacred or profane." For, Smith continues, "these are not substantive categories, but rather situational or relational categories, mobile boundaries which shift according to the map being employed" (Smith 1982, 55). So it is, then, in recognition of its shifting and fluid quality, that the maps we use to locate the whereabouts of the sacred must be redrawn.

Morley Callaghan illustrates such a remapping, a relocation of the sacred, in one of several continuing attempts to revise the story that eventually appeared in his novel of 1985, *Our Lady of the Snows*. (At the same time, incidentally, while displaying his characteristic hardboiled directness, he shows none of the embarrassment or terminological distaste of his former companion and newspaper colleague Ernest Hemingway for certain abstract or religious terms.) In *The Enchanted Pimp* Callaghan has Ilona Tomory, a prostitute, in conversation with Jay Dubuque, a jealous would-be pimp. Ilona acknowledges, in answer to Dubuque's questioning about her evening with a young man named Sills, that she went to bed with Sills. Moreover, Sills told her that the experience was "sacramental." But Dubuque cannot understand how sex can be sacramental, for in his lexicon that particular word refers to what he calls "a religious thing": "Fucking is fucking, Ilona," . . . "How can it be a religious thing?" Ilona's reply: "If fucking can't be a religious thing," she said softly, "what can be religious?" (Callaghan 1978, 139; cf. Callaghan 1985, 164). Compare the description of a kind of "post-religious" or desacralized sexual ritual by a couple in American novelist Richard Ford's *The Womanizer:* "Theirs was practiced, undramatic love-making, a set of protocols and assumptions lovingly followed like a liturgy which points to but really has little connection with the mysteries and chaos which had once made it a breathless necessity" (in *Granta* 40 [Summer 1992]:38).

Carol Shields' *The Stone Diaries*, winner of the 1993 Governor General's Award for fiction in English, in some respects returns the Canadian novel to its conventional voice and subject. In form, however, her work represents an experimental fictional probing of the limitations of autobiography, exhibiting a relocative disintegration of the boundaries between the genres of fiction and autobiography. (Some of the narrative texts considered in the essays below also do their part to break down this distinction between fiction and nonfiction.) *The Stone Diaries* is the story of the life of Daisy Goodwill, from her birth in southern Manitoba in 1905 to her death in Florida in the 1990s.

After Daisy's mother dies in childbirth her father, Cuyler Goodwill, finds God "waiting in the form of a rainbow" (Shields 1993, 56). Goodwill does not become a churchgoer, but rather develops "a mode of sustained personal meditation," "an ecstatic communion" comparable to Asian meditative practices and to the kind of trance "which was to become fashionable in our own culture later in the century, the foolish sixties, the seventies" (ibid., 63). Goodwill begins to build a stone tower in memory of his departed wife, having "come to believe that the earth's rough minerals are the signature of the spiritual" (ibid.).

A little further on the narrator (at this point Daisy Goodwill herself) tries to pin down what she terms "the religious impulse." Daisy identifies her father as one "addicted to the rarefied air of spiritual communion" and for whom there is "one unified mind" (ibid., 65). Thus, "the human and the divine are balanced across a dazzling equation" in which the human creation of the divine equals the divine creation of the human (ibid., 66). Then, in a remarkable catalogue extending over the succeeding seven paragraphs, she charts various locations of the sacred for a variety of people in 1916, bringing the list progressively closer to lives intimately connected with her own.

Through her narrative persona Shields begins her list with seven Methodist pacifists for whom "religion finds its net worth between the hard rock of private conscience and the equally hard place of the political platform," implicitly contrasting them with a Quaker congregation for whom "religion is the cement that seals shut their door on the world" (ibid., 66). She identifies, perhaps punningly, that religion for her stepmother, Clarentine Flett, the victim of a bicycle accident, "is a soft flurry of petals." Meanwhile, for the teenaged cyclist "religion is the bottled broth" of forgiveness that he sucks in the middle of the night. And for the man who sold the bike "religion is an open window, as well as the curtain with which he darkens the window."

Daisy next turns to the abandoned Magnus Flett, husband of her deceased stepmother, for whom "religion is both the container and water of remembrance" (ibid., 66-67), and then to a college principal who finds that "religion is the physic for right thinking, correct living, and earnest praying." For one of the students of that college in love with her botany professor "religion is a painful obstruction that forms in her throat when she whispers his name against her pillow." Barker Flett, the botany professor in question—also Daisy's stepbrother and, twenty years later, her husband—"believes religion to be a glorious metaphor for the soul's desire." What Professor Barker Flett himself desires may be perfection or self-knowledge or sleep and forgetfulness or his fraudulent longings for "rapturous union" (ibid.), including (presumably) his own "unnatural yearning" for the eleven-year-old Daisy.

The Stone Diaries gives its readers no single unitary view of what for its characters religion is. Shields does not impose on them any kind of blanket metaphysic. Her positionings of the locations of sacrality span the range from the everyday problematic of the mundane and domestic to the intricate mysteries of cosmic meaning. The multilocational situation of religion in Shields' writing is true to and consonant with the variegations of the sacred in contemporary Canadian life. In the spirit of Carol Shields, then, we might summarize where some of the examples explored in this book locate the sacred.

For some the sacred lies beyond, in a transcendent reality representing something larger than the self. For novelists regarded as

classic exemplars of small-town Canadian Protestantism (Robertson Davies, Hugh MacLennan, and Margaret Laurence are the
prime exhibits here) religion is as much problem as solution—and
perhaps even more problem than solution. For them what we
might term the religious lies beyond religion. For them the sacred
is located beyond the confining isolation of selfhood, whether that
"something larger than the self" takes the form of community or
nature or history or myth. In the fictional mappings of Davies,
MacLennan, and Laurence the sacred is located somewhere beyond
the conventional religious foreground of the world taken-for-
granted. In more specific terms A. M. Klein and Hugh MacLennan
demonstrate the effort to remap the sacred within, as well as in
reaction to, their inherited religious traditions of Judaism and Presbyterianism. Klein and MacLennan, faced with the Holocaust and
the death of a spouse respectively, confront the age-old problem of
theodicy. For both these authors the sacred must reside beyond
tragedy, as Klein wrests the meaning of God's presence in history
from the discovery that good comes out of evil while MacLennan
comes to affirm that all life must be accepted as a gift.

For others the sacred resides in ordinary experience. The
search for transcendence in Canadian fiction is focussed on this-
worldly reality or presence. Though the numinous is resituated in
the mundane rather than overhead, it retains an ineffable quality
beyond conceptualization. Sometimes the experience of death,
madness, wonders, or the uncanny is an encounter with the numinous; at other times a transcendence or transformation of the ordinary establishes a new domain of the sacred. The quest for
coherence and meaning can lead to the development of a personal
myth to live by or to a life enriched by art until it bears intimations
of sacrality. In this view the sacred is generally located in the here-
and-now (though perhaps at the margins and edges of ordinary
experience)—in everyday life rather than beyond the world in eternity. Morley Callaghan's *Such Is My Beloved* sacralizes human love
by conjoining sexuality and spirituality in an incarnational fashion.
Callaghan endeavours to break down the barriers between the ordinary and the sacred.

Still others locate sacrality within the natural world. Whereas
nature is a principal locus of the sacred for Canadian native peoples, it has not traditionally been so for Canadians of European
descent. Nature has not always been for non-natives a source of

numinosity, though occasionally it becomes the locale of rebirth or in its cyclic rhythms a remedy for death's finality. But increasingly today the sacred has been found not only to be within nature, but actually to be nature itself. In general, Canadians have found nature and landscape to be a more fruitful source for national and individual self-understanding than historical events or figures. Various nature mystics (perhaps Sharon Butala is a foremost contemporary example) have in their writings furthered this locative reappraisal. For such authors the importance of indigenous peoples in advancing this kind of consciousness is paramount. Margaret Atwood's *Surfacing* and Marian Engel's *Bear* illustrate a sacralized nature in a female initiatory quest following an indigenous pattern. Yet for both novelists' protagonists no simple reenactment of the native model is possible, because as modern urbanized women they must find a balance between extreme possibilities and eventually return to their lives in the city.

For some people the quest for the sacred is itself a discovery of the sacred. In the instance of the canoe trip, where nature is obviously the backdrop or domain, the quest becomes a paradigm for the search for the sacred. Even more, the modes and shape of the quest become paradigmatic of various forms of sacrality: a return to a lost unity of perfection, a pilgrimage onwards to some ideal heavenly city, or a transformative initiation. For Tom York, in his autobiography *And Sleep in the Woods*, such ambiguities amidst the sacred are pursued, though they are never exactly reconciled or harmonized, in a fugitive northward quest. Both flight and search, this quest is finally away from the engulfing earth-mother and towards a sacrality that eventually resides in some provisional, in-the-meantime, location. Yet, like the journeys of Aritha van Herk's fugitive heroine in *No Fixed Address*, York's flight may be to some nowhere beyond space and time, whether in obedience to a transcendent principle or in fidelity to one's inner self.

And for others—especially members of cultural minorities—the sacred is located in the gaps between what was and what is not yet. The Belcher Islands massacre of 1941 manifests a tragic instance of a group of Inuit on Hudson Bay attempting, by supplementing shamanism with Christianity, to find a bridge between a disappearing past and a viable future. Here a cultural crisis prompts an endeavour to move between two conflicting modes of life. Similarly, in Joy Kogawa's fiction the sacred is embodied in what could be called "religious dimorphism," as Japanese Canadians intermingle truths and practices from their past religious traditions in encounter with a present reality. Amidst absence and loss, as Joy Kogawa explores the history of Japanese Canadians she exhibits how they marshalled their past cultural and religious values in combination with their more recently adopted Christianity. Kogawa herself thereby engages mutuality and acceptance, and seeks justice.

Where is the sacred finally to be found? Above or below? Beyond the self or here within the ordinary? Within a numinous nature or as goal and form of the quest? In the gaps between the already and the not-yet, or perhaps in the interstices of cultural crisis? The here's of God as immanent and the there's of God as transcendent give way to what Mark Taylor calls the reinscription of "the sacred in the midst of the so-called concept of God" (1994, 595). For Taylor the sacred is the "denegation" of God: "While I no longer believe in God, I can no longer avoid believing in the sacred. Belief in God becomes impossible and belief in the impossible unavoidable when a certain piety of thinking brings one to the edge of the unthinkable where the sacred approaches by withdrawing and withdraws by approaching" (ibid., 594-95).

The attempt of the essays in this book to find in Canadian literature and culture the locations of the sacred leads finally to no map or chart, to no precise siting nor even to persistent and consistent rumours of the exact or exclusive whereabouts of sacrality. In the famous medieval definition God was geometrically described as a circle of indefinite ubiquity, whose centre was nowhere and whose circumference was everywhere. Amidst our postmodern uncertainties—and our literature has played a pre-eminent role in decertaintizing us—the sacred is similarly nowhere and everywhere. But for Canadians for whom even the question "Where is here?" raises a puzzle, it is not surprising that the sacred should be equally, or even more, difficult to locate.

ACKNOWLEDGMENTS

S OME BOOKS, A COLLEAGUE RECENTLY REMARKED, are solo efforts to such a degree that no extensive acknowledgments of debts or gratitude to other people are given nor are they necessary. Other books are such collaborative affairs—or else their contents have been exposed and tested in so many various scholarly milieus—that there are scores of individuals to thank. This present collection of essays, as a Flannery O'Connor character might have observed, is closer to being "one of them latters." To express fully my thanks to all the people who have given me the benefit of their help and advice would mean naming scores of names. But rather than attempting the near-impossible task of expressing my gratitude to a lengthy list of individuals here—one that expands in my mind as I think about it—my thanks will go primarily to groups, communities, and organizations within the scholarly community. I hope that the many unnamed persons who work and study within these communities will understand that I am thanking them.

Most of the contents of this book were initially, in one way or another, "user-tested" in the classroom, with undergraduate students at Queen's University and with graduate students while I was a visiting professor at the University of Toronto and at Kwansei Gakuin University in Japan. As I discovered at a workshop on teaching and learning, the person who explains is the one who learns. In much of my teaching, then—perhaps because I have done too much explaining—I have been a learner. Yet I realize, not only how much my own thinking has been formulated in the struggle to articulate and interpret to students, but how much they have changed my mind as I read their essays and tests and listened to their views in classroom discussions.

Some of these essays originated as papers given at scholarly conferences over the years in North America and (once) in England, as invited lectures at Canadian or Japanese universities, or in the context of departmental colloquia in religious studies departments at five Ontario universities. Many of the often lively and always helpful comments of colleagues and peers have had their effect on my thought, and probably by now have been absorbed into it. My thanks for that collaboration, and for the invitations to visit other campuses. Earlier versions of some of these essays have been further field-tested through their appearance in books and journals. I am grateful to the editors and (usually anonymous) readers who assisted me towards better formulation of my ideas and to those who responded in various ways to the published versions. I appreciate too the care and attention of the director and staff of Wilfrid Laurier University Press in all of the various stages leading to the publication of this book.

Support for my research towards this book was provided at various stages by funds from the Advisory Research Committee of Queen's University and Queen's Theological College. The Theological College granted my applications for sabbatical leaves in 1989 and 1995, and supported my request for a negotiated leave in 1992-93 while I was a visiting professor in Japan. Along the way my colleagues in the Department of Religious Studies at Queen's have provided me with a kind of postdoctoral education in their areas of expertise—their helpful comments and unfailing support have been a mainstay of my professional life. This book was published with the aid of a grant from the Humanities and Social Sciences Federation of Canada, using funds provided by the Social Sciences and Humanities Research Council of Canada.

If I come now to the point where I feel I must name some names, it is because I want to honour some of the authors whose writings are the subject of this present book. Their works have helped to shape my understanding of religion in Canada—perhaps most of my understanding of religion has come from literature. Some of them generously made themselves available to student and academic audiences during visits to Queen's University, freely talking about their writing in classrooms and lecture halls. In a few other cases writers whom I first met through their works became personal friends—that's a harder kind of debt to acknowledge in a place like this. My reading of and writing about some of the authors who figure in these pages goes back thirty years. As a graduate student in the 1960s I wrote extended papers on the work of Hugh MacLennan and Northrop Frye. When my paper on Hugh MacLennan ended up in his hands he wrote to thank me "for writing the only thing on my work I ever read which told me in plain English what I had been doing in such a way that I could believe I had done it" (15 October 1969). Elated as I was then by such encouragement, I suspect now that I was not the only young graduate student to have received that kind of support from him. At this point I want to pause and offer a memorial of gratitude to those Canadian authors, so prominent in the pages below, who have died since I first began to read their books: Morley Callaghan, 1903-90; Robertson Davies, 1913-95; Marian Engel, 1933-85; Northrop Frye, 1912-91; A. M. Klein, 1909-72; Margaret Laurence, 1926-87; Hugh MacLennan, 1907-90; W. O. Mitchell, 1914-98; and Tom York, 1940-88. Their words, and the spirit within and behind those words, live on. In some measure all of them shared, I think, the insight expressed by Hugh MacLennan's George Stewart at the end of *The Watch that Ends the Night*: "To be able to love the mystery surrounding us is the final and only sanction of human existence."

Speaking of living words, the ones whose challenge and inspiration I hear and heed daily are those of my dear wife, Carolyn Kirkup, my friend and companion, to whom I dedicate this book. Her love makes concrete and actual for me one of the primary locations of the sacred in my life. Her daughter, Lisa Prentice, designed the cover for this book.

Parts of chapters 2 to 4 and 6 to 8 have been published previously in different form. In all cases previously published material has been revised and expanded for this present collection of essays. Sometimes (chap. 2) new material predominates; elsewhere (chaps. 3, 7, and 8), where initial publication occurred in the 1990s, the essay was already conceived as part of this present collection.

Some of the material comprising chapter 2 was earlier published as "Religious Symbolism in Recent English Canadian Fiction," in *Religion/Culture: Comparative Canadian Studies/Études canadiennes comparées*, Canadian Issues, vol. 7, edited by William Westfall, Louis Rousseau, Fernand Harvey, and John Simpson (Ottawa: Association for Canadian Studies, 1985), 246-59.

An earlier and different version of chapter 3 appeared as "Nature and the Sacred in Canada," in *Studies in Religion/Sciences Religieuses* 21(4) (1992): 403-17.

Chapter 4 is a substantial revision of an article that first appeared as "The Canoe Trip as Religious Quest," in *Studies in Religion/Sciences Religieuses* 10(2) (1981): 151-66. A few pages of chapter 4 are derived from "Canoeing and Gender Roles," in

Canexus: The Canoe in Canadian Culture, edited by James Raffan and Bert Horwood (Toronto: Betelgeuse Books, 1988), 27-43.

Chapter 6 has its origins in two previously published essays: "Two Montreal Theodicies: Hugh MacLennan's *The Watch that Ends the Night* and A. M. Klein's *The Second Scroll*," in *Literature and Theology* 7(2) (1993): 198-206, and "A Voyage into Selfhood: Hugh MacLennan's *The Watch that Ends the Night*," in *Religion and Culture in Canada/Religion et Culture au Canada*, edited by Peter Slater (Waterloo, ON: Wilfrid Laurier University Press for the Canadian Corporation for Studies in Religion, 1977), 315-22.

Chapter 7 was originally published as "The Ambiguities of Love in Morley Callaghan's *Such Is My Beloved*," in *Canadian Literature* 138/139 (Fall-Winter 1993): 35-51.

Chapter 8 has already appeared in slightly different form as " 'You have to discover it in some other way': Native Symbols as Appropriated by Margaret Atwood and Marian Engel," in *"And the Birds Began to Sing": Religion and Literature in Post-Colonial Cultures*, edited by Jamie S. Scott (Amsterdam: Rodopi, 1996), 33-46.

No part of chapters 1, 5, 9, and 10 has been published before and no part of any chapter has appeared in print before in exactly its present form.

The lines from the poems "Canoe-Trip" and "*Coureur de Bois*" are quoted from *Weathering It: Complete Poems, 1948-1987* by Douglas LePan. Used by permission, McClelland & Stewart, Inc. *The Canadian Publishers*.

INTRODUCTION

THE CIRCUMSTANCES ATTENDING THE STUDY of religion in Canada, from the vantage point of the late 1990s, include the approaching end of a millennium, the uncertain future of Québec within Canada, and a general weakening of the role of religious institutions, both in terms of their influence in the public sphere and their hold on individuals. With all that, it would be easy to overstress the critical state of religion in Canada, seizing upon the decline of religion in the context of a pivotal period in Canada's national identity. Instead, given the potentially ambiguous and shifting ground being staked out here, it is preferable to establish with some care the conceptual framework for these essays. Which aspects of religion in Canada are dealt with here, and which ones are not? At the outset, then, I want to indicate something of the terrain to be considered in my attempts to delineate the locations of the sacred in the Canadian context, as well as the methods by which the exploration is undertaken.

In 1965 Northrop Frye, in his well-known "Conclusion" to *Literary History of Canada*, claimed that "religion has been a major—perhaps the major—cultural force in Canada, at least down to the last generation or two." He went on to state, citing the example of Ralph Connor (the pen name for Charles Gordon, the Presbyterian minister who was Canada's most influential novelist in the early twentieth century), that churches had actively pro-duced literature and had influenced the cultural climate in a more general way too. Frye emphasized that within this period "the effective religious factors in Canada were doctrinal and evangelical, those that stressed the arguments of religion at the expense of its imagery" (Frye 1971, 227). One of Robertson Davies' characters claims, with this kind of religious milieu in mind, that the "worst" Christians are those who "have the cruelty of doctrine without the poetic grace of myth" (1970, 226). Frye's point, it seems, is that

Notes to the Introduction are on pp. 15-17.

religion in Canada, at least from the nineteenth century through the first third of the twentieth century, was primarily a matter of individual intellect and conscience set in the context of moral and social values. For example, as one author has shown, in Ontario between 1820 and 1870 religion operated as a powerful component, shaping society and resulting in the formation of a "Protestant culture" (Westfall 1989, esp. chap. 1).

Though the ten essays comprising this present book examine religion in Canadian life and culture, the focus is hardly on religion as a "cultural force" in the sense Frye probably intended. In fact, little attention is paid to organized religion at all, especially not in terms of doctrinal beliefs and attitudes, nor institutional affiliation and attendance at worship. Neither is the spotlight on the literature churches have produced or even necessarily influenced. In short, not much time is spent on the "doctrinal and evangelical" factors Frye affirms as important in Canadian religion of previous generations.[1] And clearly these essays pay little attention to "the arguments of religion," understood as referring to Christian apologetics, the intellectual defensibility of belief in God, or the general credibility of religious faith amidst technological culture or in a largely secular world.

Perhaps the neglected factor that Frye terms "the imagery of religion"—a phrase that I think could be broadened a bit to refer to or include the religious imagination—is the subject under review in this consideration of "the locations of the sacred" in Canada. But the imagination, regrettably, does not seem to be a faculty highly valued in Canada, especially by religious people. Reginald Bibby, a sociologist at the University of Lethbridge, reports the persistence into the mid-1980s of such "traditional middle-class virtues" as honesty, reliability, cleanliness, and politeness (1987, 168). By contrast, imagination is valued much less, scoring lowest on the list. While more than 90 percent of Canadians in general, as well as those with ties to the major religious groups, view honesty as "very important," only 33 percent of United Church people value imagination highly. This low endorsement of the imagination hardly improves outside churches—only 51 percent of Canadians with no religion see it as a "very important" value (ibid., 168-69). While Bibby offers no explanation as to how those surveyed might have interpreted the term "imagination," we might wonder if people took it as referring to daydreaming, idle wishes, and fancy rather than to, say, creativity, inventiveness, and vision. Whatever explains this low valuation in some quarters, the imagination is significant in these essays as a vitally important link between the sacred and literary art. Other scholars, by the way, similarly find this terminology congenial (see Lynn Ross-Bryant, *Imagination and the Life of the Spirit: An Introduction to the Study of Religion and Literature* [1980]).

From another standpoint the contextual boundaries of "religion in Canada" need further definition. What comprises the "Canada" of this study? The subject here is "English Canada," to the extent, at least, that these essays, to a greater or lesser degree, examine Canadian narrative written in English, though not in French (nor, indeed, in any other language than English). The literary and cultural and religious conditions these essays explore are almost exclusively those of English Canada (though several instances of English fiction written and set in Québec are examined). While parallels and analogies (as well as contrasts) could doubtless be drawn with French Canada, its culture and history and literature, restricting the investigation to one linguistic community seems a necessary limitation, especially given the range of this exploration in other respects. The principles of breadth and inclusivity in the following essays derive from other sources.

Another qualification is that the understanding of religion, sometimes taken to refer to formal religious traditions, and principally to Christianity, is here much more ample in scope than that. *Maclean's* magazine, reporting the results of an Angus Reid poll, proclaimed that Canada is "an overwhelmingly Christian nation, not only in name, but in belief" ("God Is Alive," 12 April 1993, 32). According to the poll, 78 percent of Canadians define themselves as Christians, while only 1 percent are Jews. Other groups—such as Hindus, Muslims, and Buddhists—each comprise only about 0.5 percent of the population. The number belonging to New Religious Movements or following New Age philosophies is even lower. The remainder, almost 20 percent, say they have no religion. Paradoxically, these "Religious Nones" (a term that sociologists seem to take a wicked delight in using) are the fastest growing religious group in Canada. The largest part of the sixteen-page *Maclean's* article considers the range of Christianity in Canada, including its presence or absence, the decline in churchgoing, and the rise in private faith. It pays no attention to any other religious tradition. The present essays quite deliberately aim at extending the range of traditions considered to include Judaism, native religious traditions, and Buddhism in the Canadian setting.

Especially in the view of several recent sociologists of religion, for whom the statistically significant is what counts most, the fact that 80 to 90 percent of Canadians are Christian—the exact proportion varies depending on how the count is taken—allows them to focus exclusively on the Christian church. One essay in a recent collection on the sociology of religion in Canada simply distinguishes between two groups of Canadians, those having "church membership" and "the unchurched" (Hewitt 1993, 109). Another essay in the same volume categorizes the totality of "Religious Life in Canada" according to a typology of "Churches, Denominations, Sects, and Cults" (ibid., 41-63). Often "religion" is reduced to matters of belief and worship within the context of Christianity, frequency of church attendance becoming a prime determinant of religiosity (see Bibby 1987, chap. 1). But religion, even if one's attention is limited to Christianity, means much more than institutional affiliation. And religion in Canada necessarily includes much more than Christianity.

While religion in Canada involves other recognizable "religions" or communities of faith than Christian ones (for example, those of Jews and native peoples and ethnic minorities of non-European and non-Christian origins), it also extends beyond such definable traditions. To urge such an extension of the term is, however, to run counter to recent popular usage where "religion" usually means a formal faith community with specific traditions and history. One "has" a religion such as Judaism or Christianity or Islam. An alternative term, "spirituality" (though sometimes encumbered with a prefix such "New Age"), denotes, in the course of its developing usage, an inner and personal faith or mode of being religious that lacks such a connection. If someone explains that they are not religious but have their own spirituality, most people would grasp the nuance.[2] This distinction between religion and spirituality is assumed in a bestselling book of the 1990s, *The Celestine Prophecy*, about a mysterious manuscript predicting "a massive transformation in human society," described as "a kind of renaissance in consciousness." This impending transformation is defined further: "It's not religious in nature, but it is spiritual" (Redfield 1993, 4).

At the present these terms seem to be fluid indeed. The word "spirituality" has problematic overtones, suggesting not only inwardness and private faith, but something not entirely to be taken seriously, perhaps because of the implied association with New Age movements.[3] Confusion grows when some *Globe and Mail* writers employ the word "spiritualism" (which usually refers to contacting the spirits of the dead through a medium) when they clearly mean "spirituality."[4] Perhaps psychotherapist and Holocaust survivor Viktor Frankl, in his 1984 revision of *Man's Search for Meaning*, hoped to bypass such jumble when he replaced the word "spiritual," which dated back to an earlier edition of 1964, with terms such as "human" or "existential" (see 123 and 125).

In part to avoid this disarray of meaning the term "sacred" seems preferable.[5] Peter Slater begins his article on "Religion" for *The Canadian Encyclopedia* with its derivation from the Latin *religio*, "respect for what is sacred." Slater points out that in some traditions (Judaism, Christianity, Islam, Sikhism, and Bahá'í are his examples) the "sense of the sacred" is found in historic events, whereas in others (e.g., Hinduism, Taoism, and aspects of Buddhism) the focus is on the natural cycle and the rhythms of life. Against this background of whether the locus of the sacred is history or nature Slater states that Protestant Christianity influences the understanding of religion in North America, especially with its understanding of the centrality of faith, so that religion comes to mean a system of beliefs. But in primal traditions, having no scriptures or creeds, the contrast between sacred and secular breaks down, myth and ritual become more important, and the sacred is now defined as "whatever is of foundational value in a given society, its point of reference for bringing order out of chaos." In this light, Slater thinks, only the expectation that religion necessarily involves God or supernaturalism precludes such movements as Marxism or feminism from consideration. They too critique the present culture in favour of some future hope.

The locations of the sacred in the following pages are not restricted to the foundational values of Canadian society at large, chiefly because multiculturalism, religious pluralism, and other aspects of the Canadian context mitigate against locating any such unitary reference point. Instead, here following Mircea Eliade, the sacred may be located anywhere that groups or individuals have discovered "the Wholly Other," a numinous power that Eliade states is equivalent to being (1959, 8-13). Eliade would say that those discovering that power or being endeavour to place themselves at its centre or in its presence, thereby "founding" their world upon it. In this sense the sacred is whatever is of foundational value, what is distinguished from the profane, and what brings order of chaos.

Saskatchewan author Sharon Butala, reflecting on the response to her autobiographical *The Perfection of the Morning* (1994), wonders why she should write about her life. Why should she open up her own heart and express what she finds there? Butala's answer is that she believes in books "as a tool to lift humanity out of darkness and fear." She continues: "I believe in the role of the artist/ shaman, who achieves sometimes, in an instant's lightning flash, a bond with the powers that create the universe" (1995, 11). Butala here expresses, on the basis of her own experience as a nature mystic and given her own mode of autobiographical writing, how the writer functions as a kind of shaman or priest facilitating a connection with the sacred. Professor Tom Marshall, himself a poet and novelist, referred in a book published close to the time of his death to the poet as "heir of the shaman, a magician whose function in the tribe is to express mythically the character of vast, mysterious, more or less uncontrollable phenomena" (1992, 13). Both Butala and Marshall are indicating how the writer may fulfil the role, to borrow Heidegger's phrase, as "a shepherd of Being" (see Scott 1971, 74).

If this book falls within the general category of being about religion in Canada it is also, in a more specific way, about literature and the sacred in the Canadian context. However, not all kinds or genres of literature are dealt with (nor, as I have already indicated, with Canadian literature written in languages other than English). The fact that poetry appears only in a limited way and in a minor role in these pages does not derive from a negative appraisal of its religious significance. But this book is not exclusively about literature either. Sometimes my focus is on materials that are extraliterary or nonliterary (see esp. chaps. 3-5 below). While the major emphasis is on fiction, usually the novel, at some points it is on autobiographical narrative, which, though a form of literature, is usually considered to be nonfiction. Tom York's *And Sleep in the Woods* (chap. 9) is an autobiography by an author otherwise known as a novelist, while Joy Kogawa's *Obasan* (chap. 10) is a novel deeply and fundamentally autobiographical. Though there is some resemblance in her last novel to the outer features of her life, Margaret Laurence prefers to term *The Diviners* as "certainly a spiritual autobiography" (1989, 6). No great effort is made here to venture into complex and perhaps tedious generic questions. Suffice it to say, however, that in several of the essays below the boundaries between novel and autobiography, between fiction and nonfiction, break down or become indistinct.

Even when a novel is not directly or obviously autobiographical, the biographical connections between the fiction and the author's life are sometimes examined. A biographical approach—derived from what authors say about their own writing or from links between their writings and their lives—frequently characterizes my method of getting at the texts under review here. For instance, there are parallels and echoes of the author's life easily detectable in works to which considerable space is devoted, such as *The Watch that Ends the Night*, *The Second Scroll*, and *Surfacing*, as well as ones that receive less attention (*Fifth Business*, *Lives of Girls and Women*, *The Diviners*, *Who Has Seen the Wind*). In chapter 1 there is extensive reference to and ample quotation from the non-fictional writings or biographies of Davies, MacLennan, and Laurence. Again, Callaghan's own words are quoted in chapter 7, and his friendship with Jacques Maritain becomes at least a partial basis for explicating his "neothomism." Similarly, chapter 10 draws upon interviews with Joy Kogawa, television programs about her, and lecture material by her, revealing the autobiographical background to *Obasan* and to some extent interpreting the novel in the light of her own comments on it. Acknowledging this approach may amount to pleading guilty to committing critical misdemeanours bordering on what New Critics called the "intentional" or "biographical" fallacy—that is, reading a fictional work as if it were the expression of the views of its author (see the relevant entries in Frye, Baker, and Perkins 1985).

Of course literature should not be reduced to second-rate metaphysics, philosophy, or sociology, as if it were just a different way of saying something about life and society. Nor should literary interpretation be so governed by the intentionality of its author as to make it no more than a special form of self-expression. Yet absolute avoidance of Neocritical "fallacies" can make the literary work so self-contained, so self-referential and autotelic, as to disconnect it both from the world outside itself and from the author who wrote it. Contemporary structuralism continues the tradition in literary criticism of the New Criticism begun by John Crowe Ransom and Robert Penn Warren and Cleanth Brooks in the 1930s of separating the text from the author and from authorial intentions (Frye, Baker, and Perkins 1985, 445-46). The same distrust of any considerations from outside the text is there. Terry Eagleton asks (1983, 111): "Was the structuralist view of the literary text as a closed system really much different from the New Critical treatment of it as an isolated object?" Poststructuralism goes further: "The New Criticism deletes the authors and their intentions, concentrating on the text. Poststructuralism deletes the author and demotes the text, since the loopholes in language itself throw both into question" (Frye, Baker, and Perkins 1985, 365).

The chief opponents of the New Critics were the Chicago School (or Neo-Aristotelians), the orientation of many of the professors in the University of Chicago's English department where I did most of my doctoral coursework. They favoured a pluralistic approach to literature, using different methods for different texts.[6] (My own critical approach might be described as a "principled eclecticism.") Critics biassed towards autotelic views of literature—in the sense that a text contains entirely within itself its own purposes and ends—are generally unsympathetic to interdisciplinary work (such as "religion and literature" approaches) because they threaten the text's autonomy. While respecting the integrity of the text, I do not agree that literature has nothing to do with life, that it should be read as if disconnected from author or world (or reader either).

The niceties of a literary text as literature, and especially where the focus is on its language, elevating the poem or novel or play into a self-contained aesthetic object to be admired for the perfected beauties of its linguistic properties or for the energies of its verbal pyrotechnics, hold little interest for most readers and authors. For me, reading a book is more like communion with a person than contact with an object, as Walter Ong has put it (1971, 76). Ong asks (ibid., 70): "Would an illiterate society, where verbal expression could be given no vicarious existence in space through writing or printing, be able to think easily of songs or orations as objects?" Literature embodies what Paul Tillich calls the "ultimate concern" of an author (or hypothetical author), and as such relates to the "ground" and "depth" of the human experience of the sacred.[7] Not only does every text have a "context," and as a form of expression have something to say about the world and about the nature of being human in the world, but in its "religious aspect points to that which is ultimate, infinite, and unconditioned" in human life (Tillich 1959, 7).

Most of us, at least those of us who like me went to high school in Ontario in the 1950s and 1960s, are long since familiar with the position that literature is autotelic, serving no nonliterary purpose. Though we might not have been explicitly taught such hackneyed dicta as "Poetry is poetry and not another thing" or "A poem must not mean but be," we remember well the attention given to the "literary" properties of texts in high school English classes thirty-five or forty years ago—rhyme scheme and metre, poetic devices (onomatopoeia, synecdoche, etc.), examples of pathetic fallacy and irony, the differences between a Petrarchan and Shakespearean sonnet, and so on and on. Those approaches to literature, carried out with little or no consideration of what the novel or poem or play might mean or be saying about life, I find outmoded and unfruitful. In *Fifth Business* Dunstan Ramsay recalls a similar emphasis on form over substance in a university undergraduate course in Religious Knowledge: "It was not much of a course, relying too heavily on St Paul's journeys for my taste, and avoiding any discussion of what St Paul was really journeying in aid of" (Davies 1970, 110). My own critical approach is, in part, humanistic (or personalistic) and evaluative. But I also employ biographical and generic approaches, archetypal and source criticism, and historical and analytical modes.[8]

Some explanation of the emphasis on narrative in the chapters of this book is called for. Narrative, the presence of a story and a storyteller (or a tale and a teller), distinguishes autobiography and fiction from drama and lyric (see Scholes and Kellogg 1966, 4). Narrative, then, becomes a common link for the consideration of both novel and autobiography in these pages which, at the same time, explains the omission of lyric poetry and drama. In addition, what is variously called narrative theology or religion as story (or autobiographical theology or religion and story) has for almost a generation been a predominant emphasis within theology and religious studies. Nathan Scott charted its significance at about the point, or perhaps just beyond the point, when the trend had reached its zenith (Scott 1983).[9] Perhaps partly in reaction to the persistent emphasis in Western religious life and practice on doctrines and beliefs (as indicated above), narrative theology emphasizes the experiential and imaginative aspects of existence, the way stories and myths are foundational in religious traditions—how people interpret their lives in the guise of a story or under the aegis of a master narrative. Narrative theology also enables women, whose stories have been excluded from or made inconsequential in religions, to discover or recover an understanding of their own relation to the transcendent. Carol Christ states: "stories shape experience; experience shapes stories." She indicates that "men's deepest stories orient them to what they perceive as the ultimate powers and realities of the universe," while "we women have not told our own stories" (1979, 229). Part of the feminist project in contemporary religion has been to discover, or recover, the stories of women.

Several consequences flow from this line of thought. First, contemporary literary theory lends little support to this emphasis on story. As Nathan Scott states, contemporary theory "conceives narrative as such to represent an essential weightlessness and worldlessness, since it is held to be incapable of making any contact with what Innocence takes to be 'the ordinary universe'" (1983, 150). The structuralist movement centred around Jacques Derrida, Roland Barthes, and Michel Foucault views stories, Scott suggests, as unable "to deal referentially with the circumambient world," because language is tautological. Thus, "stories are not about life but only about other stories" (ibid., 148). Structuralism is distinguished by its claim that "stories, like all other products of the literary imagination, do not have any meaning apart from the codes and grammars which generate them" (ibid., 149). Someone interested in narrative and the sacred might reasonably expect contemporary literary theory to provide "a theory of imagination that is prepared to posit some genuinely cognitive import for story," and yet, as Scott laments, "this is precisely what cannot be expected from the reigning disposition in poetics" (ibid., 150).

The second (and more positive) thing stemming from the focus on narrative, borrowing Carol Christ's dictum that "stories shape experience and experience shapes stories," is the use of narrative structures to comprehend the incidents and events of our ordinary lives. In a general sense, the shaping of experience by stories is an example of life imitating art; a more specific example might be Joseph Gold's version of "bibliotherapy" (1990) or the kind of application Robert Coles makes of stories to people's moral lives (1989). Chapter 3 below gives extended consideration to the way an overarching narrative pattern, such as the quest, can be used as a means of grasping and managing (or as Carol Christ would have it, "shaping") an experience of the canoe trip. Concerning the tragic events comprising the subject of chapter 5, the religious murders among Hudson Bay Inuit in the early 1940s, a plethora of imaginative narratives of the events have emerged, in striking contrast with the dearth of any extended scholarly analysis of them.

The focus on narrative, in the third place, comes from my longstanding interest in literature where the dimension of story is strong. Harry Rasky, interviewing Robertson Davies, mentions that critics complained that he wrote "in an old-fashioned way," and goes on to comment: "Of course, the thing that is said most is that you are a great storyteller." Davies explains the source of that impulse: "It comes from my conviction, which I share by the way with Morley Callaghan, that narrative is the life-blood of fiction" (National Film Board 1991). My selection of fiction—and of such authors as Davies and Callaghan for consideration—may seem to be, in some ways, old-fashioned, but probably an underlying principle of selection is this preference for story, for a strong plot. That too may explain the attention paid here to some "classic" works of Canadian fiction, including a number of those appearing on an infamous list of the ten "most important" novels developed for the Calgary Conference on the Canadian Novel in 1978 (see Lecker 1991, 151). In other respects there is a disjunction between some of the authors examined here who have been identified as proponents of realism (e.g., Morley Callaghan and Hugh MacLennan) while others are said to employ "fantasy, magic, mysticism, or the uncanny" (e.g., Robertson Davies and Margaret Atwood) (see Lecker 1991, 24).

After the initial theoretical groundwork is set forth, the sacred as the preferred term for uncovering the religious meanings of literature is examined and tested. Some of the close readings of particular novels treat three exemplars from the front ranks of Canadian fiction, each associated with a specific religious tradition: Abraham Moses Klein with Orthodox Judaism, Hugh MacLennan with

Reformed Protestantism, and Morley Callaghan with Roman
Catholicism. Each one of them began his writing career in the
1930s or 1940s (that is, at the beginning of the period when
Northrop Frye says that religion ceased to be a "cultural force" in
Canada). These authors are identifiably "religious" (or have been
interpreted as such); their fiction tackles issues of faith and belief
in a social and historical context.

Perhaps examining authors so well known is to risk going back
over familiar old texts and authors by now all too well known in
Canada. Yet the case can be made, I think, that some of them have
not been adequately explored from the standpoint of religious
studies, or else that exploration has been predominantly "doctrinal" in nature. Another aspect of my approach, therefore, evident
in several of the essays below, is the use of contemporary biblical
scholarship to elucidate literary texts—and vice versa. This kind of
work is at the very forefront of interdisciplinary work in Bible and
literature, yet it seems to have gone mostly unremarked by Canadian literary critics, notwithstanding the importance of Northrop
Frye's efforts to establish the centrality of the Bible for Western literature generally. An entire recent book, *The Daemonic Imagination* (Detweiler and Doty 1990), consists of more than a dozen
essays (none of them by a Canadian, by the way) exploring Margaret Atwood's short story "The Sin Eater" alongside the account
of the Gadarene demoniac in the Gospel of Mark. If the intertextu-
ality of *Such Is My Beloved* and the Song of Songs, or of *Obasan*
and Revelation, or of *The Watch that Ends the Night* and the Psalms
(or biblical thought generally), had been appropriately and suffi-
ciently dealt with by literary critics before now, there would have
been no need to undertake it in these pages. I do not wish to carve
out a territory for myself by dwelling in a negative way on the inad-
equacies of Canadian literary critics in matters of religion: one
could complain of an impoverished theological vocabulary and
inexact religious terminology or a tendency towards moralism and
pietism (or, conversely, ignorance and disdain). Unfortunately all
these characteristics of what might be termed a "doctrinal"
approach to literature are too thoroughly evident. A Canadian colleague in religious studies once remarked about acting as an external examiner for Ph.D. dissertations in literature, usually having
been summoned when the project somehow related to religion.
The comment was that the student often lacked the kind of rudi-

mentary systematic knowledge of the study of religion that could be got from a good undergraduate course in religious studies.

Even when the following essays situate some of the locations of the sacred in Canadian culture outside the strict boundaries of what might properly be termed the literary, Canadian narrative written in English is never far from the foreground of the discussion. The initial essays "dislocate" the sacred from the domain customarily assigned it in traditional Christian metaphysics, that is, beyond the earth, or reserved as one of the properties of a transcendent deity. The sacred is "relocated" in ordinary experience, in the here-and-now, and not in the kinds of activities usually conceived of as being "religious." In fiction written in English, "religion" (especially Protestantism) is portrayed as inhospitable to "the religious," which is then relocated elsewhere and by other means. The sacred (understood primarily as "transcendence") incorporates what Thomas Luckmann has termed "invisible religion" or Edward Bailey "implicit religion." It is in this vein that Nathan Scott defines "secular transcendence" as "secularity, as it were, surpassing itself, into a modality at least incipiently religious" (1966, ix).

The essays where the focus is less exclusively literary chart how the sacred is dislocated and relocated in Canadian culture by examining, respectively, Canadian views of the natural world, the quest pattern as applied to the canoe trip, and the origins and impact of religious murders among a group of Inuit. In these three instances, the location of the sacred becomes progressively more removed from domains usually thought to be "religious," as the potentially demonic, a secular initiatory ritual, and an apocalyptic crisis cult themselves become revelatory of sacrality. Yet in each of these instances, though their locations may be more historical and cultural than literary, a narrative means is at least partially determinative of or affects the locative strategy.

The last half of this book attempts to delineate the locations of the sacred in some individual texts of modern Canadian literature written in English. This effort begins with such well-known Canadian authors as A. M. Klein, Hugh MacLennan, and Morley Callaghan, each of whom wrestles in a quite definite way with an incommensurability between his inherited religious tradition (whether Judaism, Protestantism, or Roman Catholicism) and the brute facts of contemporary life. These essays quite intentionally follow up and illustrate the locative techniques charted earlier in a more general and preliminary way.

The essay on Margaret Atwood and Marian Engel examines two works of fiction in which an initiation takes place in a natural setting, affording the opportunity to explore further the sacrality of nature as understood within native religious traditions. The consideration of Tom York's spiritual autobiography returns to the quest theme, evident in the essay on the canoe trip. The quest assumes a paradigmatic role once more in its manifestation in York's narration of a classic spiritual pilgrimage and (to a lesser extent) in a parodic quest novel by Aritha van Herk. The final essay, on Joy Kogawa, explores (as did the essay on the Inuit massacre) the relationship to Christianity of an ethnic minority group within Canada, in effect examining the liabilities and possibilities of the crosscultural use of Christian symbols. For Japanese Canadians, as for the Inuit of the Belcher Islands, this crossing of religious frontiers occurs in the context of cultural crisis and where survival necessitates alternation between ancestral religious traditions and those of the dominant culture.

In all of these instances the theme, while in one way or another dealing with religion in Canada, is hardly about religion as a "cultural force" in the sense that Northrop Frye said it prevailed in an earlier era. The doctrinal, argumentative, and evangelical factors of that previous phase of Canadian life are present, if at all, in a mostly negative way in the material explored in the essays below. Instead, these essays examine the religious imagination as manifested in various products of Canadian literary culture and in certain moments and episodes in Canadian life, whether recreational experiences or an individual's search for meaning or the historic crisis of a particular group. The result of this investigation is no large-scale generalization about the nature and role of religion in Canada. Being aware of religious diversity and pluralism precludes such a summing up. The essays in this book are intended to expand, not reduce, the domain of the religious, to add to its variety, not restrict its appearances.

If my explorations into the manifestations of religion in Canadian culture are governed by any single interpretive principle, it is, as Paul Tillich put it so well, that "religion is the substance of culture and culture the form of religion" (1957, 57). Tillich explained, in an essay entitled "Religion and Secular Culture," that religion is not just "a system of special symbols, rites and emotions, directed towards a highest being" (ibid., 59). Invoking again his own notion of religion as "ultimate concern," he emphasized that religion "is the state of being grasped by something unconditional, holy, absolute" that gives "meaning, seriousness, and depth to all culture" (ibid.). What Tillich called "autonomous culture" (as contrasted with "theonomous culture") is secularized because of the loss of its ultimate reference point or spiritual centre of meaning.

To the extent that our culture is secular, or to the extent that we exist amid a plurality of cultural forms infused with disparate religious material, to that extent it is impossible to generalize about a single sacred anchoring point for Canadian culture, as if there were only one. That is why I prefer to speak in the plural of "locations of the sacred" in Canadian life and culture, and why I regard these locations as multiple, fluid, and impossible to fix in any permanent or lasting way. To locate the sacred in Canadian culture means examining specific artists and artistic works, studying and interpreting concrete cultural forms and situations and expressions, and finding what in each instance beckons toward an unconditioned source of meaning.

NOTES

1 John G. Stackhouse, Jr., says evangelicalism in Canada includes such Protestant Reformation emphases as Scripture's unique authority, salvation through faith alone in Christ, "warm piety," and universal evangelism (1993, 7). Those kinds of evangelical factors are not part of my subject.

2 Recently a student of mine, whose parents raised her to be a Roman Catholic, wrote that she was "taught to adhere to all the beliefs of the Catholic church." This background, she says, "turned me off religion itself. I am more attracted now to spirituality." Another student, in an essay on Canadian singer Loreena McKennitt, quotes a *Maclean's* interview of 28 March 1994 in which McKennitt states that she wants "to point people in different directions . . . by asking questions like, 'What is God?' and, 'How does spirituality differ from religion?'"

In one study a woman stated that "with religion you have to choose one, you have to be locked in," whereas "spiritual" meant "an individual definition of your relationship to God and nature and religion and family and humanity." She agreed with the interviewer—"absolutely"—that being spiritual allowed her "to draw from different sources and traditions" (Roof 1993, 80).

3 In the early 1980s Walter Principe examined definitions of spirituality,
  primarily understood as an aspect of personal piety and devotion, but
  becoming a branch of study within theology and religious studies (since
  there can be a Hindu or Buddhist spirituality). He shows how the term
  first began to be used in English (initially in translation from French)
  only in the twentieth century. For Principe spirituality refers to how a
  person understands and lives that facet of their religion, philosophy, or
  ethic that for them would lead to fulness or perfection. For him,
  "spirituality . . . points to those aspects of a person's living a faith or
  commitment that concern his or her striving to attain the highest ideal
  or goal" (1983, 139; cf. 137). Since the publication of that article the
  term probably has become less specific and provisional in its ordinary
  usage. It seems to allude to the way in which various commitments and
  values are lived and worked out, these being derived from different
  sources.
      Recently Marguerite Van Die has noted that "informed Christian
  leadership and interest have largely been lacking" from the baby
  boomers' eclectic piecing together of "a highly personalized religious
  structure out of therapeutic techniques and strands of religious traditions, especially meditation sessions and support groups" (1996, 9). She
  seeks to restore "authentic Christian spirituality" by drawing attention
  to the resources available in the writings of Julian of Norwich, Martin
  Luther, and John Wesley.
4 Such crucial distinctions are not dealt with in the newspaper's *Style
  Book* (McFarlane and Clements 1994). One *Globe and Mail* article
  ("The sweatlodge and the cross") fairly consistently and correctly uses
  terms such as "native spirituality," "spiritual religion," and "spiritual
  practices," though in one place making a reference to "some native spir-
  itualists" (3 October 1994). Another article ("Indian mentor provided
  solution") refers to native people "seeking strength in revived Indian
  spiritualism." This article quotes a criminologist as saying that the
  revival of the Plains Indian Sun Dance "is as much a ritual of politiciza-
  tion as it is a religious ceremony." The same individual claims that it
  can, like "an encounter group," be "highly manipulative." The author
  of the piece goes on to refer to "the most senior Sundancer" as "effectively the pope of the tradition" (19 September 1995). Disparaging references in Canadian newspapers of the 1940s to native religious
  traditions are considered below in chapter 5.
5 Westfall makes the "important assertion" that "the sacred must be
  returned to the history of religion in Canada, for it is the sacred that
  makes religion a meaningful category of historical analysis" (1989, 18).
6 In the Preface to the abridged edition of *Critics and Criticism*, the book
  that had established the Chicago critics' reputation as a kind of
  "school," R. S. Crane wrote that although the essays in that collection

represented "Aristotelian" poetics, "the only critical philosophy that underlies them all is contained in the very un-Aristotelian attitude toward criticism, including the criticism of Aristotle, which they have called 'Pluralism' " (1957, iv).

7 "Religion, in the largest and most basic sense of the word, is ultimate concern. And ultimate concern is manifest in all creative functions of the human spirit. . . . Ultimate concern is manifest in the aesthetic function of the human spirit as the infinite desire to express ultimate meaning" (Tillich 1959, 7-8).

8 In some respects I am here defending myself against the possibility of being reduced to a mere "thematic critic," a group that was the chief target of Frank Davey's essay "Surviving the Paraphrase." Davey notes the "humanistic bias" and "tendency toward sociology" in thematic critics, who regard language as "a tool employed not for its own intrinsic qualities but for the expression of ideas and vision" (Davey 1983, 2). While I do not want to reduce literature to sociology, especially to the extent that its chief value would lie in facilitating generalizations about Canadian culture, neither do I have much interest in literature whose language is used or appreciated solely for "its own intrinsic qualities."

9 Peter Slater, at the beginning of a chapter entitled "Ways and Stories," writes: "The category of 'story' is rapidly being overworked in contemporary religious thought. To use it now is to invite the charge of catering to current enthusiasms rather than serious scholarship" (1978, 48).

CHAPTER 1

DISLOCATING THE SACRED: THE PROTESTANT VOICE

THE PROTESTANT VOICE

Novelist Matt Cohen, in a lecture given at the Canadian Embassy in Tokyo in January 1993, surveyed some of the recent significant changes in Canadian fiction. He summarized for his largely Japanese audience the new pluralistic and international outlook in Canadian literature, along the way observing that until recently the dominant voice in Canadian fiction written in English had been that of small-town Protestantism. Such authors as Hugh MacLennan, Robertson Davies, Alice Munro, Margaret Laurence, Margaret Atwood, and W. O. Mitchell, whose names dominated the Canadian literary landscape twenty and more years ago, demonstrate the seemingly inescapable significance of such a comment. While Cohen may not have been staking very much on this perhaps casual remark, and though others may have said the same kind of thing in a more formal and systematic way, his observation launched me into some reflection on the place and role of Protestantism in Canadian fiction written in English.[1]

Several prize-winning Canadian novels of the 1990s, considered in their relation to religion, illustrate the current dislocation of that imputed Protestant voice from its place of centrality. The 1990 Governor General's Award for fiction in English was awarded to Nino Ricci for *Lives of the Saints*, a novel that takes place almost entirely within the confines of a remote village in Italy; the villagers, of course, are all Italian Catholics. In 1991 the same award went to another first novel, Rohinton Mistry's *Such a Long Journey*. That novel begins with a Parsi man in Bombay praying: "The first light of morning barely illumined the sky as Gustad Noble faced eastward to offer his orisons to Ahura Mazda." In 1992 Michael Ondaatje shared the Booker prize for his novel *The English Patient*, mostly set in a villa in Italy. Kip, the bomb-disposal expert who is probably foremost among the four central characters, is a Sikh from the Punjab.

One notices immediately several things about these three prominent Canadian works of fiction from the early 1990s. Their authors were either born abroad or born of immigrant parents; their settings are outside the borders of Canada; and, if religion is important in these works at all, then that religion is something other than the Protestantism of English Canada. To examine religion in Canadian fiction, therefore, exclusively or even primarily in terms of the Protestant influence on the fiction of English Canada, appears at the outset to be an artificially restricted, even anachronistic, enterprise.

Nonetheless Matt Cohen seemed to be suggesting that, although the situation has changed, at one time Protestantism constituted a kind of exclusive and unified dominance or hegemony on the Canadian literary scene. But it might be worth asking whether that small-town Protestant voice—which can hardly be said to be a voice in advocacy of Protestantism though that might have been its context—was ever as representative or as commanding as Cohen suggested. In any event, what was that voice saying? How, in its own characteristic nuances and out of its own unarticulated assumptions, was the sacred specified and located by that Protestant voice?

My own response, initially a reaction to Matt Cohen but now developed more broadly in response to this general view, is, first, that the sacred even as depicted in its earlier Canadian "Protestant" literary modalities is both dislocated and decentred. Such Protestantism is characterized by diversity (as Protestantism so often is denominationally), exhibiting an inherently dialectical quality, and illustrating what Northrop Frye termed its revolutionary rather than its conservative tendencies. The Protestant voice in Canadian fiction cannot be said to have been a voice for or on behalf of Protestantism, certainly not in any propagandistic sense. Against the position that Canadian Protestantism is (or was) something monolithic, a central aspect of the Canadian Anglo-Tory tradition, an alternative view needs some elaboration. In the second place, therefore, in addition to clarifying the nature of Protestantism within the context of Canada's literary culture, we need to consider how some features attributed to Protestantism may be characteristics of Roman Catholicism and Judaism as well, and perhaps even of Canadian culture and identity at large.

We might recall here Northrop Frye's comment (considered above in the Introduction) about religion as perhaps the "major . . . cultural force" in Canada until the early part of the twentieth century (Frye 1971, 227). While Frye specified doctrinal argument as central then, today it is through the agency of religious symbol that the sacred has its force and import in the prose narratives of English Canada. Another retrospective view of the situation of religion in Canadian literature, similar to Frye's, is found in a centennial year essay written by historian Arthur R. M. Lower entitled "Canadian Values and Canadian Writing" (Lower 1967). Lower maintained that Canadians had drawn "their sustenance both from their formal public institutions and from the medley of beliefs, customs and convictions," in the forefront of which he placed "the Christian religion" (ibid., 86).

Canada, claimed Lower, was "a strong church-going country," and "a country of intense religiosity." Then, in a single sentence, Lower confirms exactly what Frye had said of the role of religion in Canada of a bygone era: "Until about the period of the First World War, religion, or at least denomination and church affairs, occupied a larger part in the preoccupations of the average citizen than did politics and almost as large as earning a living" (ibid., 86-87). Lower quickly went on to indicate that Christianity in English Canada (which he defined as "non-French") meant Protestantism, the Christianity of about 80 percent of the population. Furthermore, with a kind of imperial sweep in contradiction of what today we accept as a tapestry of ecumenical diversity, even English Catholics appeared to him to be little more than another Protestant denomination (ibid., 87).[2]

While Northrop Frye and Arthur Lower were looking back, from a vantage point in the 1960s, to an era that ended in the early decades of the twentieth century, we might still wonder how this Protestantism manifests itself in the subsequent literature of English Canada, written, say, in the last two-thirds of the twentieth century? Historian William Westfall, with Louis Rousseau introducing the proceedings of a conference on Canadian religion and culture, notices how the institutions and ethical values of English

Canada produced a "heavy moral atmosphere that seemed to stifle individual freedom and creativity." This Victorian legacy, Westfall argues, "has become one of the very staples of English Canadian literature, so that in the novels of Robertson Davies, Hugh MacLennan, and Margaret Laurence the heroes must surmount not only the traditional obstacles to self-awareness, they must also overcome the oppressive qualities of their own Protestant environment" (Westfall et al. 1985, 2).

Westfall, however, also refers to a "deeper pattern of the imagination" evident in these same authors who view institutional religion so negatively. The result is that religion in their fiction manifests itself, paradoxically, as both restrictive and emancipating: "Religion provides a structure of metaphors that serves as a means of liberating the central characters from the very prison house that religion seems to have done so much to create" (ibid., 3). That statement with its suggestion of a dialectical principle strikes me as full of insight, and not only because it summarizes part of the argument of my own contribution to the very volume these comments introduced (see James 1985b; cf. chap. 2 below).

A PROTESTANT TRIO: DAVIES, MACLENNAN, AND LAURENCE

THOUGH THESE ISSUES ARE NOT EXPLORED FURTHER in Westfall's brief introduction to these conference proceedings, and although the selection of the Protestant trio of Davies, MacLennan, and Laurence may be somewhat arbitrary (no mention being made of such commonalities as a Scottish or Presbyterian inheritance), their writings and biographies deserve some closer examination in that light. How does the Protestantism of Davies, MacLennan, and Laurence exhibit this duality of imprisonment and liberation, comparable to what I have called its inherently dialectical quality? Let us choose, therefore, to make what may be a gratuitous and accidental selection by William Westfall a fortuitous one for our present purposes, by taking Davies, MacLennan, and Laurence as representative. Since all three of them have a Scottish or Presbyterian past and since all three come from a small-town Canadian background, they conform to Matt Cohen's general characterization of that Protestant voice.

In the one-hundredth anniversary issue of *Saturday Night* magazine Robertson Davies contributed a brilliant and sometimes cranky concluding essay in which he attempts to locate "the soul of Canada" (Davies 1987). He notes the troublesome nature of the word "religious," pointing out that it gets defined in two different ways. Derived from the Latin *religare*, it means "to reconnect, or link back; in fact, to restrain or bind," suggesting the authority and power of churches to bind their members to codes of conduct and doctrinal forms (ibid., 187). The other derivation, and according to Davies the one preferred in classical etymology, is from *religere*, referring to "a careful observation and heedfulness toward the numinous—whatever inspires awe or reverence" (ibid.).

Davies does not find much religion in the sense of a binding code in Canada, except among Sikhs, Doukhobors, fundamentalists, and Orthodox Jews. He contends that the United Church offers "no firm theology," having long ago, like other Protestant churches, abandoned faith for good works. As a benchmark against which to measure this lamentable recent slippage from doctrinal standards Davies recalls how the Shorter Catechism of his Presbyterian childhood had been "a rock at my back and a sword in my hand." Numinosity, on the other hand, evident in robes and processions, he finds still cherished in Catholic churches and to a lesser extent by Anglicans and Lutherans (though they too give signs of having caved in to the demands for "relevance"). Otherwise, for Davies the longing of the soul for the numinous today finds its outlet in "astrology, or spiritualism, or some half-understood version of an Eastern faith" and in various forms of superstition (ibid., 190).

Against the alternatives of the empirical sciences and materialism Davies poses the possibility of depth psychology with its revolutionary rescue of the old idea that God is within the self (though raising at the same time the prospect of the gnostic heresy). In psychological introversion Davies offers an attractive though difficult Canadian route to the numinous, by taking heed of the sacred wherever it is to be found, even within nature for instance. He suggests that this intellectually demanding introspection may provide Canadians a means to discover their own soul and an alternative to American problem-solving extroversion. Readers of Davies' fiction, especially those works from *Fifth Business* on, will recognize his characteristic views in this account. For our present purposes the opposition he sets up between the two meanings of the religious, *religare* and *religere*, between binding codes and numinous heedfulness, is consonant with the dialectic opposition between the conservative and revolutionary, the doctrinal and imaginative, or the imprisoning and liberating aspects of Protestantism.

According to his biographer Davies abandoned the Presbyterianism of his own childhood for three reasons: because "he resented the doctrine of predestination"; because "he disliked the didacticism of the Presbyterian church service and the dull cadence of their discursive prayers"; and because, at Oxford, he found "the English strain of Presbyterianism particularly harsh" (Grant 1994, 187-88). These confining and narrow aspects of religion he escaped in favour of the numinosity and formal beauty of Anglicanism and the Book of Common Prayer. But his Presbyterian coreligionist Hugh MacLennan found such escape more difficult.

MacLennan begins his well-known essay "Scotchman's Return" with the comment that "the knowledge that I am three-quarters Scotch, and Highland at that, seems like a kind of doom from which I am too Scotch even to think of praying for deliverance" (MacLennan 1960a, 1). In this essay MacLennan describes a trip he made to the Highlands where, his father had cryptically predicted, he "would understand." MacLennan lists some temperamental baggage his ancestors carried to Canada 150 years earlier: "With them they brought—no doubt of this—that nameless haunting guilt they never understood, and the feeling of failure, and the loneliness of all the warm-hearted, not very intelligent folk . . ." (ibid., 8). His father's reaction to his winning a Rhodes Scholarship, long after his chances were thought to be over, is revealing: "My father had risen to this occasion in the spirit of his ancestors. 'Go out and shovel the snow,' he said, and it was the only occasion when he ever ordered me to work on the Sabbath Day" (ibid., 136).

In his "Author's Note" to the American edition of *Each Man's Son* MacLennan had commented on a similar inheritance which he termed "an ancient curse," that is, the conviction derived from Calvin and Knox of an inherited human nature so sinful that there is no hope for the individual (MacLennan 1951, viii). Daniel Ainslie, says MacLennan, "did not know—how many of us can understand such a thing—that every day of his life was haunted by a sense of sin, a legacy of the ancient curse" (ibid., ix). The Highland immigrants to Cape Breton Island, he explains, tried to escape this curse by turning to alcohol, the pursuit of knowledge, or by leaving for other places.

Some commentators, Robert Fulford for instance, claimed that MacLennan himself never escaped this ancient curse. In 1960 MacLennan had had a dream that he was fighting John Calvin, trying to kill him, but unable to do so (Cameron 1981, 229-30). Fulford, renewing a quarrel that went back to his review of *The Return of the Sphinx* in 1967, asserts that MacLennan was "permanently burdened with a Puritan conscience," and instead of fulfilling his real talent he wrote didactic novels of ideas. He concludes his brief, severe assessment written shortly after MacLennan's death: "The more MacLennan resisted Calvin (at one point he called him the most evil man in history), the more he was pursued by the demands of Calvinism. The best of his talent was sacrificed to the mean Protestant God" (Fulford 1990, 37).

The relation of Hugh MacLennan to Calvinism needs some further clarification. He wrote to John Gray that "Calvinism is not as absurd a theology as it appears to be," explaining that while he deplored teaching children "the idea that God was each man's personal enemy" and although he disagreed "that a man committed a sin merely by existing," he nonetheless found in this theology a realistic assessment of the individual's personal fate. I think MacLennan means, considering the examples he uses, that the Calvinistic view of God's judgment affirms the self-reflexive nature of evil, or put more aphoristically, your sins will find you out, or as you sow so shall you reap, or that God is not mocked. He avows of the characters in *Each Man's Son*, in terms similar (as we will see) to those employed by Margaret Laurence, that "I respected them as I dealt with them because none of them ever denied his experience as it came, or invented new phrases or jargons to pretend it was other than it was" (Cameron 1981, 229).

In 1987, in one of his last public appearances, Hugh MacLennan honoured Margaret Laurence's memory and inaugurated a lecture series established by the Writers' Union of Canada. MacLennan remarked on the similarities they shared, including their small-town roots (true of Robertson Davies too) and that "both of us were of Scottish origin" (hers in County Angus and his in the North Highlands) (Gibson 1991, 349).

Margaret Laurence seems to share Davies' view of the dual meaning of the religious when she states, in a 1982 convocation address at Emmanuel College, that "faith must mean not only a *holding on to* but also a *reaching out*" (Woodcock 1983, 60). However, here Laurence conjoins religious faith with social justice, the "reaching out" referring to the alleviation of human suffering, a note not much found in Davies (and in fact usually scorned by him as a concern for relevance or doing good works).[3] For Laurence, I suspect, the numinous resides not so much in a divinity within the depths of the psyche as it does in something fundamentally relational, in the presence and reality of other human beings. The "other" is for her the domain of the sacred.

Laurence writes of how her own social and religious faith—in particular, her left-wing reformist outlook and the recognition of the need for God's grace coupled with human responsibilities—was formed in childhood and then consolidated at Winnipeg's United College. She continues: "It is no coincidence, I believe, that two of the major threads running throughout all my work have been, in some form or another, religious and socio-political themes, or that one of my main concerns has been to show the uniqueness, the value, and the reality of the human individual" (Laurence 1989, 99).

Margaret Laurence has experienced too the strictures of Protestant moral and doctrinal codes. She was deeply hurt in 1976 when *The Diviners* was banned in the Peterborough area (where she was living) after being attacked as supposedly pornographic and blasphemous. Her opponents, Laurence said, were mostly Christian fundamentalists who as unskilled readers of the Bible failed to see the biblical allusions in her writing: "With my sense of being a Christian, or at least an aspiring Christian with an ecumenical outlook, I felt extraordinarily damaged" (Laurence 1989, 214). Of her adversaries Laurence stated: "I wish they would learn to hear what my novels are truly saying, which is a celebration of life itself and of the mystery at the core of life" ("Why Pick on Margaret Laurence?" 1980, 10).

When asked further, in a dialogue sermon with United Church minister Lois Wilson, about how her experience as a female novelist had informed her view of God, Laurence replied: "We cannot really define the informing spirit of the Universe because that is the mystery at the core of life. Whatever that spirit is and however we receive it into our lives, there must be a male and female principle

involved; there must be the father and the mother" (ibid., 11). In
her memoirs Laurence develops further this necessity of imaging
ultimate reality, at least in part, in female terms (cf. Laurence 1989,
13-16), a view shared incidentally by Robertson Davies.

The Diviners, which she terms "not precisely an autobiography, but certainly a spiritual autobiography" (ibid., 6), was for Laurence "an honouring of my own people," and being able to write it
"had felt like a gift of grace to me" (ibid., 214). Asked why she felt
it necessary to "use all those four-letter words in *The Diviners*,"
Laurence replied that "the writer's first, and perhaps only, responsibility is to be true to her or his own characters, human individuals
that the writer cares about very deeply" (ibid., 215). Laurence has
affirmed her faith "in the unique and irreplaceable value of the
human individual" ("Why Pick on Margaret Laurence?" 1980, 4).

A burden of guilt is not necessarily a specifically Protestant
legacy. British novelist Graham Greene, himself an adult convert to
Catholicism, maintains that the distinguishing marks of a Christian
civilization are "the divided mind, the uneasy conscience, and the
sense of personal failure" (Stratford 1973, 587). Clearly the literary
characters of Robertson Davies, Hugh MacLennan, and Margaret
Laurence all bear those haunting blemishes, even though we need
not restrict them to Scots, Presbyterians, or even Protestants.
Occasionally in *The Diviners* Morag Gunn summons up the ghost
of Catharine Parr Traill, that competent exemplar of the nineteenth-century pioneering woman in Upper Canada, for a chat. On
the last such occasion Morag promises "CPT" that "I'm going to
stop feeling guilty that I'll never be as hardworking or knowledgeable or all-round terrific as you were. . . . I'm not built like you,
Saint C." (Laurence 1974, 406). As Morag dismisses her "sweet
saint," Traill's fading voice can be heard: "In cases of emergency, it
is folly to fold one's hand and sit down to bewail in abject terror: it
is better to be up and doing" (ibid.).

Joseph McLelland, considering the portrayal of Presbyterians
in Canadian literature, finds that they do not emerge as the defenders of divine sovereignty and human vocation that one might
expect. Instead, they appear to be "burdened with an insoluble
problem of evil." Because they persist in believing in a benevolent
deity despite the obvious injustice of things, Presbyterians are
depicted as "restless and grieving." The Calvinist attempt at theodicy has failed; in its place a lamentation, or threnody, is raised about

this unjustifiable God (McLelland 1994, 112). For McLelland, "theodicy and threnody are the two chief themes literature sees in Calvinism" (ibid.). I would argue for the presence of a third theme, if not in the view Canadian literature has of Presbyterians, then at least in authors influenced by Calvinism who have struggled beyond it. Beyond the failed attempt to argue God's justice or the inability to solve the problem of evil, and beyond a despairing pessimistic view of human nature, authors like Robertson Davies, Hugh MacLennan, and Margaret Laurence, having burst the confines of their inherited traditions, explore in their fiction various ways of liberation.

IMPRISONMENT AND LIBERATION

A S A SECOND PART OF THE REACTION to the supposed centrality of the Protestant voice, it could be stated that some features attributed exclusively to Protestantism may typify Canadian culture generally. A heavy moral atmosphere, binding codes, and a sense of guilt could be described as necessary but not sufficient conditions for defining the characteristics of the Protestant legacy. Portrayals of confinement, victimization, and imprisonment have been seen as central to the understanding of the Canadian character and psyche. In 1972 Margaret Atwood, in *Survival*, subtitled a *Thematic Guide to Canadian Literature*, said that the central guiding image of survival is about "hanging on, staying alive" (Atwood 1972, 33). Admittedly, to maintain and sustain something (one's own life, for instance) is a more conservative and restrained tendency than is an adventuresome quest. The Canadian concern for "survival" Atwood contrasted with the sense of danger and excitement generated by the corresponding metaphor of the Frontier in American literature, this search for something *new* originating in part from "a crop of disaffected Protestants." Here the effects of the American Protestant experience are considered revolutionary. Atwood titled her final chapter in *Survival* "Jail-Breaks and Re-creations," suggesting ways of exploring the tradition and of imagining beyond it. Atwood's own writing shows ways in which she herself has imagined possibilities beyond the Anglo-Tory conservatism of the Canadian psyche.

    Another example of Canadians exploring their inherited tradition to imagine ways beyond it is found in journalist Charles Taylor's book *Six Journeys: A Canadian Pattern*. There Taylor examines the lives of a half-dozen Canadian figures of British stock, each quintessentially Canadian though also Victorian, devoted to "something that transcends the narrow secularity of their time" (Taylor 1977, iv). He investigates individuals such as James Houston and Emily Carr for whom Canada's native peoples provided a means of breaking with modernity, and Bishop William White for whom China did the same, and Edward Norman, the famed scholar and diplomat, whose acquaintance with Japan opened new possibilities for him. They were all directed by a conservative though not merely orthodox religious impulse, journeying into "spiritual realms which modern Canada either ignores or denigrates" (ibid.) to find life-enhancing insights in some older culture. Each person Taylor studies is representative of the mainstream Canadian establishment, but each also turned to some other and older cultural tradition to envisage a way beyond modernity. Taylor's conclusion is reminiscent of *Survival*: each of these six individuals wins no clear-cut triumph; each journey entails loneliness and frustration; "in the end there is a feeling of tremendous waste" (ibid., 243), yet each quest is heroic, pointing to paths still open to us.

Northrop Frye has written about "a curious schizophrenia" evident, for example, in nineteenth-century Canadian poetry where "the sense of loneliness and alienation" exists alongside a sense of "energetic optimism" about the challenges of the new land (1977, 31). Tracing some of the currents of Canadian literature Frye suggests that our earlier Cartesian introversion before a hostile landscape has lately become "an intensely centred vision" (ibid., 44) with a possibility of rebirth into "something better than the ghost of an ego haunting himself" (ibid., 45). This double movement parallels what Frye elsewhere terms contrasting centrifugal and centripetal movements in the Canadian psyche, extending both outwards towards nature and the world and inwards in a motion of descent into the self.

In his last published book, *The Double Vision*, Northrop Frye speaks of the cyclical rhythms of history, of how movements exhaust themselves and then reappear in a new context. Frye also speaks of the difference between primary and spiritual concerns and of the difference in religion between doctrine and myth (Davies' distinction between binding codes and the numinous comes to mind again). He says that "the supremacy of social authority over the individual" (1991, 10) can be practised not only within the tyranny of the state but by religious groups professing to believe above all things in spiritual freedom.

Hans Mol, a sociologist of religion, employs an explicitly dialectical model not just of Protestantism but of religion generally. Mol suggests that religion may either sacralize society by reinforcing particular social units or provide a transcendental frame of reference that changes the balance of power (see Mol 1985 and Mol 1976). Religion may therefore either bolster the identity bestowed by the state or challenge and correct that identity. Mol states that Canadians whose primary allegiance is to some transcendent vision beyond the nation are likely to question and criticize its shortcomings rather than be blindly patriotic and loyal.

As a sociologist of religion Mol applies this scheme to Canadian society. The presence of the Canadian flag in churches and prayers for the Queen and royal family reinforce national loyalties. Churches and clergy further link Christianity and democracy with God's plan for history when they represent Canada as "God's dominion" and affirm "a transcendental purpose behind the nation's affairs" (1985, 261). This side of things Mol terms "sacralization from without." But equally, he claims, legitimation is balanced with critique when churches denounce unsafe working conditions, demonic nationalism, and the compromises of political life. Thus, churches stress God's judgment of the nation as much as God's care. Theologian Paul Tillich's "Protestant Principle"—that is, the ability to expose the foundations of one's own beliefs and values to severe scrutiny—carries the matter of self-critique and self-judgment one step further. The application of the Protestant principle means that no ideology or system is sacred or beyond critical examination.

How Is Canadian Literature "Religious"?

FIRST, GIVEN THE MULTICULTURALISM of contemporary Canada, its bilingual character, its two founding cultures, and its indigenous peoples, restricting religion in Canadian literature to Protestantism in English fiction would be extremely limiting. Such a partial examination neglects French Canadian literature, genres other than the novel and short story, and native Canadians. It puts aside literatures in other than French or English. It also ignores the significant tradition of Jewish writing in Canada, characterized by such well-known writers as A. M. Klein, Irving Layton, Mordecai Richler, Matt Cohen, Eli Mandel, Adele Wiseman, and many others. Michael Greenstein, in a book whose subtitle alludes to struggles with "tradition and discontinuity," examines how Jewish-Canadian writers are decentred in various ways while believing "that the answers to all quests and questions is always over the next horizon" (1989, 12).

Second, to side with the statistical majority and restrict oneself in religious matters to the study of English Protestantism (even if Protestants still were the statistical majority among Canadian Christians, which they are not) conforms neither to the Canadian reality nor character. Our religious pluralism and traditional concern for the underdog, the bystander, the person on the sidelines, the watcher at the window, the one at the margins, opposes such limitation. Nonetheless, some attention to this supposedly dominant Protestant voice may be worthwhile, if we listen to its other accents, mutations, and variations, and even better, to its exceptions and lack of unity. Although Protestantism is the milieu or background of many of our prominent writers, they are more "in" this world (having something assimilable to Canadian Protestantism as an immediate context), rather than "of" it (in the sense of "originating from" it, speaking for it, or "characterized by" it). A version of the genetic fallacy (limiting a thing to an account of its origins) is a danger here.

Patricia Morley suggests some of this context, referring to a roughly equivalent "Puritanism" rather than to Protestantism: "*many* Canadians, whether their origins be Scottish, United Empire Loyalist, or French Catholic, have emerged from this Puritan tradition, either in its stricter or more liberal versions. And *all* have felt its influence in a host of ways" (Morley 1972, 3). Drawing upon Hugh MacLennan's work she defines three traits essential to Puritanism: "a rejection of beauty and pleasure, a condemnation of man's sexual nature, and a compulsion to work" (ibid., 5). Ronald Sutherland argues that both English and French Canada "share a common fundamental theology" because Jansenism influences French-Canadian Catholicism in the way Calvinism has been central to Protestantism in English Canada. Jansenism and Calvinism share common views about the divine-human relationship and humanity's duty on earth: hell is deserved; Christian resignation is required; idleness and personal pleasure are condemned; love of art is suspicious (1971, 63; cf. "The Calvinist-Jansenist Pantomime," 60-87). Sutherland quotes Jean-Charles Harvey's novel of 1934, *Les Demi-civilisés*, in support of the "trans-Canada nature of the Calvinist-Jansenist influence": "Nous avons des affinités . . . avec les puritans de Toronto, qui pèchent en jouant au bridge le dimanche, mais qui ne se feront pas scrupule de passer cette journée ivres au fond d'une chambre, volets clos" (1971, 83).

If not through a unified voice speaking on behalf of English Protestantism then how is Canadian literature religious? That is a separate question from asking how authors—or their characters— are religious. The initial answer rejects the position that literature is religious because of its religious subject matter or because it proposes classically religious answers to the problems of life. Canadian literature will not necessarily be religious in the way that such classics of Christian literature as Bunyan's *Pilgrim's Progress* or Sheldon's *In His Steps* might be said to be religious—or even Milton's *Paradise Lost* or Dante's *Divine Comedy*. Neither content nor subject matter nor conformity with a doctrinal stance or orthodox position—nor even grappling with a Protestant, puritan, Roman Catholic, or Jewish legacy—makes literature religious.

Consider a preliminary example (investigated at length in chap. 7 below), one that also challenges the alleged centrality of the Protestant voice in Canadian fiction. Morley Callaghan's three novels of the mid-1930s, widely regarded as representing the best of a long lifetime of work that continued right up until his death in 1990, all have titles derived from biblical sources (*Such Is My Beloved, They Shall Inherit the Earth, More Joy in Heaven*). *Such Is My Beloved* (1934), probably foremost among this trio, is an excellent example for our purposes. The central character is a priest who sacrifices himself for the souls of two prostitutes whom he has befriended. He prays at various times, shares with them a "last supper" of sandwiches and wine, runs into conflict with various influential church people who betray him, and at last has a breakdown and is placed in a mental institution.

Even this brief summary of the novel's content and plot shows it to be steeped in Christian background and practice. The novel is fraught with allusions to the biblical book of the Song of Songs and shows a strong reliance on the thought of the major twentieth-century Catholic thinker and neothomist, Jacques Maritain. However, it is highly debatable, and difficult to ascertain, whether Callaghan is taking up a position as author easily conformable to classic Catholic Christianity. Even to interpret *Such Is My Beloved* as a denunciation of the Roman Catholic church need not imply a view of Christianity or eternity transcending the church. One Jesuit professor of English from the University of Toronto has complained that Callaghan's fiction is highly ambiguous (Dooley 1979, chap. 6). This novel, others would argue, is at best ironic in its use of Christian motifs.

As T. S. Eliot says in his essay on "Shakespeare and the Stoicism of Seneca," the poet takes ideas and makes poetry out of them. Eliot claims: "I can see no reason for believing that either Dante or Shakespeare did any thinking on his own"; or, again: "In truth, neither Shakespeare nor Dante did any real thinking—that was not their job" (Eliot 1964, 116). In a related vein (and relevant to chap. 2 below), Eliot doubts "whether belief proper enters into the activity of a great poet, *qua* poet" (ibid., 118). So it is not, or at least not necessarily, in the overt religiousness of its ideational content that the religious meaning of a work of literature lies. My own conviction is that Callaghan's sensibilities are deeply Christian, and that *Such Is My Beloved* is a deeply religious work. This conclusion, however, cannot be reached by the superficial examination of the novel's issues that many commentators have conducted. The religious meaning of fiction cannot be determined or measured by the degree to which its subject is overtly religious, nor by the extent to which it espouses a view of life congenial to some religious outlook or other.

Let me say, perhaps provisionally, that a novel's religiousness derives from its concern with ultimate questions of meaning, truth, and value—implicitly set forth in an imaginative structure embodying those central concerns. Such a statement opposes views of literary art that would have the work's coherence exist only in the mind of the reader or interpreter, independent of the work itself. My view is that a verbal structure can itself communicate meaning, reflecting in part (though not limited by) the intentions of the author (see the above Introduction). Textual interpretation is thus an ongoing enterprise of collaboration between reader and text in the effort to hone and refine a view of what the text means.

THE PROTESTANT PRINCIPLE IN
ENGLISH-CANADIAN FICTION

IN CHAPTER 2 I ARGUE THAT Canadian fiction often locates a transcendent "otherness," that is, a "supernatural" dimension of reality beyond the ordinary "world-taken-for-granted." Furthermore, many fictional characters find themselves, in encounters with death or sex or madness, face-to-face with an experience where another realm beyond everyday reality opens to them. Paradoxically, the Christian church often comprises part of the everyday reality in which they live: the church exhibits the "profane" world, not the sacred one. Churches—like schools, courts, stores, newspapers, and governments—represent a world that for these characters is entrapping or stultifying, that keeps them from developing into full or free individuals, or that somehow becomes something problematic for them. Therefore, if the protagonists of Canadian fiction are seeking liberation, religion is often one of the things they are seeking liberation from. By means of some transcendent or liberating principle that might be said to be *religious* those characters often find their liberation from the confines of *religion*. Let me give some examples of how the religious dislocates religion by "decentring" it in the sacred.

In Hugh MacLennan's *The Watch that Ends the Night* (dealt with at length in chap. 6 below) the major problem facing the three characters, especially George Stewart the narrator, is the uneven distribution of suffering and death—what is sometimes called theodicy or the problem of evil. Perplexed and ridden with anxiety Stewart watches his wife die, and ponders the question of the meaning of life. In the context of a Western, and specifically Christian, view of history this question takes on special urgency for him. George Stewart regards life as meaningful and purposeful, with a beginning, middle, and end superintended by a providential God who watches over each individual. In some ways his release from what Mircea Eliade calls "the terror of history" comes from a more Eastern and cyclical view. There life is a series of ends and beginnings, of climaxes of destruction superseded by new beginnings. George Stewart comes to an awareness that life is a gift, a religious answer to be sure. Then he understands the question of the length of one's life in a new way. MacLennan's inherited Calvinism, where grace and punishment relate to the will of an omniscient God who predestines all things, is scrapped in favour of a view of life where there is more mystery and less certainty, and where life itself becomes precious.

A similar discarding and revisioning of the Canadian puritan tradition occurs in the fiction of Robertson Davies. In *Fifth Business* Dunstan Ramsay, in true Canadian Protestant fashion, shoulders his lifelong guilty burden for Mary Dempster's madness and the premature birth of her son Paul. Ramsay becomes a historian and amateur scholar of mythology in order to understand miracles and sainthood, something his Protestant upbringing had not equipped him for. He believes Mrs. Dempster has saved his brother from the dead and saved his own life. Finally, he casts aside much of his childhood religion during a trip to Mexico when the ogress Liesl instructs him to confront his personal devil and derive strength for living from that encounter. In a way Ramsay abandons a Protestant view of providence for a Jungian view of the psyche and collective unconscious. He has to learn what his role is in life's drama instead of playing understudy to someone else, or trying to live his life according to the script provided by other people.

Again, in the work of women writers such as Alice Munro or Margaret Laurence the religion of Protestant Christianity represents an entire system excluding their central characters or inhibiting their growth and freedom. Yet, to take a superficial example, consider the paradoxically religious terminology in the chapter titles in *Lives of Girls and Women*: "Heirs of the Living Body," "Age of Faith," "Changes and Ceremonies," and "Baptizing." Similarly, in *The Diviners*, there are chapter titles such as "Rites of Passage" and "Halls of Sion," in addition to the novel's title which is also the title of the fifth and last chapter. For Munro's Del Jordan the (to her) exotic ritual mysteries of Anglican Christianity are but one temporary way of trying to transcend the restrictions of her United Church background, along with other avenues such as aesthetic experience, intellectual pursuits, sex and love, and so on. For Laurence's Morag Gunn there is the double burden of exploring a personal and family past in her more remote Scottish heritage and also in her immediate Manawaka past with Christie and Prin, her foster parents.

In these novels by Munro and Laurence female protagonists struggle to escape a small-town Protestant upbringing. They do so by somehow reincorporating within themselves their own histories while drawing on the wisdom and possibilities embodied in some marginal character or group. For Laurence's Morag Gunn the Métis people, especially as represented by her lover Jules Tonnerre and their daughter Pique, depict these marginal possibilities. Through them her history becomes enlarged to include a broader vision of promise than had been available before. For Munro's Del Jordan the eccentric character Bobby Sherriff personifies, in the final chapter, potentially liberating marginality. He helps Del see that Jubilee is something she can both escape from and take with her as she becomes a writer concerned to capture its texture and detail.

The narrator of Margaret Atwood's *Surfacing* (treated more fully in chap. 8 below) also escapes from a personal history that is restricting and confining. None of the worldviews available to her through her own culture or her family are adequate to deal with the crises she faces. Neither her father's scientific rationalism nor the Christianity of her childhood enable her to cope with the death, evil, and personal failure that have become so evident to her. Instead, an inner psychic journey that simultaneously unites her with nature according to the rites of passage of Canadian Indians provides her release and transcendence.

W. O. Mitchell's *Who Has Seen the Wind* represents a very clear instance of how traditional Protestant Christianity is experienced by the central character as problem rather than solution, as prison rather than freedom, and as inhibiting rather than liberating. For Brian O'Connal life in the town is judgmental and excluding. The school board and most of its teachers, the police and the courts, and the people who control and operate most of the town's institutions and businesses are presented as narrow, bigoted, stiff, and opposing freedom and growth. People or things outside the town mostly represent possibilities for escape and autonomy—the prophet Saint Sammy, certain other characters like the Bens, and the prairie and nature in general. Through nature mysticism, reminiscent of the experience of the Holy as described by Rudolf Otto, and represented particularly by the wind, young Brian finds something beyond the town and its institutions.

A TENTATIVE CONCLUSION

WHILE THERE IS NO ATTEMPT to make a full case at this point, my argument is going in the following direction. In Canadian novels informed by Protestant Christianity the characters, at first glance, seem to have to do battle with their religious past. It is part of the problem for them, not the solution. Protestantism is confining, not liberating, and if their experience of transcendence or liberation appears within their story, then it is not always obvious that some revised form of Protestant Christianity provides that experience of resolution. So, if the Protestant voice has been thought to be somehow central to Canadian fiction, that voice has actually been decentred, and the sacred correspondingly relocated, in the work of some of the foremost literary exemplars of that Protestantism.

If one were to generalize about how Protestant Christianity is problematic for numerous characters in Canadian fiction in the kinds of works we have been looking at, then it appears that they experience a dreadful isolation, being cut off from some nourishing source of vitality. They are alone in their guilt, their terrors, their failures, and their confrontation with death. To state it simply, what seems often to have driven these characters to such a position of complete isolation is a kind of Protestant (or at least Western) individualism. To use some of the language of Hugh MacLennan's narrator George Stewart, each one of them yearns to belong to something larger than the self, but for each one of them the God of traditional Protestant Christianity is no longer available to serve as that "something larger" to which they might belong.

The search for something larger is a religious quest. Maybe it is even a Protestant or Christian quest—though perhaps just as likely is the possibility of its being a more broadly Canadian one. But these characters seem to find their answers in community with other people, in union with nature or in the wisdom of the natural world, in the recovery of a part of a personal or family or human past that had been ignored or neglected, or in some larger myth about who they are and where they are going. This quest or search for something larger than the self may be launched by Protestantism, or even be encouraged by Protestantism's religious ethos and engaged in those terms. However, it is not always immediately obvious that the solution or resolution is a Christian or Protestant one. But the quest and its resolution is religious in the sense that it is a quest to situate some of the abodes of ultimate meaning, to discover new locations of the sacred.

NOTES

1 My initial reaction was in an unpublished paper presented to the Canadian Literary Society of Japan at Tokyo University, 5 June 1993, entitled "Canadian Literature and Religion: The Protestant Voice in English Fiction."

2 Lower also supports some of the other views of religion in Canada set forth in the Introduction and in this present chapter. Commenting on the contribution of Methodism to literature, he says it gave rise to "religious and descriptive" prose, while providing "discouraging soil for the imaginative writer, whom it could easily put down as a mere dreamer, or worse, a teller of tales that were not true!" (1967, 90-91). One can see here the origins of the low view of the imagination in the United Church, the denomination continuing Methodism in Canada since 1925. He also states, along the lines of what I shall be saying about Presbyterianism, that in Canada a type of Calvinism—"practical," not "doctrinal"—"lies just under the surface of so much of Protestantism" (ibid., 88).

3 W. J. Keith defends Robertson Davies against charges of "elitism," stating that "it is a part, surely, of his realistic clearsightedness" (1989, 91). He does not, however, address the brunt of such accusations. At its worst Davies' elitism is evident in condescending putdowns of people viewed as incapable of inhabiting rarefied spiritual and academic realms. Thus, he claims that doing good (by helping the boat people for instance) is not religious but an escape from a confrontation with ultimate reality. Or, he says that middle-class WASP students are excluded from Ontario universities because of incentives for low-income students and those from other ethnic groups. Are such views the expression of "discriminating value-judgments," as Keith says, or dedication to excellence, or merely another way of keeping out undesirables?

CHAPTER 2

RELOCATING THE SACRED: THE HUMAN GROUND OF TRANSCENDENCE

ETERNITY AND TRANSCENDENCE

IN AN ESSAY FIRST PUBLISHED in 1949 the Scottish poet Edwin Muir proposed that the decay of the religious sense meant the decline of the novel. Muir argued that for novelists of an earlier era "life obediently fell into the mould of a story" because "everybody possessed without thinking about it very much the feeling for a permanence above the permanence of one human existence, and believed that the ceaseless flux of life passed against an unchangeable background" (Muir 1975, 176). This correlation of faith with fiction maintains that imaginative literature depends on "the belief in eternity," contrasted with temporality and understood in the popular sense of everlasting existence. When that belief fails, imagination is eclipsed. The disappearance of the widespread assumption of such an "unchangeable background" dooms any attempt to find meaning in the world. With the collapse of the belief in eternity the location of the sacred has altered.

Although hardly conceived as a response to Muir despite its title, Alain Robbe-Grillet's 1956 essay "A Future for the Novel" argued that because "it is chiefly in its presence that the world's reality resides," writers must "create a literature which takes that presence into account" (Robbe-Grillet 1965, 23). Further, he maintained that a fundamental alteration had taken place in our relation with the universe: "a new element that separates us radically this time from Balzac as from Gide or from Mme. de La Fayette: it is the destitution of the old myths of 'depth'" (ibid.).

This alteration is an aspect of the problem of "literature and belief," described by M. H. Abrams as the "perennial concern

---

Notes to Chapter 2 are on p. 60.

about the clash between what poets say and what their readers believe to be true" (Abrams 1958, 1). Do I have to share the medieval worldview to read medieval literature with full appreciation? Stanley Romaine Hopper wonders whether religious faith need imply a particular cosmology: Does the breaking of an older conceptual mirror mean that the reality whose image was caught there is also broken (Gunn 1971, 221-35)? Still others (Nathan Scott and Hillis Miller stand as prominent examples) consider the religious meaning of contemporary literature after the collapse of traditional theism when a kind of nihilism, a sense of the absurdity of existence, or the apparent disappearance of God becomes widely taken for granted (Scott 1966; Miller 1965). Speaking of what he terms a "defiguralized" world, Nathan Scott describes it as "a world in which all the gods honored by archaic spirituality have been dethroned—a world, indeed, which, being independent of any *other*worldly plan or scheme of meaning, has ceased to be a *figura* of anything extrinsic to itself and is sealed off against any transcendental ingression from without" (Scott 1971, 25).

According to one account the Canadian scene is more perilous for the contemporary writer of fiction than the Anglo-European one. D. J. Dooley suggests that Canadian fiction has been more deeply affected by "Nietzscheanism" because our authors lack "gigantic forerunners" who might have reminded them of the religious basis of moral demands and of the "great disciplines of humanity" (1979, 178 n. 36). Surveying some of the landmarks in Canadian fiction written before 1970, Dooley reiterates his complaint that our novelists lack a consistent philosophical, moral, or religious framework to sustain them and to make convincing their portrayal of a context for making choices. The common argument is—and examples could be multiplied—that the novel depends upon an ordered universe for its coherence of plot and structure. If, for example, the world is chaotic or meaningless, is it possible to propose a moral law? Again, does it not seem that the traditional plot with a beginning, a middle, and an end is a kind of false imposition, if most modern individuals experience their lives as other than linear and teleological? In Muir's terms again, if people stop believing in an eternity existing as a kind of backdrop to this temporal world, can the writing of fiction persist? One answer—Frank Kermode's—is that fiction fulfills a human need, that of giving order and design to the world: "Novels, then, have beginnings, ends, and potentiality, even if the world has not" (Kermode 1967, 138). The book is a world-model, or bibliocosm (ibid., 52).

Towards the end of his essay "The Decline of the Novel" Edwin Muir asserts that the religious sense—and literature too—can never disappear because "the belief in eternity is natural to man" (1975, 177). By proposing an alteration of terminology (perhaps well beyond anything Muir himself would have accepted) that general view can be supported further. Applying the canons of a more inclusive language, and moving beyond strictly theological categories in favour of nomenclature customary within religious studies, we might read "people" or "humankind" for "man"; for "eternity" we might substitute "transcendent"; and for "belief" we might propose "faith." This proposal would be resisted by the theologian-critic David Jasper as part of a tendency "to banish the entire theological enterprise..., its philosophy, spirituality and sense of the finite and infinite, to vague terms like 'otherness' and 'alterity.'" Such a tendency, reflecting a movement away from the doctrinal and apologetic approaches of "theology and literature," Jasper castigates as "religion (and literature) without commitment" (1989, 1-2). Acknowledging, then, that my reformulation of Muir's statement moves it away from its original strictly theological context to a humanistic one, the proposition that "faith in the transcendent is natural to people" can now be endorsed and argued further.[1]

In his book *A Rumour of Angels* the sociologist of religion Peter Berger speaks of "The Alleged Demise of the Supernatural." He maintains that although the "supernatural" realm, thought of as a sphere inhabited by divine beings and forces, has pretty well disappeared from the modern consciousness, the phrase continues to denote a fundamental category of religion. For Berger the term "supernatural" means simply the "belief that there is *an other reality*, and one of ultimate significance for man, which transcends the reality within which our everyday experience unfolds" (Berger 1969, 14). In other words, the *Lebenswelt* or taken-for-granted world in which modern men and women live out their ordinary lives may be broken through in various ways. Berger turns his attention to certain "prototypical human gestures" in which he discerns "signals of transcendence," that is, reiterated acts and experiences which, although grounded in the everyday world, point beyond it to a transcendent order. On the basis of such gestures, Berger offers a series of arguments—from order, from play, from hope, from damnation, and from humour—having discovered "a basic ontological ground in human experience for the affirmation of transcendence" (Harvey and Neale 1979, 9 n. 1). As Joseph Campbell conveniently states it, "transcendent" may, in the first instance, refer to "God as being beyond or outside the field of nature"; but it has a second meaning—"'transcendent' properly means that which is beyond all concepts" (Campbell 1988, 62).

Various arguments have been made on such a basis for the religious meaning of literary art. Vincent Buckley, drawing on the work of Rudolf Otto and Mircea Eliade, has shown how poetry performs a "sacralising act" by specifying the sacred through its symbols, setting aside "certain experiences or places or people or memories as representatively revealing ones—in however attenuated a form, sacred ones" (Buckley 1968, 21). Similarly, it could be maintained that novels, poems, and plays express and represent those prototypical human gestures which Berger calls "signals of transcendence." In the same vein R. W. B. Lewis argues that literature intensifies "the human drama to the moment where it [gives] off intimations of the sacred" (Gunn 1971, 100). Important in all these instances is the heightening of ordinary experience through which one encounters gestures towards the transcendent—reality is whole, with no breaks or gaps. The location of the sacred is more likely to be found *within* (a kind of transcendence in immanence) or in a dimension of depth than it is in some overhead realm, in eternity, or infinity. Canadian fiction of the past few decades illustrates this relocation of the sacred in the movement towards the representation of this-worldly transcendence.

"ETERNITY" IN CALLAGHAN AND MACLENNAN

AT FIRST IT MIGHT APPEAR that the course of the twentieth-century Canadian novel displays a shift from the depiction of eternity as the backdrop to the temporal world to the representation of life as an interplay between everyday reality and transcendence. Before turning to more recent fiction a consideration of a few better-known older novelists shows how their works have been interpreted as displaying a dualistic split between heaven and earth. Hugo McPherson terms Morley Callaghan a religious writer because he had "concluded that the temporal world cannot be self-redeemed; that human frailty is bearable only in the light of divine perfection" (Conron 1975, 61). There are "Two Worlds" in Morley Callaghan's fiction (as even the title of McPherson's essay has it), designated as the "empirical" and the "spiritual," or "an imperfect world of time" and "a larger reality *out of time*" (ibid., 62). Of course, to raise again the question of literature and belief (discussed above), whether Callaghan actually believed in these two distinct worlds is beside the point—his fiction, at least in this view of it, lends itself to that kind of reading. In chapter 7 below I show how *Such Is My Beloved* operates seen in terms of immanent categories or this-worldly transcendence.

At the end of *Such Is My Beloved* (1934) Father Dowling sacrificially offers his insanity for the souls of the two prostitutes, Midge and Ronnie. He looks across "the calm, eternal water" to the three stars high in the sky, and identifies his love in its steadfastness with the stars. Callaghan's *More Joy in Heaven* (1937) likewise seems amenable to interpretation from the standpoint of classic Christian metaphysics, similar to David Jasper's reading of the ending of Dostoyevsky's *Crime and Punishment* (Jasper 1989, 43-44, 104-106). The relationship between Kip and Julie in *More Joy in Heaven* (Callaghan 1937), lacking the conditions for its fulfilment within the society where the novel's action is set, is taken up at the end to some realm beyond the earth. Though they have both been shot by the police and are dying, Kip "had made a private peace with her; it held them together, it touched everything they had wanted." Kip "could feel their dream still in her," getting larger, until "the dream got so big it was death for her" (ibid., 156). Kip dies without speaking three days later, but "he had made his peace with Julie and the things he knew were good that night on the stairs when they shot him" (ibid., 159). It is the familiar story of a love too good for this rotten world, or in Dostoyevsky's words, "of ... gradual passing from one world to another, of ... acquaintance with a new and hitherto unknown reality" (cited in Jasper 1989, 44).

W. J. Keith, in a recent book-length study of Hugh MacLennan's *The Watch that Ends the Night*, states his agreement with Malcolm Ross, who had reviewed the novel for the *Queen's Quarterly*, "in seeing the book primarily—if not exclusively—as a religious novel" (Keith 1993, 17). Ross emphasized that the novel's "innermost theme is death and resurrection" (ibid.). At the conclusion of *The Watch* George Stewart speaks of the unreality of the surrounding world as his wife Catherine's death approaches. "I knew then," George says, "that the loves she had known and inspired had not cancelled one another out, were not perishable absolutely, would not entirely end with her but would be translated into the mysterious directions of the spirit which breathed upon the void" (MacLennan 1958, 370). This spiritual illumination—Edmund Wilson calls it "a spasm of revelation" (1965, 72), while George Woodcock alludes to its "flavour of pietistic smugness" (Smith, 1961, 139)—enables George to surrender his earlier wrestlings with the problem of theodicy and to accept all of life as a gift. Here it seems, as in many older novels, that one leaves the temporal world behind at the end as the action moves beyond the terrestrial plane to an eternal realm. As Edwin Muir commented about the traditional novel, it appears that the circle of the story is closed in the work of Callaghan and MacLennan because the unchangeable background of eternity stands behind the flux of human life. Once again, here I am citing these critical readings for the sake of developing my own view. Below, in chapters 6 and 7, I advance my own interpretation of Callaghan and MacLennan, less dependent than these others on traditional Christian theism or on a dualistic earth-heaven split.

In those examples (considering that Callaghan's Father Dowling in his insanity undergoes psychic death) death becomes, in the words of Amos Wilder, "a catalyst of transcendence" (1969, 219). Terrence Des Pres points out that in Western religion and literature our highest praise is reserved for "action which culminates in death" (1976, 5). Our greatest heroes resolve conflict by dying or become heroic in a death sanctioned by the belief in eternity. Once again problems set in motion by the novelist in terrestrial terms are resolved or have their culmination or explanation in some eternal or extra-terrestrial realm.

Criticism has been levelled against Christianity by both Elie Wiesel and Albert Camus at this point. Wiesel states that "in Christianity, because of its beginnings, death became part of the decorum" (Bonisteel 1980, 54). Wiesel disagrees that Judaism and Christianity are one religion and suggests that Christians who regard life as somehow penultimate may not take the Holocaust and the deaths of six million Jews seriously. Camus argues that eternity is an illegitimate solution to the problem of the absurd: "Within the limits of the human condition, what greater hope than the hope that allows an escape from that condition?" (Camus 1955,

100). From a feminist theological standpoint Rosemary Ruether says that a "communal world view of humanity and nature, male and female" broke down in the first millennium as "the old religions of the earth became private cults for the individual, no longer anticipating the renewal of the earth and society but rather expecting an otherworldly salvation of the individual soul after death." Men longed "for a heavenly home to release them from their enslavement within the physical cosmos" (Ruether 1979, 47).

THE ORDINARY AND THE SACRED
IN MITCHELL AND MUNRO

DEATH CAN BECOME A CATALYST of transcendence in fiction even where traditional modes of heroism or the prospect of eternity are not evident. In W. O. Mitchell's *Who Has Seen the Wind* (1949) young Brian's search for some clue to the riddle of existence is prompted, deepened, and paradoxically answered by a succession of experiences of death, ranging from a pigeon or gopher, to that of his dog, then to his father and finally to his grandmother. Each of the four parts of the novel ends with a burial and with Brian walking on the prairie. There is, however, no promise of immortality to alleviate his loss: "People were forever born; people forever died, and never were again." For Brian death is one location of the sacred. An uncanny experience of otherness comes too from other sources such as the prairie, the wind, certain persons like Saint Sammy or the Young Ben, and his strange excited feeling at a meadowlark's song or a dewdrop on a spirea leaf.

All these glimpses of transcendence contrast with the world-taken-for-granted represented by the conventional folk of the prairie town. Their lives exclude mystery, questions, and longing; their educational, judicial, and religious institutions restrict freedom and inhibit growth. At the end Brian walks out on the prairie with the sun glinting on a wild rosebush covered with frost crystals. There he experiences a realization of the nature of the cycle of life and death. From that vantage point he looks back at the town: "And the town was dim—gray and low upon the horizon, it lay, not real, swathed in bodiless mist—quite sunless in the rest of the dazzling prairie" (Mitchell 1949, 299).

Although in Mitchell's novel clearly an-other reality stands over and against the *Lebenswelt* of everyday experience, the transcendence is horizontal rather than vertical, the sacred located within the temporal world rather than requiring a leap beyond it. In Alice Munro's *Lives of Girls and Women*, however, no stable reality, not even a fixed and dependable version of the "ordinary," presents itself. There are no role models for Munro's protagonist, Del Jordan, either. As a result Del finds herself negotiating a world of shifting, various, and unreliable surfaces where exotic, dangerous, and threatening possibilities beckon with their enchantments. In the novel's Epilogue Del comments that "people's lives, in Jubilee as elsewhere, were dull, simple, amazing and unfathomable—deep caves paved with kitchen linoleum" (Munro 1971, 210). In *Who Has Seen the Wind* Brian has the simpler task of reconciling the conflicting alternatives represented by the town and the prairie. Brian's resolution is his decision to become an agricultural scientist, by that following the pattern of his mentors who have previously incorporated the values of both rural and urban realms. Del rejects the domestic entrapments exemplified in her friend Naomi's decision to have a family and her mother's assumption that "of course you will want children." She also avoids the enticing aspects of the bizarre (the "amazing and unfathomable") that may take her too far away from the ordinary.

Del Jordan's growing up in Alice Munro's *Lives of Girls and Women* is in many respects similar to Brian's. A conventional town, Jubilee, comprises the ordinary world. Outside the town on the Flats Road, Del's father has a fox-farming venture, fitting in well with neighbours who raise donkeys or goats. The Flats Road is also the domain of such oddities as Uncle Benny, who catches frogs for bait, keeps turtles to sell to Americans for soup, and values "debris for its own sake." Benny's tabloid newspapers are filled with "revelations of evil, of its versatility and grand invention and horrific playfulness" (ibid., 4). These papers stand in contrast with the humdrum reportage of the Jubilee or city newspapers or with the *Family Herald* or *Saturday Evening Post*: "This was a world unlike the one my parents read about in the paper, or heard about on the daily news" (ibid.). After Benny's trip to Toronto to find his wife, a "journey without maps" (to borrow the title of one of Graham Greene's books) because Benny relies on directions asked from strangers, he tells the story of his expedition in meticulous detail, everything remembered. Del comments: "So lying alongside our world was Uncle Benny's world like a troubling distorted reflection, the same but never at all the same" (ibid., 22). Del imagines that in Benny's world "luck and wickedness were gigantic and predictable; nothing was deserved, anything might happen; defeats were met with crazy satisfaction" (ibid.).

Throughout the novel's initial chapter other parallel, reflected worlds are evident. Since reality is shifting and unstable, available in different versions dependent on one's situation and perspective, Del encounters various possibilities and differences. Her mother differentiates the Flats Road people with their drunkenness, their "sexual looseness, dirty language, haphazard lives, contented ignorance" from "the real poor whom she loved" (ibid., 7). Her father is liked and accepted on the Flats Road; her mother is not. Del's mother thinks their family does not belong among the bootleggers, idiots, and weird folk who share the Flats Road with them.

Among other distinctions *Lives of Girls and Women* draws a contrast between the world of men and the world of women, the country and the town, and the house experienced upstairs in bed and the house downstairs around the kitchen table. The "Flats Road" chapter ends with Del's assumption of a connection between her parents. Though her father sits in a wooden chair and her mother in a canvas one, they share a common world, linked in turn with that of Uncle Benny. At first Del remains confident of some degree of continuity among different competing versions of the world. She assumes that "this connection was plain as a fence," though, it seems, acknowledging a boundary as well: "it would stay between us and anything" (22). Del, about to enter grade four, finds that the reality of Benny's tabloids fades and becomes doubtful when she returns from his house to her own. At the same time her retention of a coherent world picture requires some nexus between these different worlds.

Similarly, when Del places Benny's name and address within an expanding universe radiating outwards from the Flats Road to include the western hemisphere, the solar system, and the world, he extends it even further to include heaven, "because the Lord is there!" (10). Benny's version of the world reaches infinity; it also extends Del's attempt at a complete return address—though he is connected to her reality, he goes beyond it. His wife-seeking Toronto trip, a journey to one of those "terrible ordinary cities" where "anything might happen," is not a journey (contrary to what Del's mother says) that "proves you have to have a map!" Though

Benny's journey cannot be mapped, it can be narrated by him, as Del realizes: "it was his triumph, that he couldn't know about, to make us see" (22).

While the young Del appreciates Benny's artistry in his presentation of his world, she has yet to reckon fully with the sheer subjectivity of his eccentric interpretation. Del's mother would prefer to believe that Benny might have concocted the accounts of the child, Diane, being beaten. Del recognizes that even Madeline, whom they have all seen and whom they "remembered . . . like a story," nonetheless "was like something he might have made up" (23). In the novel's conclusion Del's fictional version of Jubilee's Sherriff family selectively incorporates various features of the town. "The main thing," she reflects, "was that it seemed true to me, not real but true, as if I had discovered, not made up, such people and such a story, as if that town was lying close behind the one I walked through every day" (206). An encounter with an actual member of the Sherriff family, Bobby, destroys Del's "faith" in her own fictional transformation of Jubilee, revealing her novel as an "unreliable structure" (208). The challenge reality poses to artistic truth makes Del fear that "the hope of accuracy we bring to such tasks is crazy, heart-breaking," as if her own unreliable version of reality might represent madness surpassing Bobby Sherriff's.

Lives of Girls and Women, then, begins and ends with Del's reflections on the correspondences between various aesthetic transformations and the world's actuality. As a grade four student she grasps Benny's artistry in enabling the Jordans to visualize the world as he encountered and experienced it. As a high school graduate Del receives an offering—"I wish you well in your life"—graciously held out by Bobby Sherriff with a movement like "a plump ballerina." To the would-be writer that gesture seems to have its own "stylized meaning . . . in an alphabet I did not know" (211). Instead of thanking him, she affirms his blessing with a simple "yes" of acceptance and confirmation. With that the world returns to her in all its actuality and facticity after she has been "sabotaged by love" (207), performed badly in her final exams, and apparently lost her scholarship.

Del's realization stands as a commitment to accuracy and reality: "What I wanted was every last thing, every layer of speech and thought, stroke of light on bark or walls, every smell, pothole, pain, crack, delusion, held still and held together—radiant, everlasting"

(210). As Lorraine York (1988) points out, Del commits herself to a photographic realism of fidelity to ordinary appearances and to the mystery of things themselves, not to an unrealistic rendering of things into an artistic object fantastically disconnected from its source. A reversal takes place when the photographer's pictures, transcending the temporal limitations of their aesthetic medium, are prophetic portraits of what will be. Meanwhile, the supposedly mad Bobby Sherriff restores Del to the sanity of the world as it is, while retaining all the mysteries of an aesthetic rendition of it.

The tensions between art and reality run throughout the intervening chapters too. Del, growing towards becoming an artist, finds this tension complicated by the unstable and changing aspects of reality, or, better, by the apparent impossibility of finding "ordinary reality" at all. Is there anything reliable and consistent to be found underlying the different competing versions of ordinary reality? The elusive "normal" is not incarnated for Del in anyone she knows. Further, she has ample demonstration of the perils and pitfalls of a too-fantastic artistic transformation of reality into some alternative version, however "true" it might subjectively appear to be.

In the chapter "Heirs of the Living Body" Del inherits the chronicle of Wawanash County compiled by her Uncle Craig—"He would not leave anything out" (27). But Del, contrary to her aunt's dictums, has ambitions to produce a writer's masterpiece. She aspires to surpass her uncle's catalogue of the county, scorned as "so dead to me, so heavy and dull and useless" (52). Like other dead things (his corpse in the parlour or a dead cow's body) Del wants to avoid the cumbersome substance of Uncle Craig's opus. So Del neglects the manuscript, leaving it lying in the basement until water ruins it. With mixed remorse and satisfaction she contemplates the destruction the flood has made of that "dead body." Though Del's neglect ruins this formidable and unread local history, she at least frees herself of her aunt's urging her to "copy his way" and continue his efforts beyond the terminal date of 1909. Like Uncle Craig, though, Del has a compulsion to get everything down; like him she wants accuracy and completeness. His files and drawers housed "a great accumulation of the most ordinary facts, which it was his business to get in order. Everything had to get into his history. . . . He would not leave anything out" (27).

While Del spurns a factual approach to ordinary life, scoffing at her uncle's concern for historical detail and his seemingly pointless lists, she nonetheless wants as a writer to have "death pinned down and isolated behind a wall of particular facts and circumstances" (39), to turn the mysterious into something mundane. Within the family she is in terror of being regarded as "highly strung, erratic, or badly brought up, or a *borderline case*" (48). In the chapter "Princess Ida" Del feels "the weight of my mother's eccentricities," the sense of there being "something absurd and embarrassing about her" (54), while appreciating too that from her conventional aunts' viewpoint her "mother did seem a wildwoman." Discovering that after all she herself "was not so different" from her mother, Del feels obliged to conceal it, knowing the dangers (68). When her mother's brother visits them Del discovers an entirely different fund of stories and memories from the home her mother and her uncle had shared as siblings, presenting yet more competing versions of reality for her to chose among. In the chapter "Age of Faith" Del begins to venture into some of these other possibilities on her own. She tries out the United Church and then, beginning with her attendance at the Anglican Church, discovers "the theatrical in religion."

Munro's fiction is much more elusive in its meanings than Mitchell's. Yet Del, like Brian, struggles with the multiple options in the baffling, ordinary world of Jubilee and the various possibilities of transcending it. The possibilities include the aesthetic ritual of the Anglican Church (assigned the resonance of the numinous by Robertson Davies), the dizzying escapes of adolescent sexuality and romance, the glamour of a school dramatic production, and the elevating power of knowledge and academic achievement. Each appeals to Del at one or another stage of her life. Each offers escape from the limits of her own selfhood to become other than what she is, a way of achieving a different kind of humanity.

As the Epilogue suggests, the danger in this "portrait of the girl as a young artist" is that Del may lose touch with the conventional and very ordinary world of Jubilee and succumb to a kind of mythomania. Instead of writing her intended fantastic "black fable," Del, brought up short by "the ordinariness of everything," settles instead for the reality of the ordinary, wants to make up lists and get it all down—"every last thing, every layer of speech and thought." Del has discovered that "people's lives, in Jubilee as elsewhere, were dull, simple, amazing and unfathomable" (210). Like Mitchell's Brian who hopes to reconcile his two opposing worlds—

town and prairie, knowledge and nature—by becoming a "dirt doctor," Munro's Del completes her transcendence of the ordinary world of Jubilee with a return to its ordinariness, retaining her vision of possibility.

DIVINING THE DEPTHS IN DAVIES, LAURENCE, AND ATWOOD

LOUIS MACKENDRICK IDENTIFIES one of the two predominant themes in Alice Munro's work as "the provocative elaboration and mystery beyond the seemingly 'real'" (1983, 2). Robertson Davies, speaking through the narrative persona of Dunstan Ramsay in *Fifth Business*, the first novel of his Deptford trilogy, says: "I have been sometimes praised, sometimes mocked, for my way of pointing out the mythical elements that seem to me to underlie our apparently ordinary lives" (1970, 46). Ramsay, incensed at a colleague's patronizing portrait of him as a doddering old schoolmaster, writes his *apologia* to his headmaster to demonstrate that "the sources from which [his] larger life were nourished were elsewhere" (118). He wants to show how all his life he has inhabited "a strange world that showed very little of itself on the surface" (36). In Ramsay's world, invisible to the unpractised eye of his superficial younger colleague, are romance and marvels, conjuring and madness, saints and legends, miracles and the devil. Religion is "psychologically rather than literally true" (71), and the "worst" Christians are those who "have the cruelty of doctrine without the poetic grace of myth" (226). It is a world of coincidence (or Jungian synchronicity) and of spiritual adventures.

Yet Davies' world of wonders shares some aspects of the transcendent with Mitchell's and Munro's fictional realms. The bizarre and initiatory aspects of death and the uncanny otherness of madness, perhaps more than anything else, mark off the transcendent or numinous from the ordinary taken-for-granted realm. Mary Dempster brings both Dunstable Ramsay and his brother Willie back to life. The auspices of this apparent madwoman save him from death at Passchendaele in November 1917, though Dunstable enters a long coma that lasts until May. He completes his second birth when Diana renames him Dunstan the following Christmas. Convinced that Mrs. Dempster has vicariously suffered his fate, figuratively died for him in the process, and thus enabled him to enjoy his present good life, Ramsay embarks on the effort to canonize her and ends up, in the manner of his namesake, grappling with his personal devil.

In the second novel of the trilogy the death of his father and fear for his own sanity launches David Staunton on his quest for "an-other reality." Staunton takes himself to an analyst in Zurich (*The Manticore* being much more explicitly Jungian than *Fifth Business*) and under her guidance learns how underdeveloped his emotional side is. Staunton explores a previously hidden reality through the analysis of his dreams and figures from his past. David Staunton's "rebirth" occurs in a cave high in the Swiss Alps, inhabited in a prehistoric time by the practitioners of bear cult rituals. As he crawls out through the narrow passage (the imagery of a birth canal is unmistakable), a roar in the darkness unnerves the exhausted and struggling Staunton: "I knew in that instant the sharpness of death" (Davies 1976, 304). Both these novels by Davies share the motifs of death and rebirth and the exploration of a mythic realm just below the surfaces of ordinary life. The movement towards integration is different from that in Mitchell and Munro where the protagonists reconcile the demands of two conflicting worlds, one ordinary and the other transcendent, lying alongside each other. Instead, in Davies there is a descent into the mythic inner world to fight one's trolls or accept one's personal devil.

In *What's Bred in the Bone* (1985), probably Davies' best work since *Fifth Business*, the action spreads out on a world stage again. The story takes its readers from the Ottawa Valley to Toronto, England, Bavaria, and Rome. Like the Deptford Trilogy, *What's Bred in the Bone* portrays, from the vantage point of a boy growing up, life in an Ontario town (this time Blairlogie, an Ottawa Valley town derived from Davies' recollections of Renfrew). All the ingredients of the earlier Davies are here. The story begins with an obituary notice and its attendant puzzles, and the wrangling over the terms of a will. It goes on to chart the unseen and unrecognized events in the secret life of the deceased man, the prominent critic and restorer of works of art, Arthur Cornish. And it shows how, in a more ambitious way than with Dunstan Ramsay, the nourishing sources of that life are "elsewhere."

As with many of Davies' other works, *What's Bred in the Bone* is set in motion by a public event accompanying an individual's coming to or going from this world. *Fifth Business* began with the snowball that hastened the birth of Paul Dempster; it ended with the question "Who killed Boy Staunton?" *The Cunning Man* (1994) begins with Father Hobbes' death in church on Good Friday morning under circumstances clarified only a few pages from the end. *What's Bred in the Bone* similarly delves into the mysteries attending birth, copulation, and death. No puzzle accompanies the actual circumstances of the death of Arthur Cornish. Rather, the problem here is to plumb the secrets, from the time of his conception, of the private life of the public figure who has died. The novel charts the course of the personal myth that Cornish has discovered, acted out, and fulfilled.

What's Bred in the Bone is a kind of *bildungsroman* told from the supernatural vantage point of the Lesser Zadkiel, the Angel of Biography, and of the Daimon Maimas, Cornish's personal "daimon." Their perspective, of course, goes beyond any obituary notice or proposed biography, transcending the knowledge of anyone who actually knew him in the flesh or even of Cornish himself. As with so much of his earlier work, Davies wants us to know once again that there is more here than meets the eye—much more. If in *Fifth Business* hagiography opens this "world of wonders" for Dunstan Ramsay (as Jungian psychology later was the key for David Staunton and magic for Paul Dempster), here astrology and alchemy make accessible and then intensify the mysteries.

Robertson Davies is both a debunker and a "rebunker." He debunks once again modern science, liberalism, the cult of the therapeutic, personalism, the shallowness of contemporary Christianity. He rebunks—that is, he restores to our contemporary sceptical age—the old wisdom of saints' lore, classical and Celtic mythology, and the great secret things of sex, art, and religion. In *What's Bred in the Bone* Davies disowns, if anyone had been thinking of holding him to it, any final reliance upon a single mythology such as that of Jung. Cornish's mentor maintains that whereas the "inner vision" of earlier art "presented itself in a coherent language of mythological or religious terms," now it comes from what the psychoanalysts (the "great magicians of our day") call the Unconscious ("though it is actually the Most Conscious"). Modern artists speak a private language that is "perilously easy to fake." What they reveal, Davies seems to think, is revelation only to themselves.

The title comes from an English proverb: "What's Bred in the Bone will not / Out of the Flesh." What that cryptic statement means is that what's bred in the bone will not *escape* from—indeed, will inevitably come out in—the flesh. But modern individuals, as the Lesser Zadkiel and the Daimon Maimas comment, cherish their free will and believe in chance. Though science may show them evidence of a pattern in the rest of nature, humans like to think themselves above all that. But destiny—and reckoning with it—is not any simple affair of coming to terms with one's heredity. The two supernatural guardians (and their creator, Davies) allow for choice within the meaning-pattern of people's lives. They also scorn people who, unable to bear the thought of anything external to themselves shaping their lives, use the dismissive term "coincidence" to refer to any chance occurrences. Here, like Hugh MacLennan, the former Presbyterian Davies undertakes a new exploration of what the Calvinist view of predestination might mean in a demythologized or remythologized form.

What's bred in the bone of Francis Cornish is the shadow of his older half-brother (also named Francis, but nicknamed the Looner because, in the cruel parlance of his hometown, he remained an "idjit" all his short life long). The shadow cast by madness across a boy's life, absent or ineffectual parents (and the difficulty of knowing one's parents, especially one's mother), the cruelty of children to each other, the struggle to find one's personal myth, an inside look at an arcane art that may be a kind of alchemy (such as embalming or art restoration), deception, and, yes, coincidence and chance—all these are familiar motifs in the Davies canon.

If the things Davies does well (such as the portrayal of a strange childhood in a small town) shine forth in *What's Bred in the Bone*, some of those things that he either avoids or does less well become equally clear. Like Dunstan Ramsay and David Staunton— and like Dr. Jonathan Hullah in *The Cunning Man*—Cornish finds marriage impossible. Though married for a short time, he remains a functional bachelor. As with others among Davies' fictional creations "the yearning for a girl companion, and for the mystery and tenderness ... he might find in such a creature," is unfulfilled. Small-town eccentrics (the undertaker, the doctor, a maiden aunt) are portrayed well; but other minor characters from Cornish's adult life (especially his friend Aylwin Ross) resist coming to life under Davies' hand. In fact, a friendship that goes beyond an archetypal relationship such as that of mentor to disciple or shadow to self remains elusive.

Although Davies skilfully recreates the past life of his chief characters in his novels, he has difficulty getting them back to the present. The endings of *Fifth Business* and *The Manticore* have something of contrivance about them, as if the return to ordinary reality from the mythic world of wonders is difficult for him to manage. *What's Bred in the Bone* again belabours the reentry. The last fifty pages seem hasty, plotted, condensed. Perhaps Davies' mythomania (or, more charitably, his mythophilia) makes the elaboration of a sequel easier for him than the closure of a particular work. What's bred in the bone and marrow of the fiction of this unsurpassed Canadian mythographer is a sense of otherness, of rich possibilities, and of marvellous depths lurking beneath the surfaces of things.

Margaret Atwood's *Surfacing* is even more obviously an archetypal narrative of rebirth than Davies' work. The heroine of the female rebirth narrative will have greater difficulty in reintegrating herself into culture than her male counterpart—her adventures "increase her chances for death, madness, self-sacrifice, and accusations of 'deviance'" (Pratt 1981, 141). Many of the stages outlined by Mircea Eliade for the mysteries of initiation—examined extensively in chapter 8 below—apply to Atwood's narrator in *Surfacing*, especially the central motif of "the symbolism of death as the ground of all spiritual birth" (Eliade 1967, 200). The deaths of her parents, her abortion, the destruction of the natural world, and the numbing death of feeling (described as the separation of head from body), have their completion in her ritualized initiatory death at the end of the novel.

Surfacing, capable of being explored fruitfully from so many angles, illustrates the features Carol Christ outlines as central to the spiritual quest of a modern woman (Christ 1979). That journey "begins in the experience of nothingness, the experience of being without an adequate image of self," for the narrator the result of domination by a succession of males including her rationalist father, her married lover, her predatory brother, and her boss. Getting beyond the resulting nothingness demands what Carol Christ calls "a vision..., however fleeting, of transcendence." Indeed, the sight of her father's dead body underwater, at first interpreted as an image of her aborted fetus, constitutes a gift from him. Supplementing this vision is a gift from her mother—a picture the narrator herself had drawn as a child—that she accepts as an injunction

to atone for the abortion. The succeeding redemptive act of "conception" may correspond to Christ's reference to learning "from
motherhood to gain detachment from all her past struggles." In her
integration with the natural world, a kind of descent into madness,
the narrator "explores a reality underlying ordinary reality" and
finally emerges as "a seer, a prophet" (Christ 1979, 238).

Apart from its specifically feminist or nationalist or ecological
implications, *Surfacing* exemplifies the basic initiatory pattern of
rebirth into a new reality, given special impetus by several experiences of death, and involving madness as part of the exploration
into a transcendent reality. More epic in scope than Atwood's
novel, yet surprisingly similar in many respects, is Margaret Laurence's *The Diviners*. Michel Fabre calls it "an archetypal quest for
salvation and meaning," an accurate though not immediately obvious characterization of the novel (1983, 247). Like Atwood's narrator's, Morag's quest (though beginning much earlier in her life) has
its initial impetus in the deaths of her parents. Though it follows a
somewhat different route, and ranges over more space and time,
Morag's journey also involves an exploration of the past, and
emerges finally with a similar insight. As Marian Engel effectively
puts it, Morag "achieves the apocalypse of knowing what her life
has been about, not through the agency of a man, but through her
own experience" (Engel 1983, 240).

Like Munro's Del, Morag is at many points excluded by the
conventional world, or else does not wish to identify with it. Moreover, there might not be a consistent single alternative world—a
consistent and stable "other" reality—available to her from beginning to end. Like many of the protagonists considered here, she has
an unlikely mentor in the person of her stepfather, Christie. He,
along with Jules Tonnerre, opens for her the possibility of an-other
reality, an alternative way of being. But the novel's vision of transcendence is most clearly alluded to in the complex of meanings
suggested by its title. "Divining" refers in a literal way to the
water-witching activity of Royland and to Christie's ability to
prophesy through plumbing the depths of the community's
garbage. By easy extension, it comes to mean Morag's writing of
fiction and Jules' composition of songs. Finally, divining suggests
the ability to probe beneath the surfaces of a visible reality, to read
its hidden meaning, to have, in a sense, a shamanistic gift of second
sight. Those who possess the gift are frequently loony or clowns or

otherwise outside society's mainstream, so that visionary powers are associated once more with madness. From that transcendent other realm Christie bears to the orphaned Morag a fund of stories from a mythic past, providing her with the ancestors and history she needs to sustain her. In comparison, Brian O'Connal's mentor, his grandmother, imparts stories to him; Del clarifies her relation to her Uncle Craig's writing of history; and, David Staunton in his extremity summons up the memory of Maria Dymock. For the orphaned Morag, as for others, parental death launches the protagonist on the quest for a "real" past.

CONCLUSION

THE KIND OF ANALYSIS ACCORDED here to five authors undeniably in the front rank of Canada's writers of fiction could be extended to others. The experience of motherhood, the threat of madness, the fragmentation of the self almost to the point of nothingness, the alienation of a woman from the mainstream of conventional culture, and the loss of a parent in death are all themes predominant in Adele Wiseman's novel *Crackpot* (Wiseman 1974). These thematic similarities make her work comparable to that of her friend Margaret Laurence, especially in the way ancestral stories function to provide her protagonist, the obese prostitute Hoda, with a potentially transformative model. But Wiseman's Jewishness shows that the transformative religious perspective identified here in Canadian fiction cannot be restricted to novelists whose background is Christian.

The cosmology and structure of *Crackpot* derives from a Lurianic or Kabbalistic view of creation with its major phases of the divine exile and darkness, the fragmentation of the vessel and proliferation of the shards, and the final restoration of the universe into a harmony (see Margaret Laurence, "Introduction," in Wiseman 1974, 3-8). In *Crackpot* everything can be redeemed, gathered up, and incorporated. Wiseman's worldview comes largely from her mother who regards nature as inherently good—"take what nature gives"—combined equally with her sense of a responsibility to improve it. The elder Wiseman, famed in her own right as someone who even in her eighties made folk dolls out of other people's discards, is a recycler of waste, someone who gathers up other people's garbage, and incorporates it into her own creation—"Why should junk lay around and not be used?" (Wiseman 1978, 43).

In *Old Woman at Play*, a book that is as much an exploration of the meaning of art as a description of doll-making, Adele Wiseman catalogues her mother's inventory of buttons, plastic lids and bottles, scraps and bones, jewellery, seeds, cardboard packages, and concludes: "Redeemer of waste, champion of leftovers, saviour of non-biodegradables, apostle of continuous creation, she has this hunger to find and establish new relations between things, and so create new things" (ibid., 8). Wiseman attributes to Judaism her parents' "utter faith in and submission to nature," defined as "that aspect of the unknowable which allows itself to be known; it is divinity revealing itself in action, and man is a part of that revelation, a part which can, to some extent, shape its own contribution to the continuous process" (ibid., 40). And, speaking of her own literary creations, Wiseman states: "I still adhere to the hope that I may yet be able to create my own true magic model for the spirit of a more humane world" (Wiseman 1987, 30).

Two further examples provide possibilities for extending this analysis. Clark Blaise in *Lunar Attractions*, winner of the 1979 Books in Canada Award for a first novel, deals with conflicting realities in the consciousness of a boy growing up in the United States. Again, as the title suggests, madness lurks in wait as a chaotic dream world intrudes upon an otherwise ordinary world. Death is here much more violent than in the other fictions, since a murder is central to the work. Throughout this *bildungsroman* the young protagonist struggles to retain his grip on himself, and to find some pattern of meaning in the chaos of his experience. A different blend of violence and spirituality occurs in Thomas York's *Trapper* (York 1981), a fictional attempt to chronicle the inner life of the famed "mad trapper," Albert Johnson. Again, death in this novel is brutal, beginning with Johnson shooting a policeman whose fault lies in his obligation to bring the lawless Johnson within the net of law and order. *Trapper* concludes, after Johnson's own literal and figurative "ascent," in his own death at the hands of the posse that carried out an extensive manhunt. The conventions of an ordered society opposing the possibility of the attainment of inner freedom are the "two worlds" of this fiction. Clearly York wants his readers to know that Johnson has, like Callaghan's Kip Caley in *More Joy in Heaven* (Callaghan 1937), asserted the primacy of the inner world over the outer, achieved a transcendence of the ordinary world in so doing, though paid the (perhaps necessary) price of dying for the sake of its accomplishment. The various locations of the sacred charted here derive from fiction's creation of "an-other reality," a world that transcends the taken-for-granted world of ordinary reality. Whether lying alongside the ordinary world, or above or below it, or within the individual self, in one way or another these transcendent dimensions, these locations of the sacred, are explored by the protagonists of the fictions examined here. Indeed, the pattern corresponds in many respects to Joseph Campbell's composite "monomyth" of the heroic quest (a pattern examined in chap. 4 below with respect to the canoe trip).

While the transcendent or the sacred resembles somewhat what an earlier age called "eternity," perhaps its contemporary character lies in fiction's locating the sacred in the structures of negation or absence. That is, the search for ultimate meaning may bring one into critical confrontation with the void or with the darkness of the eclipse of God rather than with divine presence. In that respect the sacrality located in Canadian fiction resembles Rudolf Otto's characterization of "the holy" as the *"mysterium tremendum,"* the awe-inspiring, uncanny mystery that is the sacred minus its rational or moral qualities (Otto 1950, 1-30 passim). The fictional protagonists looked at here are transported beyond the usual realm of ordinary experience by an experience of something unconditioned and unfamiliar, of death or madness, of nothingness or non-being, that takes on the character of the numinous.

If Flannery O'Connor is right that "all good stories are about conversion, about a character's changing" (1979, 275), and if religions "induce a selfhood in which a transformation is effected from an old self perceived as broken and awry to a new identity of ultimate integration and well-being," then the sort of "passage from plight to redemption," from "chaos to meaning" (Gualtieri 1977, 508) examined here is central to literature and to religion and to their point of intersection. But the question remains about how this exploration brings to light anything specifically Canadian.

Death and madness and transcendence—and, yes, even survival—are not after all exclusively Canadian themes. Canadian literature has moved well beyond a literature dramatizing failure (as Margaret Atwood characterized it in 1972) to depicting the possible "jailbreaks and re-creations" of transformative possibilities. Perhaps the typical Canadian is not so much the loser or victim as the ironic onlooker standing apart from the mainstream. Because the literary protagonists examined here seek an-other reality, eventually locating the sacred beyond the *Lebenswelt* of the conventional, perhaps they share a typically Canadian consciousness. The case could be made that the "centre" of Canadian culture is, in fact, in marginality, that is, on the outside, on the periphery.[2] And that appears, too, to be one of the relocated domains of the sacred.

NOTES

1 Whereas others might want to support Muir's original statement in strictly theological terms, my own approach is not necessarily compatible with "theology and literature." The philosophical and theological problems attending the word "eternity" are conveniently outlined by William C. Kneale (*Encyclopedia of Philosophy* 3: 63-66). While Joseph Campbell, for instance, insists that "eternity has nothing to do with time," and that "eternity is that dimension of here and now that all thinking in temporal terms cuts off" (1988, 67), it is doubtful the word can be rescued from those who, like Muir and (presumably) Jasper, use it in the sense of "everlasting" or "timelessness." Wilfred Cantwell Smith argues that "faith" is more appropriate than "belief" to convey the characteristic attitude and outlook of Christians (and other religious people) (Smith 1979). Further, Peter Berger as a Lutheran theologian is generally considered to be theologically conservative in his efforts to redefine transcendence (though its meaning might be equivalent to "eternity" for him). A recent sociological assessment of an earlier version of this essay interpreted mine as one of several efforts to uncover the "hidden gods of Canadian literature," and as such dealing with "implicit religion" (see O'Toole 1993).

2 After the bombing there in 1995 there were repeated references in the news media to Oklahoma City as "all-American" and located in the "heartland" of the United States, terminology entirely absent when New York's World Trade Center was bombed by foreign terrorists. One analysis suggested that such references conveyed that "all-American" means "white, Christian, rural, and midwestern." As one American professor put it: "The old Protestant northern European ethnic stock is somehow more American than any other" (Valerie Strauss, "Coast-to-Coast Heartland," reprinted from the *Washington Post* in the *Daily Yomiuri* [Japan], 2 June 1995, 11). I am suggesting that the difficulty of imagining any Canadian city today being described in similar terms proves that Canadians have a different view of themselves.

CHAPTER 3

NATURE AS THE LOCALE
OF THE SACRED

> THAT CONQUERING RELATION to place has left its mark
> within us. When we go into the Rockies we may have the
> sense that gods are there. But if so, they cannot manifest
> themselves to us as ours. They are the gods of another race,
> and we cannot know them because of what we are, and
> what we did. There can be nothing immemorial for us
> except the environment as object.
>
> — George Grant, *Technology and Empire*

NATIVE AND CHRISTIAN ATTITUDES

AN ETERNITY BEYOND THIS WORLD as the paramount location
of the sacred has persisted in Western religious thought and
popular attitudes alike. As the preceding essay has shown, Edwin
Muir claimed that such an eternity, contrasted with temporality,
was necessary for the existence and continuation of the novel. This
particular version of heaven, an everlasting paradise after death, has
been differentiated in Christianity from the insubstantialities of the
transitory natural world. Father Paul le Jeune, the seventeenth-
century Jesuit missionary in New France, describes his attempt to
evangelize a Montagnais Indian. He presented the natural world in
typical theistic terms not as itself intrinsically sacred but as an
orderly creation revealing a creator abiding in an eternity accessible
to humanity after death:

> When thou seest the beauty and grandeur of this world,—how the
> Sun incessantly turns round without stopping, how the seasons fol-
> low each other in their time, and how perfectly all the Stars maintain
> their order,—thou seest clearly that men have not made these won-
> ders, and that they do not govern them; hence there must be some

Notes to Chapter 3 are on p. 80.

one more noble than men, who has built and who rules this grand mansion. Now it is he whom we call God, who sees all things, and whom we do not see; but we shall see him after death, and we shall be forever happy with him, if we love and obey him (Thwaites 1897, 7:103).[1]

The Jesuit missionary follows the age-old method of the argument from design, described as always "the most popular of the theistic arguments, tending to evoke spontaneous assent in simple and sophisticated alike" (Hick 1963, 23). Beginning with the observed creation, then moving on to refer to its beneficent creator, Father le Jeune concludes with the prospect of heaven. Significantly, for this missionary, consistent with the central core of Christianity, nature is not itself inherently sacred; rather, nature is the basis on which is set up the superstructure of grace. The locale of the sacred is eternity, not the earth. The Montagnais man, unimpressed by what he heard, gave nothing like the "spontaneous assent" that the Jesuit might have anticipated, and moved quickly to end the conversation. " 'Thou dost not know what thou art talking about,' he answered, 'learn to talk and we will listen to thee' " (ibid.).

Writing from the vantage point of Canadians of European ancestry, John Webster Grant comments that the "psychic shock" experienced by the Indians in their first meeting with Europeans is "comparable to that which we might feel if extraterrestrial beings set out to colonize the earth" (Grant 1984, 21). Between indigenous peoples and colonizing Europeans lay profound and irreconcilable differences. Brian Moore, in the "Author's Note" to his novel *Black Robe* (later made into a motion picture), describes his reading of *The Jesuit Relations*, the seventy-three volumes of annual reports sent from New France to Paris between 1632 and 1772 (and source of le Jeune's speech quoted above). Moore became aware "of the strange and gripping tragedy that occurred when the Indian belief in a world of night and in the power of dreams clashed with the Jesuits' preachments of Christianity and a paradise after death." Moore characterizes his novel as "an attempt to show that each of these beliefs inspired in the other fear, hostility, and despair" (Moore 1985, ix).

While the European God had acted decisively in history, in the Christian view the created world remains provisional, a temporary arrangement before the establishment of a new order and the final revelation of God's purposes. Father le Jeune looked beyond death for union with God and for full happiness. The meaning of life for him was intelligible only by reference to something outside it. For the Montagnais and other natives, the meaning of the world is to be found within this sacred cosmos, the purpose of religion being "to maintain or to restore the equilibrium inherent in nature" (Grant 1984, 24). The rationalist assumptions of the European mind made, from the Montagnais point of view, even the most basic discourse impossible. "Learn to talk" was the only possible response, even given le Jeune's acknowledged difficulties with the native language.

In the view of aboriginal peoples nature is the dwelling of supernatural power or supernatural spirits. In the native view there are persons—some of them human and some of them other than human—occupying the entire cosmos. All these persons are spirits. Consequently, spirits are found within people, within animals, and even within what we would call inanimate nature. Everything is alive in the native sacred circle of the cosmos (see Vecsey and Venables 1980, ix). By contrast Northrop Frye says that Christians regard it as a "great error" to attempt to find God or numinous presences in nature. The Bible condemns this enterprise as idolatrous. At best, one might "see the reflection of God from his works in nature" (Frye 1991, 59), but "the Bible is emphatic that nothing numinous exists in nature, that there may be devils there but no gods, and that nature is to be thought of as a fellow-creature of man" (ibid., 26). Frye's summary of Christianity's dim view of nature as a possible location of the sacred stands sharply contrasted with modern spiritualities of nature and environmental theologies that would interpret the created world in a more positive light, even to the point of making it a source of revelation.

This broad-brushed sketch of differences between native and Christian attitudes towards nature remains relevant because many Canadians live in some middle ground between the two, characterized by a kind of ambivalence towards nature as they find themselves betwixt wonder and terror, veneration and revulsion, respect and loathing. Several new movements show a changing attitude towards the natural world, some of them incorporating aspects of the native view (see the "ecological spirituality" set forth in Kinsley 1995). One thinks of ecofeminism and goddess religion or neopaganism, and of various other ways in which some women

especially see their connection to the natural world in distinction
from patriarchal religion. Much of New Age spirituality stresses a
harmonious interconnectedness with nature, as does Matthew
Fox's "creation spirituality" and Green politics (see Albanese 1990,
153-98).

SOME TYPICAL CANADIAN VIEWS

CANADIAN ATTITUDES TOWARDS NATURE, however, derive
from additional sources other than biblical theology or theism, though these Christian views may have been influential. Discussing patterns of imagery in Canadian poetry Northrop Frye lists
three "cultural imports" from seventeenth-century Europe to
North America: Christianity's revolutionary theism with its horror
of the sacred in nature, the power of mathematics with its emphasis
on geometric grids, and Cartesian egocentric consciousness that
located the essence of humanity in reason (Frye 1977, 26-27).
These imports, he goes on to say, were bound to create in the
immigrant to Canada a feeling that nature is threatening and hostile, that the "environment [is] less impressive than oppressive"
(ibid., 29). "Indifference in the landscape" creates "an identity
driven into a last stand of such total isolation, that it can define
itself only by extinction, unless it can make some effort of rebirth"
(ibid., 13). Although Frye describes the Canadian attitude towards
nature as "schizophrenic," and raises the possibility of rebirth, the
negative reaction is recoil before a malevolent or indifferent nature.
    As Margaret Atwood points out in *Survival*, Canadian litera-
ture portrays nature more frequently as ice goddess than earth
mother: "Nature seen as dead, or alive but indifferent, or alive and
actively hostile towards [the individual] is a common image in
Canadian literature" (Atwood 1972, 54). Atwood finds the central
theme of survival equally in the literature of Québec, including that
of nature as monster. Referring to *Maria Chapdelaine* she comments: "The bleak and confined life inside the wall is preferable to
the threatening emptiness that lies outside it" (ibid., 219). For the
sake of useful generalization we can ignore possible differences in
their portrayal of nature between the literatures of French and
English Canada. As a heuristic device consider the conclusion of
Ronald Sutherland, applied to the environment and other themes,
that there are "many significant parallels" (and fewer major differ-

ences than we might have thought) between the two major literary traditions of Canada (1971, 3). Dominique Clift has written that although "Canadians cultivate their differences with uncommon energy, . . . they share a common vision on many topics that constitute the vital elements of culture: nature, religion, science, economics, and art" (Clift 1989, x).

Because nature is dead, indifferent, or hostile Atwood points out that many characters in Canadian literature, at least as she surveyed them in her book of 1972, die by drowning, freezing, or getting themselves bushed. One of her own later short stories, "Death By Landscape," has Lois, a widow with grown-up children, installed in a Toronto condominium above Lake Ontario with no worries about unkempt lawn or encroaching ivy or gnawing squirrels: "the only plant life is in pots in the solarium" (Atwood 1991, 109). Lois has retreated from nature, though on the walls of her apartment hang several original landscapes by Tom Thomson, A. Y. Jackson, Lawren Harris, Arthur Lismer, J. E. H. MacDonald, and David Milne: "They are pictures of convoluted tree trunks on an island of pink wave-smoothed stone, with more islands behind; of a lake with rough, bright, sparsely wooded cliffs; of a vivid river shore with a tangle of bush" (ibid., 110). These paintings, however, bring her, instead of peace, a "wordless unease," "as if there is something, or someone, looking back out" (ibid.).

Lois remembers the time that her best friend Lucy disappeared on a canoe trip at summer camp when they were thirteen. The two girls had gone off from the rest of the group during a lunch break to climb a cliff. Inexplicably Lucy disappeared from Lois's sight, having drowned after falling or jumping off the cliff. The camp director, seeing in this event the prospects of the ruination of the camp's reputation and the loss of her own livelihood, insinuates that Lois may have pushed her. Lucy's body was never recovered.

Years later as Lois looks at her paintings, she sees them in sinister contrast to tidy European landscape scenes of gentle hills and curving rivers, with a cottage, a mountain in the background, and a golden evening sky: "Instead there's a tangle, a receding maze, in which you can become lost almost as soon as you step off the path" (ibid., 128). Her paintings have no background, only foreground that twists and turns "no matter how far back in you go" (ibid., 129). Lois sees each painting as a picture of Lucy, who is hidden behind the islands, or beneath the cliff, or behind the trees. As

Atwood comments in *Survival*, here her character Lois receives no revelation from nature because the European models provide no instructions about where to look for it. Lois remains haunted and in retreat from a hostile natural environment.

Gaile McGregor, looking at Canadian painting of a slightly earlier period, characterizes several typical features of Canadian landscape painting: dwarfed human figures; denial of any meaningful relation between the human and nature; an indistinct background; the low obstructing vantage point; a claustrophobically shortened focus; and, a generally ominous atmosphere (McGregor 1985, 16-17). The negative Canadian reaction to the environment gets extensive consideration in McGregor's bulky book, a study of what she calls the Canadian "langscape," recognizing how language shapes our relation to the landscape. She maintains that "our national response to the environment *has* been almost completely negative" (ibid., 10), in contrast to a more positive American view: "While Americans have generally viewed nature as a source of inspiration, natural wisdom, moral health, and so on, Canadian writers seemingly do not even like to look upon the face of the wilderness" (ibid., 47). Though such a generalization is often made, it seems not to be fully accurate either about the American experience or the Canadian one.

To be sure, the Transcendentalists in the nineteenth century regarded "God and nature [as] almost indistinguishable." Similarly, the Puritans looked upon the wilderness as the Promised Land of Exodus to be transformed into God's kingdom with its inhabitants as new Adams in this wilderness garden. But Lynn Ross-Bryant maintains that the understanding of the land as "a place of darkness to be dominated has been the dominant image in American culture" (1990, 340). Only as a repressed undercurrent of American experience, she argues, is nature seen as the place where one encounters the sacred. My point is that the American view of nature is neither as positive overall as McGregor suggests, nor the Canadian view of nature as negative. Despite the predominant dark view in American culture, Ross-Bryant uses as her epigraph the famous line from Robert Frost's poem, "The land was ours before we were the land's." Would a Canadian ever say that, with its American overtones of manifest destiny, or of seeing the land as a gift, or of God commissioning His people on a Puritan "errand into the wilderness?"

Northrop Frye's claim is that our national mythology actually employs two complementary versions of a pastoral myth. In the one considered so far, we recoil before, or attempt to conquer, an indifferent and hostile nature. The other more positive aspect represents our kinship and rapport with the animal and vegetable world. According to the prevailing Western religious view regarding nature as numinous is idolatry. Nature should be dominated, not worshipped or loved. Yet that conviction has been challenged by an opposite one, that the immanent natural world has a spiritual force (Frye 1971, 245), creating a "meditative shock" in the Canadian imagination (Frye 1982, 49). Frequently, for example, instead of a conflict between the human individual and nature, the individual makes an alliance with nature against society.

The affiliation of a character with nature is evocatively illustrated in W. O. Mitchell's novel of 1947, *Who Has Seen the Wind*. There, as suggested in the previous chapter, feelings prompted by the experience of nature, "most exquisite upon the prairie or when the wind blew" (Mitchell 1947, 123), help Brian O'Connal come to terms with death, especially his father's. *Who Has Seen the Wind* unambiguously manifests the sacredness of the natural world, registered in Brian's "electric tingling" (120), his "breathlessness and expectancy" (108), "as though he were on a tightrope high in the air" (176). Brian's experience of "the feeling" bears a strong resemblance to C. S. Lewis's account of *Sehnsucht* or nostalgic longing—what he termed "joy" in his spiritual autobiography, *Surprised by Joy*: "an unsatisfied desire which is itself more desirable than any satisfaction" (Lewis 1959, 20). Like Brian, Lewis experienced joy in his early childhood. For Lewis joy "was something quite different from ordinary life" (ibid., 19), a longing not to be satisfied by any of the objects evoking it: "a single, unendurable sense of desire and loss, ... which ... had already vanished, had eluded me at the very moment when I could first say *It is*" (ibid., 62-63). Lewis concludes that his experience of joy had its chief significance as a pointer towards God prior to his conversion to Christianity. Afterwards, he claimed, though he continued to experience joy just as often as previously, "the subject has lost nearly all interest for me" (ibid., 190). Brian too is left with the conviction that "the feeling had nothing to do with anything," that the knowledge he was searching for "had slipped completely and forever through his fingers" (Mitchell 1947, 206).

Brian's "feeling," especially associated with the wind and prairie, is awakened by such sights as a dewdrop or a tiny garden toad, such sounds as telephone wires humming, a bucksaw twanging, or a meadowlark singing, or such smells as baking bread, clover, leaf mold, or wolf willow.[2] Brian's experience of this feeling occurs in various manifestations of the sacred unfathomable within the ordinary categories of his young life. The sacred comes upon him at times of death or during experiences of the uncanny or incomprehensible. Physical sensations such as his heart stopping, his knees feeling weak, his throat aching accompany it. Eventually, only memory evokes the feeling until at last he seems to have lost it altogether.

In Mitchell's view, when experience replaces innocence, and knowledge supplants ignorance, then mystery, with its accompanying wonder and questions, may also be dispelled. Religious awe, identification with and sympathy for the natural world, even keeping alive questions about life's meaning—seen in the discussions between Palmer and Digby in the shoemaker's shop—all meet approval. Brian shares his experience of the feeling with these two men and asks if "a person can do it by feeling." Digby assures him, "that's the way" (294).

Mitchell identifies the non-human natural world with the sacred, contrasting it, especially the prairie, with the human world as represented in the town. The resulting dualism of nature and civilization becomes the major guide to his moral universe. While the prairie implies such values as freedom, beauty, and God, the town suggests structure, order, law, and rules, represented in the court, the school, and the church. Set in the midst of this dualism—parallel, in effect, to Robertson Davies' contrast between religion as numinosity and religion as binding doctrinal codes—Brian O'Connal experiences in his growing up the tugs and claims of both worlds. While he loves the prairie, he lives in the town. Though he becomes aware of the cyclical and mysterious aspects of nature's renewal, death, especially his father's, shakes his human and family world. The cycles of nature have a remedy for that finality not evident within the linearity of human time.

GEOGRAPHY OVER HISTORY

IN A BROADER CONTEXT, perhaps the defining aspects of Canadian character come more from shared geography and nature—or our climate—than from historical remembrance of a common past. Northrop Frye uttered what has become one of the most celebrated and puzzling pronouncements about the Canadian imagination when he wrote: "It seems to me that Canadian sensibility has been profoundly disturbed, not so much by our famous problem of identity, important as that is, as by a series of paradoxes in what confronts that identity. It is less perplexed by the question 'Who am I?' than by some such riddle as 'Where is here?'" (Frye 1971, 220). Since first hearing that revision of interrogative priorities I have wondered, both at the meaning of the question "Where is here?" and at the apparent certainty of others about what it means. Its original context and meaning has probably been aphoristically transformed as far away from the possibility of hermeneutic recovery as has Hugh MacLennan's title *Two Solitudes*.

What Frye is speaking of is the role of the landscape, and especially such dimensions of it as the wilderness, the north, and the frontier in the Canadian imagination. Canadians have regarded their country as a land unfit for humans, as an impenetrable wilderness, as a colony, as an obstacle to a Northwest passage, and so on. He continues: "One wonders if any other national consciousness has had so large an amount of the unknown, the unrealized, the humanly undigested, so built into it" (ibid., 220). Interrogation of the immediate environment and surroundings shows that the questioner is not at home, does not know his or her place, is uncertain about the environing situation. Given that, the question of identity cannot be settled until one is "in place"—located and knowledgeable about one's surroundings.

Canadian author Clark Blaise, who has written about living in Florida and Pittsburgh and Montreal, calls his semi-autobiographical book, *Resident Alien*, "a journey into my obsessions with self and place; not just the whoness and whatness of identity, but the whereness of who and what I am" (Blaise 1986, 2). As John Moss writes in his memoir, *Bellrock*, "It is essential in Canada to locate oneself with the land. . . . Geography alone is our common ancestor" (Moss 1983, 47). Moss might have meant "landscape" here because recently he opposes the terms landscape and geography, the latter defined as "the imposition of knowledge on experience in a specified landscape" (Moss 1994, 1). In the later book he asks, "Is it possible to situate yourself, except in landscape? If not, then we are lost; victims of geography" (ibid., 18). Clark Blaise situates his own obsessions with "whereness" in terms of other attempts to locate the sacred: "I was invaded by geography the way other self-conscious youngsters are invaded by God, by music, by poetry, or a butterfly's wing.... The significant blob of otherness in my life has always been Canada" (Blaise 1986, 170-71).

Though in a casual way coming to terms with identity in relation to environment may be seen as inevitably an encounter with the sacred, other responses to nature in Canada, and its impact on Canadians, are more overtly theological. Presbyterian theologian Joseph McLelland remarks that "the natural theology of Canadians is natural theology" (McLelland 1994, 112), that is to say, both a theology of nature and a doctrine of natural knowledge adapted from Scottish Common Sense and British Idealism. McLelland's United Church colleague at McGill, Douglas Hall, maintains that the Canadian experience of nature inhibits an optimistic response to the liberal vision of progress characteristic of Americans (Hall 1980, 78-79). University of Toronto theologian (and Anglican) Peter Slater asks why there is no Canadian equivalent of American civil religion, no "articulated monomyth which follows the biblical plot line of the new Promised Land" (Slater 1985, 92). He too makes the case that what Canadians have in common is our geography and climate—not history. Rather than attempting to discover a plot in our sacred story, we should search instead for its character and setting: "When we look for traces of transcendence and saving power in Canadian experience, we must look more to the land than to our divisive history" (ibid., 94).

Novelist Matt Cohen relates how he was struck in his first reading of Canadian fiction by the unarticulated bond to the land. One innovation in this predominantly realistic tradition has been the way our more visionary authors "re-see" the land, for example, in such novels as Margaret Laurence's *The Diviners*. Cohen makes the intriguing comment that, unlike European fiction where grace occurs between humans and God, in Canadian novels "grace is to be found in a redeemed relationship between [individuals] and nature" (Cohen 1984, 70). A character is thrown on the mercy of a previously violated nature, forgiven, and made whole. Canadian novelists, Cohen concludes, continually reinvent "the country in which [their] novels would take place—if there were a place for them to take place in" (ibid., 71).

Probably the foremost example in contemporary Canadian fiction of a renewed relationship with the natural world, simultaneously an instance of primal religious experience, is Margaret Atwood's novel, *Surfacing* (Atwood 1987a). The narrator's journey is a solo voyage, a descent into the depths of the self under the auspices of the animistic deities of lake and rock as she reenacts an Amerindian vision quest. The natural world, desecrated by the urban disease infecting the landscape and northern lakes, becomes sacred setting and transformative vehicle for a rite of passage. The narrator's rebirth requires a literal and metaphoric baptismal dive into the depths, a prelude to a complete psychic immersion into the wilderness of nature itself. Her initiation begins with the reenactment of the cosmic deluge, becomes a complete identification with the natural world, and concludes with the decision to live a life of "holy secularity." The return to nature in *Surfacing* is an escape from the failures of a personal history that the narrator cannot accept. Her "victimization" (a self-description repudiated in Atwood's scheme) mirrors the larger historical succession of colonial exploitations—previously of Canada by the French and British, more recently of Canada by the United States, and throughout of Québec by the rest of Canada.

A similar vision of the wilderness occurs in Marian Engel's *Bear*, a sometime infamous story about a woman who has sex with a bear—or tries to. The protagonist, Lou, travels from Toronto to an island on Georgian Bay to catalog a library in an octagonal house. But the library has no significance for the regional history of nineteenth-century northern Ontario; instead, it is a gentleman's collection full of British books. While caring for the bear that comes with the place Lou experiences the rebirth anticipated with her trip north in the spring, though like the house's legacy, the contents of this rebirth differ from her expectations. Marian Engel maintains it is not her theory of history that she derived from her mentor, Hugh MacLennan, but something else: "It's my geography I'm taking from Hugh MacLennan: that theory of his that in Canada we have to map the country" (Engel 1984, 100). Her novel *Bear* maps the country through an encounter with one of its animals, not by reckoning with a (nonexistent) historic past (see chap. 8 below).

Overtaken with mythomania Lou loses touch with the bear as a creature of nature and as something other than her. She goes from the rational extremity of methodically cataloguing the library to a passionate and imaginative involvement with the bear. When the bear claws her back in return for her presumption, she is at once wounded, healed, and restored to herself and to her senses. She realizes that there is something incommensurable between her world and the bear's. Earlier she learned this lesson in an encounter with blackflies: "a sign that nature will never capitulate, that man is red in tooth and claw but there is something that cannot be controlled by him" (Engel 1977, 78). Cleansed and renewed she returns to Toronto in September, determined to change her life.

Lou's initiation has similarities with Atwood's narrator's as an integration with the natural world, an individual transformation parallelling a cosmogonic renewal taking place on an island in the northern wilderness. Again, a woman who has experienced the insufficiencies of modern civilized life achieves completion through contact with nature. Its resolution involves balancing civilization with nature's wisdom, or better, redressing the problems and failures of civilized life by insights gleaned from the natural world.

A NEW DIRECTION

WHERE DO WE GO FROM HERE? Let us consider some possibilities from the pens of literary naturalists, taking account of their suggestions about the way we should be going. By the standards of today's ecological consciousness talk about humans dominating and exploiting the environment is abhorrent. Clearly, the attitudes that Frye says were imported from seventeenth-century Europe will no longer do. As Reinhold Niebuhr and others have affirmed, we are creatures of both nature and culture. Accordingly, we cannot find out who we are or where we should go simply by regarding ourselves as no more than part of nature; neither can we regard ourselves as exclusively creatures of spirit set apart from the natural world.

For many readers Barry Lopez's *Arctic Dreams* has become a contemporary classic, helpful from several perspectives. For some readers it is valuable for its biology—almost half of the book is about the arctic's natural environment. Three of the nine chapters are devoted successively to muskoxen and polar bears and narwhals. The remainder of the book is more history than nature, about people and the places they sought. Lopez presents accounts of the journeys of Brendan, John Davis, William Parry, John Cabot, Sir John Franklin, Robert Peary, and Vilhjálmur Stefánsson, about their quests for the Northwest Passage or their attempts to achieve the farthest north. The Irish monks emerge as most heroic among these adventurers because they were least commercial, least dominated by the lust for wealth or conquest or accomplishment. They, according to Lopez, moved "back and forth between insight and awe"; they travelled "without a thought of ownership or utility" (Lopez 1986, 358). Davis and Parry too might have shared the monks' desire for spiritual elevation, their quest for remote places in the oceans' deserts suitable for contemplation.

In the interstices between biology and history, amidst a welter of dates and numbers, *Arctic Dreams* is about relationships, about the possibility of sacrality in the fit between humans and the natural world, about the interaction between high technology and primitive cultures. Lopez has written a modern work of nature mysticism, standing in the line of such others as Annie Dillard's *Pilgrim at Tinker Creek*, Norman Maclean's *A River Runs through It*, George Whalley's *The Legend of John Hornby*, or some of the writings of Wallace Stegner and John McPhee and Peter Matthiessen.

The misguided aspirations of earlier centuries when the wealth of Cathay shaped people's dreams of a Northwest Passage have their modern counterpart in the arid, alienated lives on northern drilling rigs. At military and industrial sites in the modern Arctic there is "a sadness born of the dismalness of life . . . which no amount of red velour, free arcade games, and open snack bars can erase" (ibid., 397). In a dismissive or violent attitude towards the land, one sees dreams shaped only by drugs, alcohol, and pornography—dreams whose operative language comprises "seduction, domestication, domination, control" (ibid., 398).

In retreat from the surfeit of technological knowingness in which we have abandoned our wounded earth for the possession of the moon or the false security of a scheme such as "Star Wars," the by now almost mercifully forgotten American government's Strategic Defense Initiative, Lopez would have us discover a primal relation to the land for our salvation. In the correspondence among the Inuit of a spiritual landscape existing alongside the physical landscape lies the possibility of legitimate dreams, imaginings, and ideas that could make the northern spaces into places, that alien territory into our home. Lopez puts it this way: "Occasionally one sees something fleeting in the land, a moment when line, color, and movement intensify and something sacred is revealed, leading one to believe that there is another realm of reality corresponding to the physical one but different" (ibid., 274).

Arctic Dreams shows with passion and eloquence how the ideas in the minds of the beholders become the metaphors by which the imagination shapes the landscape to fit its dreams (also the central theme, incidentally, of Simon Schama's mammoth *Landscape and Memory* [1995]). Lopez shows the poverty and possessiveness of the modern soulscape, the resulting disregard and even hatred for the exterior landscape, and the possibility of reshaping our dreams to help us towards the congruity with reality and achieved wisdom that northern native peoples have possessed all along. While never becoming overtly pedantic or preachy, Lopez presents a persuasive argument for the coherent vision of indigenous people: European culture "has yet to understand the wisdom . . . that lies in the richness and sanctity of a wild landscape, what it can mean in the unfolding of human life, the staying of a troubled human spirit" (ibid., 406).

Another possibility for a new relationship with nature is set forth in Harold Horwood's book of 1987, *Dancing on the Shore*, subtitled "A Celebration of Life at Annapolis Basin." Horwood's account is an exaltation of the natural world in a kind of pantheistic vision. His book is filled with close-up and appreciative observations of nature—birds, seals, squirrels, flowers—near his home in Nova Scotia and of a kind familiar from the work of Annie Dillard or Barry Lopez. The difference is that Horwood sees humanity subsumed within the natural world, to the extent that he feels that the degradation to the environment caused by men and women is finally insignificant. He offers no disapproval of megaprojects such as Hydro Québec's in the region of James Bay: "I'm not a bit sure that humans modify their environment to any greater extent than earthworms, for example" (Horwood 1987, 195). Even allowing for differences in scale one finds that hard to swallow. Horwood's evolutionary naturalism provides him with no grounds for favouring humans over other species: "I'm not at all sure that the German gas ovens or the American nuclear bombing of Japan were

any more appalling than the destruction of the buffalo or the exter-
mination of the passenger pigeon" (ibid., 50). Elsewhere though he
seems to hate humans with Swiftian distaste, siding with nature
against them (or, better, us): "It is indeed difficult to believe that
any creature as atrocious as the human animal can have an evolutionary future, that anything so opposed to the very thrust of life
can be tolerated by the living universe" (ibid., 204).

In contrast to Horwood, a more sensitively balanced and
nuanced view exists in a book from the other end of the country,
from Canada's west coast—Richard Nelson's *The Island Within*.
Nelson is a cultural anthropologist who has spent twenty-five years
living and working with North American natives, especially the
Koyukon people. He considers that the Koyukon teachings do not
conceive the forest, for instance, as merely "a place to invoke the
sacred," nor as "an expression or representation of sacredness"
(1989, 52). Rather, "the forest is sacredness itself." In contrast to
the classic Christian depiction of the place and role of the natural
world, in this native understanding, "Nature is not merely created
by God; nature *is* God" (ibid.). In his book Nelson explores one
Pacific coast island using techniques learned from the natives, prov-
ing his conviction that "there are many paths to a meaningful sense
of the natural world." Eventually Nelson loses his sense of separateness from nature to the point that he can affirm: "I am the
island and the island is me" (250).

At the conclusion of *The Island Within* comes a statement that
epitomizes Nelson's approach, adapted from the Koyukons, and
pointing in one possible direction: "Expect nothing of nature,
but . . . humbly receive its mystery, beauty, food, and life. . . . show
the same respect toward nature that is shown toward humans,
acknowledging that spirit and sacredness pervade all things." The
basic principle of this native worldview is to "approach all life, of
which humans are a part, with humility and restraint. All things are
among the chosen" (ibid., 277). While deeply indebted to native
peoples and "borrowing heavily from their teachings," Nelson
affirms that he is "deeply committed to the Euro-American culture" into which he was born (Nelson 1989, xii).

However, both Frye and Atwood quote the same statement
from George Grant's declaration in *Technology and Empire* that
suggests a limit to non-native adaptation of a native understanding

of nature. In fact, Grant argues the impossibility of non-natives taking on the native position:

> That conquering relation to place has left its mark within us. When we go into the Rockies we may have the sense that gods are there. But if so, they cannot manifest themselves to us as ours. They are the gods of another race, and we cannot know them because of what we are, and what we did. There can be nothing immemorial for us except the environment as object. (Frye 1977, 28; cf. Atwood 1972, 90)

Grant seems to be saying that the historical legacy of European immigration to North America dooms non-native Canadians to continuing alienation from the natural environment, to a lack of spiritual connection with the landscape. But Northrop Frye suggests that, although Grant's statement sounds irrefutable, contemporary poets are showing how "white Canadians, in their imaginations, are no longer immigrants but are becoming indigenous" (Frye 1977, 40). And Margaret Atwood, in conversation with Graeme Gibson about *Surfacing*, calls Christianity an "imported religion" whose gods tell you to destroy the indigenous gods. She maintains, however, that the "authentic religion" that has been destroyed must be discovered "in some other way" (Ingersoll 1990, 19). For Atwood, Amerindian religious traditions represent what we have to recover by another means. Both Frye and Atwood, then, hold out the possibility of Christianity's apparently negative valuation of natural numinosity being revised or supplemented by means of some kind of synthetic adaptation or imaginative appropriation of native religious traditions. Richard Nelson therefore exemplifies the possibility put forward by Northrop Frye and Margaret Atwood of Canadians undergoing an imaginative and spiritual rebirth—though without necessarily surrendering or repudiating all of the aspects of their predominantly European religious heritage—as they are converted to a more indigenous comprehension of the natural world.

Author Sharon Butala, in her autobiographical *The Perfection of the Morning*, nominated for a Governor General's Award in 1994, writes about her spiritual journey in its southwestern Saskatchewan context, particularly as affected by her daily contact with nature. Butala comes to a realization about the inherent limitations in terms of possible affiliations to native religious traditions after her discovery of stone circles, remnants of native ceremonies. She seems almost to be observing the cautions of Grant and Atwood when she says she cannot understand the stone circles "because my history is a different one from that of the Natives of the Great Plains" (Butala 1994, 112). But, she continues, "although I do believe in spirits and in local gods, I avoid theology, even in feminism." She concludes: "Rather than reconstructing or copying Native beliefs, these understandings of the spirit world, it seems to me, come with Nature, come out of Nature itself; come with the land and are taught by it" (ibid.). Like Barry Lopez, Sharon Butala discerns an invisible spiritual dimension, a "presence," in the "emptiness" of the landscape. She continues too the widespread contemporary trend to find religious meanings within the world rather than beyond it, in immanence rather than otherworldly transcendence.

But can "theology" be avoided, as Butala prefers, in the attempt to work out the human relationship to the natural world, taking into account the history of colonial presence in North America, retaining a recognition of how our culture and thought have been shaped by those roots, while at the same time endeavouring to incorporate an indigenous view of nature? There ought to be some middle ground between a romantic or pantheistic idealization of a beneficent nature and a theistic revulsion of horror before a nature regarded as largely demonic. American writer Annie Dillard (1974) seems to me to have gone some distance towards doing justice to both the beauty and terror of nature as she tries to reckon with the coexistence of cruelty and grace. She refuses to pretend that nothing is amiss as she wrestles with the significance of human values in the face of a seemingly indifferent cosmos. The key question for her—and her posing of it is yet another foray into the age-old issues of theodicy—is: "Are my values then so diametrically opposed to those that nature preserves?" (176). Dillard, wondering whether the world ("my mother") is a monster or whether she herself is a freak, thinks that perhaps "right and wrong is a human concept" and that "we are moral creatures in an amoral world" (177). While *Pilgrim at Tinker Creek* may not adequately resolve the problematic lack of fit between humans and their environing world, Dillard relocates the conflict to another domain by retaining her insistence that the cosmos is holy or sacred, replete with both terror and beauty, cruelty and grace.

Dillard's attempt, though, to work through the collision between inherited theological dictates and her own plain experience of living in the world stands as something unfortunately too rare. More usual seems to be a compartmentalization of Christian doctrine, for instance, especially theism's estimate of the place of nature, in some place walled off from an appreciative and sensitive reaction to environment. An interesting example of such bifurcation is found in the life and work of Canadian filmmaker and canoeist Bill Mason. Mason's films, most of them well-known and highly esteemed works done for the National Film Board and remarkable for their engagement with nature, celebrate the canoe, the wilderness, and wildlife. But Mason's Plymouth Brethren and Presbyterian background, especially the evangelical influences of his early life, remain unreconciled with his growing spirituality of nature expressed more and more fully through the canon of his films. His earliest film, *Wilderness Treasure* (1959-62), was a twenty-minute promotional effort for the Manitoba Pioneer Camps where canoe camping was an inherent part of their efforts to evangelize young people. In keeping with the religious convictions of the Inter-Varsity Christian Fellowship's theology, the narrator at the film's end comments that although the hand of the Creator can be seen in the glories of the sunset, one cannot have a personal relationship with a sunset. The Creator can be known and experienced only through Jesus Christ. Here the role of nature in connection with the sacred is identical to that attested by Father le Jeune: the Creation is at best the handiwork of the Creator. Nature points to God beyond the world without itself being divine.

Among the difficulties evident in Mason's last film, a feature-length effort titled *Waterwalker* (1984), are the conflicts between the longstanding patriarchal and hierarchal relationship to the environment characterized by Christian stewardship and the insights of a feminist and native spirituality of nature. One internal NFB memo railed against the sexist Christian theology in an early version of the film: "Must they bring their male God idols into mother nature's sanctuary" (Raffan 1996, 237). Mason's response to this and other criticisms was to incorporate quotations from native sources in *Waterwalker*, partly as supplement and corrective to the use of scripture. Whatever its remaining flaws, the film in its final form reveals Mason's own sense of nature as itself inherently revelatory, especially as discovered and expressed in his enthusiasm for painting. One has the impression that Mason's own artistic and imaginative development as filmmaker and artist was taking him in rather a different direction from the one sanctioned by his explicit (though rather underdeveloped) theological convictions.[3]

To supplement or rectify the Canadian view of nature derived from European roots (as Frye suggests, theistic, geometric, and Cartesian) with native outlooks (or some other alternative view of the cosmos as itself the bearer of spiritual meaning) may be just what our present political context requires and our geographical inheritance imparts. What does our shared preoccupation with geography and landscape contribute to the Canadian character? Dominique Clift says that "unrelenting insistence on personal and social ethics is the product of Canadian concerns with survival in the face of an unfriendly and even hostile environment" (Clift 1989, 205). As Margaret Atwood, in her poem "They Are Hostile Nations," declares, the only affordable war is the battle to survive (Atwood 1971, 38).

Clift concludes that a contemporary Canadian identity is at last emerging, shared in common in both English and French Canada. He thinks that the influence of the British Crown and Empire on anglophones and of the Roman Catholic Church on francophones remained "ethical symbols located outside Canada" in the nineteenth and most of the twentieth century. Clift believes that "geography and climate contributed in creating a common political culture in spite of the conflicts that opposed them [i.e., the French and English] and in spite of their divergent traditions" (Clift 1989, 228). He predicts that this shaking off the psychological burden of the past will strengthen our national ego. Putting aside whatever might seem a bit facile or overly optimistic in this account, perhaps most remarkable is the promise here for the role of the land in furnishing Canadians with the symbols and myths to shape their futures. That opportunity becomes even more attractive if the Canadian response to the landscape incorporates at least partly the reverence of native peoples for nature rather than originating solely from "imported" attitudes and responses—if the natural world, that is to say, is understood as inherently sacred.

The intrinsic sacrality of nature does not imply that nature must be seen as without exception beautiful and benevolent. Canadians know well that human endeavours do not always conform with the purposes and conditions of our natural environment. Perhaps our difficulty in comprehending the negative manifestations of the sacred comes from the theistic tendency to identify the good with the divine, while leaving evil out of the model of ultimate reality, either unpersonified or relegated to some inherent quality of humanity alone. To experience nature as one of the locations of the sacred might mean embracing its negative and positive dipolar aspects as components of a comprehensive view of the world. This kind of dialectical quality within the cosmos, recognized by Rudolf Otto as intrinsic to the holy, gets further elaboration in chapters 4 and 5 below when nature becomes the domain of death, challenging both Western theologies of the natural world and too optimistic contemporary spiritualities of nature.

NOTES

1 The original French text of *The Jesuit Relations* is given on the facing page of Thwaites. This passage is quoted by Catherine L. Albanese as typical of attempts in communication between Europeans and native North Americans (Albanese 1990, 16). See too discussion of the conflict between Jesuit and Huron worldviews (Irwin 1990).

2 Tom Sinclair-Faulkner gave a fine rendition of Mitchell's novel from this viewpoint in a paper presented at the XIVth Congress of the International Association for the History of Religions in Winnipeg, 15-20 August 1980.

3 Much of my depiction of Bill Mason's view of nature comes from a colloquium (and the subsequent discussion) presented at Queen's Theological College on 13 November 1996 by James Raffan, Mason's biographer (Raffan 1996).

CHAPTER 4

IN QUEST OF THE SACRED:
THE CANOE TRIP

> WHAT SETS A CANOEING EXPEDITION apart is that it puri-
> fies you more rapidly and inescapably than any other. Travel
> a thousand miles by train and you are a brute; pedal five
> hundred on a bicycle and you remain a bourgeois; paddle a
> hundred in a canoe and you are already of child of nature.
> — Pierre Elliott Trudeau, "Exhaustion and Fulfilment:
> The Ascetic in a Canoe"

THE QUEST PATTERN

ONE SUMMER ON A CANOE TRIP, while paddling up the labyrinthine meanderings of a creek in Algonquin Park, our party took a wrong turn and lost the main channel. When the tributary became impassable a stranger who had been silently following us for more than an hour asked, "Have any of you read *The Lord of the Rings?*" The sympathy was immediate. Our common experience became shaped and understood through a shared narrative pattern. Like Frodo and his questing companions we had lost our way, been deflected from our goal, expended much time and energy uselessly, and now had to go back and begin again.

That episode was the beginning of my conscious reflection on the similarities between narratives of the quest in literature and the canoe trip. All the ingredients were there: the departure from the known, the voyage into the unknown, and the return to civilization; the obstacles of high winds, rough waters, brutal portages, dissension, and long dreary rainy days; the unexpected pleasures of new vistas, of wildlife seen, of achievements and minor triumphs, and the joy of one's companions; the sense of participation in a primitive reality, or the reenactment of an archetypal event, sloughing off the inessential, and the experience of renewal.

Notes to Chapter 4 are on p. 100.

My argument, briefly, is this: the primary fact of the Canadian experience is a geographical one, whose major ingredient is the presence of the Canadian Shield, dominating our country, comprising most of the "wilderness," and still best explored by canoe. Encountering that wilderness by a canoe trip repeats the quest pattern described in its most familiar form by Joseph Campbell. This version of the quest is inevitably a search for the sacred because, following the argument of chapter 3, nature in Canada may be seen as the locale of the sacred. And, as we saw in chapter 2, narrative (in this instance that of the quest) locates the this-worldly domains of sacrality. But the canoe trip even as a transformative journey into the sacred has a sometimes ambiguous religious significance that can be misapplied with often unfortunate and sometimes disastrous results.

In *The Hero with a Thousand Faces* Campbell draws upon the stories of such figures as Prometheus, Jason, Aeneas, Mohammed, the Buddha, Jesus, and Moses to set forth the "monomyth" of his composite hero: "A hero ventures forth from the world of common day into a region of supernatural wonder: fabulous forces are there encountered and a decisive victory is won: the hero comes back from this mysterious adventure with the power to bestow boons on his fellow man" (Campbell 1956, 30; cf. 36 and 245-46). The career of the hero has three main stages: separation or departure; the trials and victories of initiation; and the return and reintegration into society. Within each of these stages Campbell and others have further delineated additional elements or episodes exhibited in the lives of the heroes of folklore or legend. The three main stages of the quest will be a sufficient basis for consideration, without too specific an analysis of details. There will be no attempt, for instance, to show that within the first stage (Departure) one might find parallels in the canoe trip to "The Call to Adventure," "Refusal of the Call," or "The Crossing of the First Threshold" (to cite some of Campbell's section headings).

Although the hero of myth achieves a "world-historical, macrocosmic triumph," the canoeist's triumph is domestic and "microcosmic," like that of the fairy-tale hero. Campbell argues in his concluding chapter, "The Hero Today," that the modern hero's quest is more personal and internal than it is social. Thus, mythologies formerly socially based and visibly expressed through various formal rites have their modern counterpart within the individual, expressed in dreams. Because the canoe trip is an "objective correlative" (to use Eliot's phrase) of the monomythic quest it exhibits some external resemblances to the archetypes (for example, the canoeist makes an actual journey). Sometimes, though, we will explore internal or spiritual significance in the canoeist's quest (for example, the canoeist achieves no literal boon or spoils). For Campbell mythology has become psychology and Jungian psychoanalysis rediscovers the timeless symbols. For Northrop Frye, however, literature remains the place where myths are expressed and may be studied, especially the quest archetype.

Frye examines literature as a "central unifying myth." The archetypal narrative of romance (distinguished from tragedy, comedy, or irony) is the form of the myth closest to the quest (Frye 1957, 186-203). Elsewhere, Frye places Campbell's monomyth within "the story of the loss and regaining of identity." The archetypal hero's "adventures, death, disappearance and marriage or resurrection are the focal points of what later become romance and tragedy and satire and comedy in fiction" (Frye 1964, 55). Therefore, the focus here is on writings of two main kinds: first, literature about canoeing; and, second, texts on wilderness canoeing or magazine articles on particular canoe trips. Such writings, more imaginative than straightforward factual or historical accounts, accordingly should exhibit the quest archetype more readily. Nonetheless, even explorers' journals move beyond their ostensible factual aims "into the realms of the archetype: the quest, self-preservation, alienation, and the search for identification" (Hodgson 1967, 12).

The journey, with its image of the road, forms a familiar analogue, bearing possibilities for narrative, closely corresponding to our subjective experience of life as historical (Auden 1968, 40-61). As well as the end or destination, the journey has, like life, a beginning and a middle too: obstacles to overcome along the way; forks in the road where choices are made; and, parallel to this spatial journey, is the awareness of time as an irreversible process. Arthurian Grail Quest literature readily illustrates such features. The religious form of the journey is the pilgrimage, with the pilgrim as an image of the transitory human situation (one thinks of Bunyan).

Travel by jet is hardly comparable to travel in a pre-industrial age, when journeys were by boat or foot or horse, daily destinations were variable, and food and lodging were less certain. While a canoe trip may bear parallels to a bicycle trip, a backpacking expedition, or a cross-country ski tour, by virtue of the traveller being self-propelled and travelling light, it has several unique features too—its adaptation to Canadian conditions and its historical significance. Further, to travel by water in a canoe represents a more radical departure from the known into the unknown than any form of land travel could be.

One of Canada's eminent historians, W. L. Morton, emphasizes the centrality of the Canadian Shield—that grim precambrian horseshoe—to Canadian geography and history and, indeed, "to all understanding of Canada." He points out that in contrast to the fertile heartland of the United States the Canadian Shield is one of the world's most forbidding wildernesses, a waste of rocks and lakes and bush comprising one-half the area of Canada. In days gone by the Shield was traversed by fur traders, lumberjacks, prospectors, and miners who "wrested from it the staples by which Canada has lived," though they always had to return to their home base in southern Ontario, or in the St. Lawrence valley, or on the prairies, for there lay the sources of their food. Morton claims that "this alternate penetration of the wilderness and return to civilization is the basic rhythm of Canadian life" (Morton 1961, 5). This rhythm, of course, parallels the rites of passage in the nuclear unit of Campbell's monomyth (separation, initiation, return). It remains to consider the canoe trip, in several versions, as an exemplification of this general movement outlined by Campbell, and given a specifically Canadian context by Morton.

In 1955 Blair Fraser wrote a magazine article entitled "The Fairy Tale Romance of the Canadian Shield." Considering his reputation as an avid canoeist—he was to die in a canoeing accident on the Petawawa River in 1968—we might expect some comment on the spiritual and recreational significance of the Shield. To the contrary Fraser depicted it as Canada's "Ugly Duckling," though a vast treasure chest replete with mineral wealth, being just unlocked, and at last bringing the fulfilment of Laurier's prophecy that this century belonged to Canada. Only in the last paragraph Fraser remarked that no matter how wealthy Canada might become, the Shield would remain mostly empty, and we would "still have the cleansing wild within a hundred miles more or less" (Fraser 1955, 45). Though this version of the Canadian dream (and with it,

Laurier's prophecy) remains unfulfilled, the Shield retains different possibilities. By means of a canoe trip, interpreted through the quest pattern, the Canadian Shield becomes the setting for a less materialistic version of the fairy tale romance.

STAGES OF THE QUEST

THE FIRST MAIN STAGE OF THE QUEST is separation or departure and includes the whole business of preparation: poring over maps, perusing catalogues from outfitters, reading books and brochures describing various routes, discussing plans with the rest of the party, making lists of food and equipment, and so on. The significance of such preparation should not be missed or minimized. The careful selection of food and clothing distinct from the profane routines of ordinary life suggests a break with the usual and the familiar, like the irruption into everyday life occasioned by the sacred festivals of less secular cultures than our own. The very necessity of reducing one's baggage to a minimum requires awareness of essentials uncommon in our cluttered world. When at last the cars are loaded, the canoeist goes on to the "threshold of adventure." John and Janet Foster describe that initial occasion each spring when this threshold is crossed and the journey into the other world begins. Though the weather is still cold, the launching is a magical moment: "The canoe seems to hang suspended above the dark water, momentarily floating in space, quietly separating from the land that has held you throughout the winter months. And now the noise and tumult and vibrations of the city 200 miles away begin to fade" (Foster 1975, 88).

The Fosters stress, as do other accounts of canoe trips, the therapeutic benefits of exposure to the wilderness, its ability to release one's tensions, and the healing effects of solitude. This emphasis is not just the reaction of contemporary conservationists, for similar effects appear in nineteenth-century writings too. During leisure hours spent in their canoe Susanna Moodie and her husband experienced "a magic spell upon our spirits" and "began to feel charmed with the freedom and solitude around us." The language used by Mrs. Moodie suggests an Edenic experience: "Every object was new to us. We felt as if we were the first discoverers of every beautiful flower and stately tree that attracted our attention, and we gave names to fantastic rocks and fairy isles" (Moodie 1962, 155).

Anna Jameson, who in the summer of 1837 made a "wild expedition" from Toronto to Sault Ste. Marie and back, a large part of it by canoe, reports her experience as a travel diary. Her writing bears a strongly romantic tinge: "I cannot, I dare not, attempt to describe to you the strange sensations one has, thus thrown for a time beyond the bounds of civilized humanity, or indeed any humanity; nor the wild yet solemn reveries which come over one in the midst of this wilderness of woods and waters." Her comments upon the effects of "solitude" and of "nature unviolated" parallel Mrs. Moodie's in their suggestion of a return to paradisiacal innocence: "we its inmates . . . might have fancied ourselves alone in a newborn world" (Jameson 1965, 124-25). At the turn of the century, Egerton Young relates his travels by birchbark canoe, emphasizing travelling with an outfit "as light as possible." He continues: "There is something glorious and exhilarating in getting away from civilization for a time, and living close to the heart of nature in some of her wildest domains. Then, when it is possible to throw them off, we get some idea of the despotism of many of the customs of civilization" (Young 1907, 191). For one modern couple, throwing off the customs of civilization meant an escape from the tyranny of the watch and the calendar, as they paddled down the Yukon River without keeping track of the time and without adhering to a fixed schedule: "It was a pleasure; my watch was now my prisoner, confined to the depths of a waterproof bag. Eating, sleeping, starting and stopping whenever we felt like it—there was a freedom that we wouldn't have again for years" (Palmer 1977, 51). Accounts like these are surprisingly consistent in portraying the canoe trip as an experience of separation from civilization and a departure from the known world.

In spite of the gulf between the world of adventure and the ordinary world, the canoe trip is more than an idyllic retreat from civilization to nature. A genuine quest must achieve the integration with nature through a series of trials and ordeals. Otherwise, one suspects harmony with the natural world is something precarious, illusory, or easily lost. Most canoeists, therefore, mention the trials and ordeals following the separation from civilization and central to the initiation into the wilderness. And so it should be if Campbell's scheme is applicable. To reach the interior of Algonquin Park, one must escape the crowded Highway 60 corridor and get away from the busy access points at Canoe and Opeongo Lakes. Then you must traverse at least one major portage of several thousand metres to achieve something like the solitude sought. The Fosters' experience is typical, as they struggle across overgrown portages, beaver dams, and downed trees to reach an almost impassable river with low water and deep mud: "But every obstacle passed was another psychological barrier between us and the city we had left behind, and the photographic and spiritual rewards were remarkable" (Foster 1975, 89).

Canoeing literature is full of tales of hardships endured, especially on an initial journey: the first lengthy portage over rough terrain; an upset that soaks all the gear; a miscalculation resulting in a shortage of provisions or losing one's way; the impossibility of starting a fire to cook supper; the interruption of a journey by winds or rain. Such difficulties are significant chiefly as ordeals demanding a reorientation of the self or one's values. The skills cherished and fostered in the classroom, office, or marketplace are worthless under these conditions, and that realization is itself a humiliating experience. Thus, the perilous journey may lead to a purification of the self, or the dissolution of past images of the self.

Grey Owl's books epitomize the notion of an ordeal undergone to penetrate the wilderness. In his characteristically colourful style he writes of "The Trail," where "the soul of man is stripped bare and naked, exposed for all to see, and [where] his true nature will come out, let him dissemble never so wisely" (Grey Owl 1976, 49). According to Grey Owl (now of course known to be an Englishman who passed himself off as native), the "brooding relentless evil spirit of the Northland" presides over the wilderness, haunts the "fastnesses, with a view to the destruction of all travellers" (ibid., 76 n). On The Trail, travelling by snowshoes in the winter and canoe in summer, "newcomers must undergo the severe scrutiny of the presiding powers, and all who enter are subjected to trial by ordeal, from which only the chosen few emerge unscathed" (ibid., 51). Again: "Day by day, he penetrates deeper and deeper into the Kingdom of the Spirit of the North, where, jealous of such encroachment on his domain, with a thousand imps of mischief to do his bidding, master of all the powers of evil, the brooding Killer grimly bides his time; nor does he always wait in vain" (ibid., 64).

Grey Owl, perhaps deliberately and for rhetorical effect, overstates the evil character of this "spirit of the Northland." He must have known, from his acquaintance with the Indians of the Biscotasing area, that the powerful Ojibwa spirit of the water, *Mi-shi-pi-zhiw* or the Great Lynx, is feared but also revered in a protector role. Similarly, the "imps" or *May-may-gway-shi*, little water-dwellers residing especially near rapids, are more mischievous than malevolent, and are met as friends by Indians who bestow gifts of tobacco for good luck (Dewdney and Kidd 1967, 13-14). Sigurd Olson learned that these spirits inhabiting rapids along the Churchill River system delighted in tipping over the canoe, but ensured that it was not smashed to pieces (Olson 1974, 206).

Regardless, many canoeists testify that the real difficulties result from friction among the members of a small, isolated group thrown together in close quarters. As John McPhee notes: "When trouble comes on a canoe trip, it comes from the inside, from the fast-growing hatreds among the friends who started" (McPhee 1975, 68). Kamil Pecher preferred to journey alone by kayak along the fur-trade rivers of northern Saskatchewan. However, Pecher fell prey to "The Enemy Within" (a chapter title in his book), becoming ill from stress attributed to the tension of loneliness. At least in a group there is always someone else to care for or to compete with, and one's own weaknesses can be covered up through comparison with those of others (Pecher 1978).

One must not overemphasize the canoe trip's physical hardships alone. Whatever form the ordeal of the adventure takes—whether physical obstacles and hardships, the spirits of the wilderness, relationships within the party, or the inner enemy—the trial should culminate with some kind of victory, or perhaps insight, won by the canoeist. A. Y. Jackson describes the difficulties of this initial canoe trip, especially overturning the canoe in a strong current, and learning how to portage properly. At the end of his brief account Jackson comments laconically: "By the end of that trip we had learned a lot about getting around by canoe, how to choose a camp site, how to make fires in the rain, and how to adapt ourselves philosophically to whatever transpired" (Jackson 1964, 85). Similarly Grey Owl speaks of "the spiritual satisfaction, the intellectual pleasure, and the knowledge of power that comes with a victory over the valiant but ruthless adversary . . ." (Grey Owl 1976, 51-52). Probably more common than increased competence or victory over a ruthless enemy (and strongly implied by both A. Y. Jackson and Grey Owl) is the change wrought within by the trials of the journey. The foreword to *Still Waters, White Waters* describes the humility and self-possession of the canoeist: "We were always the lowest object on the landscape, often vulnerable to water and weather. . . . But at the end, alone at night on a corner of the Arctic Ocean, we had confidence in our canoes and ourselves" (Abell 1977, 5). Pierre Trudeau, whose essay interprets the canoe trip as a ritual of purification viewed as an ascetic philosophy, describes its effects on the personality: "Allow me to make a fine distinction, and I would say that you return not so much a man who reasons more, but a more reasonable man" (1944, 4).

Of course, such achievements must be assessed on the basis of their continuing effects in the "ordinary" world. Let us consider, therefore, the third stage of the monomyth when the hero reemerges from "the kingdom of dread" bringing the boon that restores the world. As expected, with the internalization of the quest and the resulting emphasis on inner transformation, the return to domesticity is necessarily more prosaic. The mythic adventurer brings back the runes of wisdom, the sleeping princess, or the Golden Fleece. Campbell suggests that such tangible boons are symbolic of spiritual vision, a glimpse of the secret of the cosmos possessed by the returned hero. The adventurer has gone through a death and self-annihilation that is prerequisite to rebirth in the realization of truth—that is, religious transformation in the other world. The problem frequently arises of applying those insights to the ordinary world. Thus, the crossing of the return threshold is supremely difficult. Lemuel Gulliver undergoes such a radical transformation among the Houyhnhnms that he can barely tolerate his own family upon return: "I began last week to permit my wife to sit at dinner with me, at the farthest end of a long table." Campbell cites the story of Rip van Winkle as typical of the returning hero who (perhaps like the canoeist) has nothing to show for the experience but his whiskers.

The returning canoeist often has an experience of what G. K. Chesterton called *mooreeffoc*—the queerness of ordinary things when seen or experienced from a new angle (and that Sam Keen [1969] suggests is necessary for a sense of wonder).[1] Even today canoeists commonly spend a week in an interior wilderness without seeing a building, hearing an engine, or getting any news of the "outside." The return in such cases is often dramatic: "Your expedition, if you run it according to the Ideal, should end with a final bursting out of the pristine wilderness back to the world of men and machines" (Davidson and Rugge 1976, 239). Anna Jameson illustrates the problematic return to civilization at the end of her "summer rambles." She had looked forward to sleeping "once more on a Christian bed" at the inn at Penetanguishene ("not the worst of Canadian inns"): "But nine nights passed in the open air, or on the rocks, and on boards, had spoiled me for the comforts of civilization, and to sleep *on a bed* was impossible: I was smothered, I was suffocated, and altogether wretched and fevered;—I sighed for my rock on Lake Huron" (Jameson 1965, 165).

Contemporary accounts agree that the major change experienced by the canoeist is an inner one, the exploration of the wilderness becoming a voyage into the interior of the self. A book on canoeing written for children and published by the Canadian Red Cross Society strikes the right note: "Like the voyageurs of the past three centuries, you"ll find that the path of discovery leads, in the end, to learning about . . . yourself" (Red Cross Society 1975, 5; the ellipses are in the text). Even a story in *Outdoor Life*, a formulaic magazine about masculinity, concludes that two paddlers during their 700-mile journey down the Back River in the Northwest Territories had "certainly made marks of their own. Not on the land. But in the frontiers of their minds" (Smith 1977, 107).

A Book of Canada wisely includes as one of three short pieces comprising its Epilogue the poem "Canoe-Trip" by Douglas LePan. There the poet strings together a circuit of lakes and rivers, returning from the wilderness with its limitless "pinelands," "millions of lakes," "clearings enamelled with blueberries," and "flames of sunset." Then the question is: "Now what shall be our word as we return, / What word of this curious country?" And the answer, in part, is that "It is a good stock to own though it seldom pays dividends," that there are places for a hydro plant or a gold mine, but that "whoever comes to tame this land, beware," for there is "no hope to harness the energy here." The canoeist must circle back from the maze to "face again the complex task" and to convert "the dream to act":

> . . . here are crooked nerves made straight,
> The fracture cured no doctor could correct.
> The hand and mind, reknit, stand whole for work.

The entire poem is relevant with its theme of return and the superiority of spiritual wisdom to material boon. It also relates the change effected during the adventure to the demands of the ordinary world upon the canoeist's return (LePan 1987, 77-78).

Another of LePan's poems, *"Coureurs de Bois,"* continues the motif of inner transformation, suggesting that after the destruction of forests and the charting of rivers, then one's travel must be "Through the desperate wilderness behind your eyes, / So full of falls and glooms and desolations." The poem's final line describes the modern *coureur de bois* as "Wild Hamlet with the features of Horatio" (ibid., 73-74). "Never," claims Robertson Davies, "did anyone pack so much insight into the Canadian character in a single phrase" (Davies 1981, 214), our climate having made us a combination of moody introspection and roaring extroversion. If Campbell's scheme applies to the canoe trip, it remains to investigate further the content and nature of the canoeist's transformation as related to Canadian character.

TRANSFORMATIVE QUEST AND
CANADIAN CHARACTER

THE VALIDITY OF THE CANOE TRIP as heroic quest diminishes if the pattern derives principally from male experience, or if it promotes a masculine code of sport. A book on the history of the canoe in North America describes its users' mobility: "It put the fisherman on the water and extended the hunter's range. It carried braves to war and was freight vessel for Indian traders" (Shackleton and Roberts 1983, 2). While the authors do not ignore the canoe as an artistic object, a spiritual symbol, or even a sepulchre, its major uses relate principally to classically male endeavours: fishing, hunting, racing, making war, doing business, exploring, and migrating.

It has been remarked that Arthur R. M. Lower's experience of northern Canada shaped his view of Canadian history. In a 1932 essay he wrote about going into the woods in the spring and coming out in the fall "hard as nails," "rejoicing in your ability to carry a canoe over a two-mile portage without setting it down, or to paddle at racing speed up the length of a twenty-mile lake" (McGregor 1985, 68 n. 10). The first page of Lower's *Canadians in the Making* has this: "Canadians, if they are men of the canoe and the portage, can well enough understand the distant days when all the continent was wilderness. If they are men of trade, they can remember that traders explored a continent. If they are men of books, there have been countrymen of theirs who could wield both axe and pen" (Lower 1958, 1). Now this is history in the manly mode. It is difficult to imagine that the nouns "man" and "men" here include both sexes. Bruce Kidd argues that the "manly sports" of the nineteenth century developed traits associated with dominant norms of maleness: "courage and stamina, ingenuity, close friendships, and leadership" (Kidd 1987, 253).

Similarly W. L. Morton argues that the rhythm of penetration into the wilderness and return to civilization "forms the basic elements of Canadian character": "the violence necessary to contend with the wilderness, the restraint necessary to preserve civilization from the wilderness violence, and the puritanism which is the offspring of the wedding of violence to restraint" (Morton 1961, 5). Yet the idea of contending violently with the wilderness (or anything else) is disquieting today, given not just environmental degradation, but the brutal effects of violence evident in war-torn countries, our city streets, and domestic lives (especially children's and women's). The discomfort increases if violence is inevitably an aspect of the quest, and if the quest is an essentially male activity. The comments about prospectors and fur traders and miners and lumberjacks wresting treasures from the grim expanses of the rocky Canadian Shield have the same masculine ring about them. Morton describes the basic rhythms of Canadian life entirely from the perspective of male experience ("penetration of the wilderness" is a telling phrase).

Asked by Bill Moyers if women could be heroes, Joseph Campbell replied that giving birth is a heroic deed although the male "is out there in the world, and the woman is in the home" (1988, 125). But there ought to be other, nonessentialist possibilities for a woman to fulfil a heroic quest, ones that do not relegate her to the home and keep her out of the world. In canoeing literature other images offset the typical turn-of-the-century photograph of a woman in a canoe seated amidships in a white dress and carrying a parasol. Even in nineteenth-century accounts the testimony of female as well as male canoeists abounds. Besides Anna Jameson and Susanna Moodie and Catharine Parr Traill, Lady Dufferin has left in *My Canadian Journal* a narration of canoeing episodes when her husband was Governor General of Canada. We have as well the story of the canoe journey by four Grey Nuns from Montreal to the Red River in 1844. Among Indians, women as well as men paddle canoes (Mrs. Jameson describes a canoe race involving women at Manitoulin Island). Of a dozen poets cited in *The Romance of the Canadian Canoe* who celebrate the canoe in poetry, one-half are women, most notably Pauline Johnson. Among artists who used the canoe to reach their subject, or painted the canoe as their subject, one thinks of Paul Kane and Tom Thomson, but also of Frances Hopkins and Emily Carr. The photographs in instructional books on canoeing now often show a woman displaying methods of paddling and portaging. Women can probably develop the ramifications of canoeing rather than prematurely abandoning it as an exclusively male preserve. Criticism of particular canoe trips may keep exclusively masculine models from becoming normative.[2]

Margaret Atwood believes that the attempt to order nature by imposing straight lines (walls and roads and fences) on the curvature of nature results in more defeat than victory (tumbledown barns and fallen fences). Religious feminists (and others) have wanted to balance or replace the male, rationalistic dominance of patriarchal religion with a more naturalistic or earth-centred religion. Ecstasy and wonder are the basis of the religion of Dionysus (or the earth-mother), contrasted with that of Apollo (or the sky-father). Chapter 8 below examines in Margaret Atwood's *Surfacing* and Marian Engel's *Bear* the wilderness encounter of a female protagonist who becomes integrated with nature. Engel's Lou and Atwood's narrator encounter the wilderness through adaptation rather than aggression before returning to civilization, in marked contrast with the male hunters of the fictional worlds of Faulkner and Hemingway. Such may be the trend as well in many writings stressing a new ethic of conservation: an adaptation to, rather than a hostility towards, nature.

Northrop Frye characterizes European settlers as having seen nature in Canada as hostile, as monster or leviathan (Frye 1977, 24-45). This "immigrant mentality" makes rationality the essential human power. Derived from a Cartesian egocentric consciousness, this mentality results in a turning away from nature. In some Canadian poetry, according to Frye, Indians symbolize a primitive mythological imagination that may be reborn in non-natives, resulting in an "indigenous mentality" replacing the "immigrant mentality." If former "immigrants" are to make this territory a home, they must form attitudes appropriate to those who belong here, by descending into the self to be reborn. Significantly, the legacy or tutelage of native peoples (our "true ancestors") in a wilderness setting brings about the transformations of the female protagonists in *Surfacing* and *Bear*.

Something like this, it seems to me, is one significance of the canoe trip seen as religious quest. In enabling us to encounter our geographical uniqueness, in making possible a completion of that circuit of separation, initiation, and return, and bequeathed to us by those peoples who were here before we were, the canoe may well be an effective vehicle, not only for the exploration of the wilderness of the Shield, but also for exploring that inner frontier, and perhaps for effecting an appropriate transformation of attitudes through a kind of indigenization. C. E. S. Franks quotes Father Brébeuf's reflection that although on his journeys by canoe he was "sometimes so weary that the body could do no more," he nonetheless experienced a deep peace in his soul, "considering that I was suffering for God." Franks concludes that the modern canoeist can also experience "a deep peace in the midst of fatigue" and "for the same reason it came to Father Brébeuf." The modern canoeist is also "converting the savage," except today the savage to be converted is the inhabitant of civilization—including the canoeist (Franks 1977, 205).

THE CANOE TRIP AS INITIATION RITE

JOSEPH CAMPBELL'S MODEL of the quest as applied to the canoe trip fits a bit too neatly, perhaps a shortcoming this analysis shares with any typological approach. Therefore let us complicate matters a little and test the model; let us see if it can take account of a problematic reality that raises questions about the kind of transformation that the canoe trip achieves. Specifically, does the version of the canoe trip as religious quest developed here have any relevance to a tragic incident of multiple deaths in a canoeing accident? In June 1978 a canoeing accident on Lake Temiskaming caused the unfortunate deaths of twelve boys and one leader. For a week the event was front-page news although it received little subsequent sustained analysis.

The questing pattern of departure, initiation, and return best describes the type of trip that begins and ends at the same place. This circular quest in which the canoeist returns to the starting point inwardly changed recalls the familiar words from Eliot's "Little Gidding" which identify the place of arrival as the previously unknown departure point. But what about a different kind of canoe trip—one that is linear rather than circular? To avoid retracing their steps or because of the impossibility of planning a circular route, many canoeists are dropped off at their point of departure or picked up at their destination, either by car or plane or train. Thus, the internal combustion engine makes easier, for example, a long trip down a river. At first it seems that such a linear canoe trip is like downhill skiing: a mechanical conveyance becomes necessary, destroying the "purity" of the original activity. Furthermore, perhaps the linear trip is more likely to be an aggressive assault on the wilderness, for instance, when would-be whitewater enthusiasts set out to "conquer" a river, as in James Dickey's *Deliverance*. Thus, it seems that the environmentalist and purist would prefer the circular trip as obviously more "natural," harmonious, and adaptive.

However, this simple dichotomy will not do: there are examples of downriver linear quests of a gentle and adaptive kind just as there are vigorous and assaultive circular canoe trips. For example, in the instructional film *Doubles Whitewater* (1977) in *The Path of the Paddle* series by the National Film Board, Bill Mason, accompanied by his son Paul, combines expertise in the demonstration of paddling strokes, the ability to read rapids, and the exhilaration of challenge and achievement with the exploration of rivers as "a spiritual link with the natural world." As Mason states at the film's end, the European way of living left little time for learning from nature, whereas Indians experienced a harmony with the natural world that we have been slow to discover. Further, the relationship between father and son as developed in the film depends upon mutual respect, constant consultation, and Paul's learning to make judgments about the wisdom of attempting to shoot particular rapids without pressure or intimidation from his father. This was an adaptive and harmonious, yet linear, trip.

By way of contrast, another NFB film, *The New Boys* (1974), depicts a circular trip of almost five hundred kilometres from the St. John's School at Selkirk, Manitoba, in 1973. This annual trip at the beginning of the school year functions as an initiation rite, a rigorous trial by ordeal, and a demonstration of the school's credo that "only by confronting the wilderness does a boy become a man." Once this trip begins the boys stop only to eat and sleep, the object being to get back to the school as quickly as possible. Here the canoe trip provides a mock battleground for adolescent boys to test themselves and toughen up their moral fibre through meeting a challenge and hard work. The boys become increasingly wet, cold, and exhausted. When the boys cross a large lake in heavy winds, their canoes shipping water, the film becomes sinister and foreboding in the light of the tragedy five years later experienced by the sister school at Claremont, Ontario. In sharp contrast to the relationship between the two Masons, here the adult leaders function as "demon-masters" presiding over a cruel rite as they spur their young charges to stretch themselves to the limits of their endurance. The trial by ordeal receives religious sanction in a chapel service with which the trip begins and ends. The muscular Christianity common to Anglican boys' boarding schools provides the explicit framework of the rite. If the adaptive quest errs in too quickly forcing a false harmony with nature while avoiding the agony of spiritual growth, the assaultive quest overstresses the trials and ordeals of initiation as ends in themselves.

The same principles and objectives shown in *The New Boys* undergirded the expedition that on the first day out resulted in death for thirteen young canoeists on Lake Temiskaming in June 1978. The Québec coroner, Stanislas Déry, criticized this trip as "an exaggerated and pointless challenge." Déry cited fifteen errors or omissions in planning committed by the St. John's School in Ontario, including the fact that the school had made no effort to find out whether the participants could swim. Moreover, one of the four leaders accompanying the twenty-seven boys was a novice with respect to canoeing. He had been swimming for only two years, had come out from England only a year before, had a minimum of canoeing experience, and had never steered a canoe before. The canoe with him at the stern was the first to founder in the high waves, setting off a chain reaction of further upsets and mishaps in the subsequent rescue attempts. In accordance with the usual St. John's practice, this neophyte was expected to "learn on the job" and, like the boys he was supervising, grow with the challenge.

This tragedy partly resulted from a school philosophy that encouraged confrontation with difficulty and danger, and at times deliberate risk-taking and even foolhardiness. No one consulted weather reports before departure, and the group had driven all night to reach their starting point. The boys had little sleep, and some leaders none. Within a day after the accident, a representative for the school was maintaining that the "best thing" for the fifteen survivors was to continue their trip: "I know these kids and their parents. They'll want to do it for the challenge." He used the analogy repeated by two others associated with the school: "It's like falling off a horse: You just get back on again." The overtly religious responses seem equally bizarre. The headmaster of the school reportedly demanded why God should have allowed such a thing to happen: "What have we done to offend you?" Billy Graham, holding a crusade at Maple Leaf Gardens, told his audience that word had come from the school's chaplain that all twelve of the drowned boys had "received Jesus": "How comforting it must be to their parents to know that their children knew our Lord." And one of the parents announced: "God can bring good out of it," a statement that became the title for a *Reader's Digest* article emphasizing parental support for the school even after the accident.[3]

At the beginning of the film *The New Boys*, the headmaster exhorts the boys to learn how to look after themselves. He tells them that "Mommy won't be there" to remind them to bring along their raincoats, and that "Mommy won't be there" if their sleeping bags get wet. Here, as in many initiation rites for male adolescents, the exclusion of the female is a prominent aspect. Significantly, when the survivors of the Lake Temiskaming accident resumed canoeing two weeks later on the relatively sheltered waters of Rice Lake, it was for a two-hour trip with their parents along, including one mother who had never been in a canoe before. The St. John's Schools, founded as "a reaction against a permissive and increasingly godless society," might be successful in producing the kind of "aggressive self-starter" cherished in the business world. It is questionable whether their formula for manhood can foster passivity and aggression, dependence and self-assertion, and kindness and courage. It is, anyway, not a formula that St. John's has sought to apply to girls as well as boys. The first observation concerning St. John's philosophy, then, is that the values it celebrates seem today to be somewhat anachronistic and aimed at producing achievers in a male-dominated world. The exclusively masculine orientation of the initiatory canoe trips suggests such a conclusion.

The second observation is that the St. John's expeditions illustrate the "immigrant" mentality towards the Canadian wilderness, cultivating rather than subjugating the ego. In contrast, Joseph

Campbell describes the model of what the returned adventurer ought to be: "His personal ambitions being totally dissolved, he no longer tries to live but willingly relaxes to whatever may come to pass in him; he becomes, that is to say, an anonymity" (Campbell 1956, 237). Kamil Pecher, describing his long kayak voyage in northern Saskatchewan, continually contrasts the white man's approach and the Indian's: "The Indian way is to yield to the natural forces and live in harmony with them. Progress is made only at the right time and in the right season. The white man's way is to conquer or be conquered. In the north the lone white man is usually a loser unless he adopts Indian ways" (Pecher 1978, 161). Often Pecher attempts to cross a lake when the water is too rough. During one such crossing, waves breaking over his kayak, he laments his impatience: "I should have waited another day—even two idle days would have been better. . . . No Indian or voyageur would be so stupid" (ibid., 33).

Pecher, a recent immigrant to Canada from Czechoslovakia, had been sent off on his voyage by his old Indian mentor with the words: "Don't hurry like a white man. There will come many things that you won't understand, but be patient. You still need to feel the country. When you return you'll be a new man" (ibid., 1). However, before the old Indian's prophecy is fulfilled and Pecher returns from his harmonious integration with the natural world, he has had to interrupt his trip for a month and to be air-lifted out of the wilderness. Because he took along his "city rush and white man's ways" he developed in the woods the classic affliction of an overworked executive, a duodenal ulcer. Pecher, after the "ordeal" of his illness, resumes his voyage with a changed approach and attitude, taking his time, allowing his mind to "drift freely," considering his life, and ceasing to strive for achievement: "From the point of view of white people I had probably become bushed; to the Indians this was harmony with nature. Here I was, returning not as a conqueror, but as a humble pilgrim" (Pecher 1977, 172). During this 1000-kilometre journey an immigrant finds the indigenous mentality appropriate to the canoe trip as religious quest, and in stark opposition to the St. John's School philosophy.

CONCLUSION

THE APPLICATION OF JOSEPH CAMPBELL'S scheme of the heroic journey-quest to the recreational canoe trip may at first seem a frivolous and pointless exercise. Searching for metaphors, finding parallels, and looking for resemblances and synchronicities is fraught with pitfalls. Is a leisurely summer paddle at the cottage a reenactment of the *Odyssey*? Straining to find superficial parallels is an inherent danger in any typological approach—the tendency to overlook differences and to stress similarities, to neglect the historical realities of time and place when one searches for mythic patterns underlying ordinary everyday reality.

Perhaps as Canadians we are never more nostalgic, never more atavistic, than when we get into a canoe. But it is well to be cautious before uncritically rhapsodizing about the transformative possibilities inherent in canoe trips seen as mythic quests. The canoe has no magical properties to purge people of their vices, change frogs into princes, or even lay anxieties to rest. It is easy to be romantic and sentimental about the restorative properties of the wilderness. But Canadians generally exhibit healthy suspicions about large claims for easy solutions or quick fixes, whether the goal is harmony with the natural world or the making of boys into men.

At the very least, then, there can be adaptive linear quests as well as assaultive circular ones. Some quests that set out with the intention of being transformative end disastrously—the old stories tell us too that sometimes things that might have been good become worse. Joseph Campbell's quest pattern applied to the canoe trip needs testing to see if it can take account of a problematic reality. Has the model anything instructive or relevant to say about a canoeing tragedy? We should be prompted to ask questions about the kinds of transformations canoe trips have been used for. Indeed, the "true wilderness" may be discovered to lie behind our own eyes, within rather than without, in the city rather than in the bush.

What we normally think of as leisure activities have important implications, implications whose importance may grow even as the time available for leisure grows. At the furthest extreme, they may become as great as matters of life and death. The application of the quest pattern to the canoe trip can illuminate the significance and gravity of canoeing, enriching our appreciation as we become aware of some of its hidden meanings; but such an application should also warn us of perils even as it holds out promise, all the while unveiling some of the ways in which our deepest concerns and most fundamental humanity display themselves.

The attempt of scholars of religion to turn their attention to the religious dimensions of leisure, as this essay has done, may appear to be a waste of time. After all, the usual business of religious studies is supposed to be the study of sacred texts, of religious communities, and of historical traditions. These are important matters to be sure, but at the very least I am suggesting that certain aspects of what we normally think of as leisure activities have important religious implications too. The application of a well-known model from religious studies to canoeing can illuminate its gravity and significance, can enrich our appreciation by making us a little more aware of its hidden meanings, and can unveil for us locations of the sacred in areas frequently thought to be outside the domain of religion traditionally conceived. Alternatively, we find that traditional forms of religion, having undergone at best an incomplete process of translation or "indigenization," display a rigidity and inflexibility in their lack of a sufficient degree of correlativity with contemporary culture. In short, examining the canoe trip as a possible religious quest serves not only to alert modern secularized individuals to the sacred dimensions inherent in one of their possible modes of self-transcendence, but also to remind those who are consciously religious of the perils and possibilities of an alliance between their faith and culture.

NOTES

1 "Mooreeffoc" is the phrase Chesterton coined to describe how things sometimes appear strange when they are seen from an unaccustomed angle. One of the examples, in his book *Orthodoxy*, is the word "coffeeroom" painted on the window glass and seen from inside.

2 Some of these issues of the relation of canoeing to women's experience are explored in my essay "Canoeing and Gender Roles" (Raffan and Horwood 1988, 27-43).

3 See Robert Collins, "God Can Bring Good Out of It," *Reader's Digest* 114 (February 1979): 183-210. Details of the Lake Temiskaming accident come from this sympathetic account and from the many often critical articles that appeared in Toronto daily newspapers in June and July 1978.

CHAPTER 5

SACRED DEATH: THE BELCHER
ISLANDS MASSACRE

THE SHADOWS OF ESKIMO PAGAN GODS laughed into the
teeth of the blizzards that swept the islands when distorted
theology led men, women and children to their death. Torngak, the Eskimo "Storm-Child-God" was believed by the
forefathers of the Belcher Eskimo to lure men, naked to a
frozen death. "Avert the wrath of Torngak," the old Eskimo
used to pray. "We hear him riding naked in the wind, laugh-
ing his deadly laugh. Turn him from our houses."
— William Kinmond, *Toronto Star 18 April 1941*

INTRODUCTION

IN THE WINTER OF 1941 on the Belcher Islands in Hudson Bay
nine Inuit people died. In the initial stage two Inuit men and a
teenaged girl were violently murdered; then, seven weeks later, two
women and four boys died of exposure after being driven or led on
to the sea ice without clothing. They all died in what the judge at
the subsequent murder trial termed an instance of "religious frenzy
or hysteria" initiated when two Inuit men declared themselves to
be God and Jesus.

The story of the Belcher Islands massacre has been told almost
entirely from a non-native perspective, through newspaper and
magazine articles, the records from coroners, police, and court officials, and in the form of fictional narratives. Commentators from
southern Canada in the early 1940s, sharing the assumptions of the
day, generally regarded Christianity as the only true religion and
were dismissive of the validity of native religious traditions.
Whereas today native myths and rituals have entered mainstream
popular spirituality or have been appropriated in Christian worship
(see chap. 8 below), then missionaries, reporters, and officials of

Notes to Chapter 5 are on pp. 129-30.

governments and fur trade companies alike tended to be suspicious of the incorporation of native traditions within Christianity. The murders on the Belchers were frequently attributed, as in the case of the reporter quoted at the outset of this essay, to "distorted theology." The Inuit involved were regarded as insufficiently civilized and christianized, their "primitive" behaviour and "pagan" views not yet having been fully supplanted. Religious murders and suicides, especially involving the larger numbers and sensational events attending the People's Temple, the Branch Davidian, and most recently the Solar Temple and Aum Shinrikyo and Heaven's Gate still leave interpreters perplexed and grasping for explanations. The Belcher Islands massacre, though smaller in scale, is just as mystifying and has been subject to similar sensational treatment.[1]

The immense difficulties for a smaller and weaker minority to maintain its traditions in the face of a more powerful dominant culture are illustrated here by the Belcher Islands Inuit and in chapter 10 below by the Japanese Canadians during (and after) their time of internment in World War Two. In both cases the eruption of a cultural crisis necessitates an innovative combination of inherited practices of indigenous or Asian origin with European Christianity. Chapters 1 and 2 above show how the dislocation of the sacred from its traditional domain prompts its contemporary relocation elsewhere, interpreted as being in the here-and-now rather than overhead. Chapters 3 and 4 examine the locations of the sacred in the understanding of nature or in the interpretation of a canoe trip as experienced by Canadians of non-native ancestry who avail themselves of locative strategies partially drawn from indigenous traditions. This present chapter picks up many of its interpretive strands from the previous four chapters, exploring how from the other side of the encounter a group of Inuit in northern Canada attempted its own relocation of the sacred in their effort to bridge two worlds. An examination of these events from the perspective of religious studies shows how among the Belcher Islands Inuit shamanism enters into combination with European Christianity as a way of maintaining continuity and ensuring the future.

Considering the sacralization of death, especially the kind of sacrificial death hallowed for centuries in Christianity, the reaction to the Belchers massacre may seem, if not contradictory, then at least ironic. Most of those killed were women and children, inno-

cent victims of the tragedy. Some of them could even be claimed to
be Christian martyrs who died for their faith. But the tendency was
to regard these Inuit deaths as occurring entirely within a sphere
apart from our own, involving people unlike us. Seen in other
terms the Belcher Islands murders are a comprehensible and even
logical reaction to cultural loss, something more than an outbreak
of hysteria or madness. At the very least these events illustrate for
us a manifestation of contact with the sacred when the resources
and devices of everyday life are experienced as lacking or having
failed.

GEOGRAPHICAL AND RELIGIOUS BACKGROUNDS

THE BELCHERS CONSIST OF about twenty islands extending
over an area approximately 60 by 120 kilometres located about
120 kilometres offshore from the community of Great Whale River
on Hudson Bay's east coast. This treeless and inhospitable welter
of rocky ridges and convoluted coastlines remained almost
unknown and unvisited by whites until the famed filmmaker
Robert Flaherty spent a year there in 1915-16 with a geological
expedition. The Belchers were not properly mapped until 1933
when RCAF planes provided aerial photography of this
archipelago, "so pocked with lakes, pools, arms, bays, inlets, so
bewildering and dizzy with all forms of sea mazes" (Twomey 1942,
184). The best and fullest account of the Belchers—the flora and
fauna and geography, as well as native life—is given by Arthur C.
Twomey, an ornithologist who spent a summer there in 1938 while
doing research for Pittsburgh's Carnegie Museum.[2]

In the early 1940s the Belcher Islands were inhabited by less
than two hundred Inuit who called themselves the "Qiqiktarmiut"
or "Island People." Until well into the twentieth century their only
contact with whites occurred during visits to the mainland when
the Qiqiktarmiut would meet traders and missionaries, representatives of the Hudson's Bay Company and of the Anglican Church,
stationed at Great Whale River. Since late in the nineteenth century
Great Whale had functioned as the principal trading centre for the
Inuit living on the east coasts of James and Hudson Bays. Some
Island People were accustomed to journeying to the post, by kayak
in the summer or in the winter by kamatik across the hazardous ice
bridge passable for about six weeks each year. Probably most of the

Qiqiktarmiut in the 1940s had never been off the islands. A permanent church building existed at Great Whale since the 1890s, served by an Anglican missionary resident at Great Whale River or Fort George several hundred kilometres to the south (see James 1985b).

In 1933 the first permanent buildings were built on the Belcher Islands when the Hudson's Bay Company established a post there. In the early 1940s a post manager and his assistant looked after the Inuit trade on the islands, taking in sealskins and white fox furs, and some items such as boots handmade by the Inuit women, while dispensing the usual HBC stock of tobacco, tea, ammunition, knives, clothing, material, flour, sugar, and biscuits. The view of one observer was that "this Post was originally established by the Company, not because it believed it would be remunerative but because it was requested so to do by the Government, as through the Post Manager a means would be afforded of extending relief and certain supplies to the Eskimos who were believed to be on the point of starvation" (Memorandum from R. A. Olmstead, 11 October 1941).

While no permanent mission station was established on the Belcher Islands until 1959, the Anglican Church was present on the Québec coast north of Fort George after 1852. Two Anglican missionaries in particular, Rev. E. J. Peck ("the Apostle to the Eskimos") and Rev. W. G. Walton (nicknamed "Reindeer Walton" because of his plan to bring reindeer into the area), were well known to the Inuit during their decades of work in the regions of James Bay and Hudson Bay, beginning in the late nineteenth century and extending well into the twentieth. Both Peck and Walton were excellent linguists who translated the New Testament, the Prayer Book, and hymns into Inuktitut syllabics (Marsh n.d. [1967?], 6, 23). The Hudson Bay Inuit travelled great distances from the north, sometimes as much as 1,000 kilometres, to assemble at Great Whale River for trading and church services. A photograph from 1902 shows a congregation of at least fifty Inuit, none of whom would have been permanent residents of the community, crowded into the little iron-clad church for worship at Great Whale River (see James 1985b, 22). Photographs and post journals originating in the early years of the twentieth century identify several visiting Inuit at Great Whale River as coming from the Belchers.

In May 1941 Inspector Martin of the RCMP reported to the Northwest Territories Council about the investigation into the nine deaths that had taken place on the Belcher Islands. (Though just off the coast of Québec the Belchers, like all Arctic islands, came under the jurisdiction of the Northwest Territories.) In reply to a question Martin stated that "no missionary had been on the Belcher islands since 1924 but the natives used the Prayer Book, New Testament and Hymnal translated for them by the Reverend E. J. Peck and the Reverend W. G. Walton" (Minutes 6 May 1941). He added that Rev. George Neilson, the missionary at Great Whale since 1940, had served as an interpreter for the police during the investigation "and afterwards circulated among the Eskimos and told them a wrong interpretation had been put on the Bible readings" (ibid.).

Because all the accounts of the deaths of the winter of 1941 come from southerners, it is difficult to describe or interpret them from an Inuit perspective. White journalists, traders, missionaries, police, and jurists made little effort to account for the murders from the native viewpoint or within a traditional Inuit worldview. The usual explanation was that the murders resulted from "distorted theology" (Kinmond) due to a lack of missionary presence. But sociologist of religion Hans Mol summarizes the threats and changes confronting Inuit religion in its traditional form: "Birth and death, sickness, the visit of a stranger, the introduction of steel knives and guns, abundance and scarcity of game, abnormally good and unusually bad weather—in short, all change tended to upset the Inuit status quo" (Mol 1985, 24). Appropriate rituals and observances kept these changes within a stable frame of reference: "The souls and the spirits, the deities and the myths, the taboos and the shamans, the magic words and the rites of passage together built a world which made a stronger whole out of the various forms of endangered integrity" (ibid.). Amid a precarious and uncertain existence, the traditional Inuit religion put great emphasis on the role of spirits in governing daily existence. The shamans would investigate the causes of scarcity of game, illness, bad weather, difficult relations, and poor hunting luck by considering how the spirits might be offended or taboos violated.

The naturalist Lucien Turner, who worked in the northern part of the Québec-Labrador peninsula from 1882-84, has been praised for his careful and astute observations of the life and activities of the Inuit, including their shamans. Turner provides detailed accounts of the shamans' mediation between their society and a supernatural world charged with spirits, especially how the shaman deals with the "Tung ak" or great spirit "who is nothing more or less than death, which ever seeks to torment and harass the lives of people that their spirits may go to dwell with him" (Turner 1894, 30). Presumably this "greatest Tungaksoak or great Tung Ak" is the same as "Torngak," referred to by William Kinmond (see the epigraph to this chapter). The designs of the Tung ak can be thwarted by fasting and abstinence and through the intercession of the shaman who learns "the secret of preserving life, or driving out the evil which causes death" (ibid.). The authority of the shamans, and their knowledge of supernatural phenomena, was considered to be enormous. They were consulted on "nearly all the important undertakings of life in order that he [or she] may manage the spirits which will insure success" (ibid., 32). Perhaps most significantly, Turner also says that it lay within the shaman's power to order "some sort of punishment or . . . an act of penance" to relieve someone of the spell of an evil spirit. He thought that conversion to Christianity for some of these Inuit was "merely nominal," and that once they found themselves beyond the range of the missionary-teacher they reverted to the shamans (ibid., 15). Concerning the Belcher Islands Inuit he specifically comments: "These people are represented as often being driven to greatest extremity for food" (ibid., 16), an observation that frequently recurs among non-native observers of the Qiqiktarmiut.

Turner also relates various Inuit stories he collected. In one of them, called "The Coming of the White People," the Inuit are on the brink of starvation, having exhausted nearly all their supplies of food and being close to death. At this point "the greatest Tungaksoak or great Tung Ak [the most powerful of all the spirits] determined to bring relief and prophesied that people having light hair and white skins would come in an immense úmiak" (Turner 1894, 97). Then a puppy was put adrift on an old sealskin boot and nearly forgotten until one day "a strange white object like an iceberg came directly toward the shore" (ibid.). "In a few moments the puppy, now a man, announced that the people had come with many curious things in their vessel. The man immediately became a dog" (ibid.). In addition to explaining the origins of whites, often said by the Inuit to be descended from dogs, this story bears strong similarities to accounts of cargo cults or apocalyptic traditions where the introduction of foreign trade items and currency initially creates an expectation of reciprocity or rescue. However, eventually the appearance of foreign goods ends up generating a crisis: "How could one enter into reciprocal relations with the white man who possesses and hoards all this 'stuff,' whose manufacture took place in some distant land which the native has never seen?" (Smith 1982, 99). A messianic anticipation by the Inuit occurs here—in time of hardship and scarcity these people with "light hair and white skins" in their large umiak would bring relief.

One more piece of background information about some of the participants in the killings helps to set the stage. Arthur Twomey's book of 1942 mentions the Belcher Islands massacre only in a brief footnote (Twomey 1942, 273), presumably because its publication was well advanced before these events became known. Peter Quarack, one of those later charged with murder, is described by Twomey (who gives his name as "Quorik") as dominating the native scene on Tukarak Island, most easterly of the larger islands making up the Belchers. Quarack's hunting territory was the eastern half of the northern part of Tukarak; the western part was hunted by an Inuk named Meeko. Peter Sala, another one of those charged with the murders, hunted entirely on the southern part of Tukarak Island. Of Quarack Twomey comments—and we must recognize this as the external, perhaps inaccurate, view of a white observer—that "many men must have wanted his death and his possessions." Twomey claims that Quarack was "the most boastful, the shrewdest hunter, the most feared and disliked man of all the natives—'Big Mouth' they called him" (Twomey 1942, 188). He also remarks that Quarack, whose territory was the finest on Tukarak, neither encroached on anyone's land nor expected his own to be violated: "He was the Tukarak symbol of justice, but of justice which was violent and strong" (ibid.).[3]

In contrast, Twomey's account of Peter Sala from his knowledge of him in 1938 mostly praises his general hunting prowess and in particular his seamanship on an expedition to capture a seal specimen. Though it was his first acquaintance with an outboard motor, Sala handled the motorized canoe so skilfully in heavy seas that it shipped very little water: "Few admirations I ever had equal my regard for Peter Sala as I saw him in those moments. Ours was dangerous sport, but Peter was an unqualified expert. . . . I felt that actually he was supremely happy through the whole thing" (ibid., 264; see also 258-73 passim). Twomey and others have commented that Inuit openness and their ability to grasp and adapt European technology, related to their marvellous ability to improvise, rendered them vulnerable to cultural incursion.

Narrative of the Events

WHAT HAPPENED WAS THIS. Early in January 1941 Charlie Ouyerack, accompanied by Peter Sala, began to announce that he was Jesus and that soon God was coming to end the world. Shortly, after some promptings by other Inuit, Peter Sala claimed that he was God. Sala told the coroner (28 July 1941) that "Kuqveet said to me, 'You are not an ordinary Eskimo you look much better than the rest of us.' Kugveet said I was untouchable? sacred?" (The question marks in the preceding sentence presumably indicate the translator's uncertainty.) Sala goes on to describe how the others "were praying to me as God," admitting that "sometimes I thought I was God." Asked directly at the trial if he had believed that he was God, Sala answered: "I did not think my body was God, only my thoughts,"[4] perhaps contrasting Christian incarnationalism (and therefore from a white perspective, a blasphemous claim to divinity) and Inuit spirit possession. The investigating RCMP officer, Inspector D. J. Martin, stated in his report that "this religious frenzy was apparently started with a discussion of the Eskimo Bible (Anglican) and the sight of either a falling meteor or shooting star that was interpreted as a sign from the Almighty" (30 April 1941). Charlie Ouyerack explained to the coroner that "when the northern lights were showing we also said Jesus was coming" (28 July 1941).

The biblical context for an apocalyptic interpretation of such phenomena as shooting stars or northern lights could be Mark 13:24-26: "But in those days, after that tribulation, . . . the stars of heaven shall fall, and . . . then they shall see the Son of man coming in the clouds with great power and glory."[5] Also, the Inuit were told "that Jesus was coming and there was no need to work any more." Further, because they believed that material things were no longer required, they destroyed a rifle and shot some of their dogs. Ouyerack testified that this shooting took place because "the dogs were bad. They were Satan." They tore out pages from hymnals and Bibles and burned them in the igloos. As Johnasie, the twenty-five-year-old chief crown witness, said at the trial, "They had burned the books because they were going to get new ones, and they were waiting for Jesus to come" (quoted in the *Toronto Star* 20 August 1941). These acts of destruction, though typical of apocalyptic movements and not inconsistent with Inuit shamanism independent of Christianity, could also be seen as obedience to Jesus' injunction, "Take no thought for your life, what ye shall eat; neither for the body, what ye shall put on" (Luke 12:2).

On 26 January about forty-five adults and children gathered for what witnesses at the trial called a "happy time" at a camp on Flaherty Island. At the meeting, presided over by Charlie Ouyerack, one of his followers, Alec Apawkok, asked his thirteen-year-old sister Sarah if she believed in the return of Jesus. When she answered that she did not, Sarah was beaten unconscious with an *enowtuk*, a stick used to knock the snow off clothing. Everyone present concurred with this action, believing that Sarah was either Satan or possessed by Satan ("Satanasee"). A witness at the trial said that those present recited the Lord's Prayer before killing Sarah. The teenaged girl was dragged to another igloo where a widow named Akeenik beat her on the head with a rifle causing her death.

After the attack on Sarah a forty-six-year-old man, Keytowieack, left the igloo following a scuffle with Ouyerack. Later, when Keytowieack looked into the igloo, Peter Sala struck him in the face with a piece of wood. The next day, 27 January, Sala found Keytowieack in his own igloo "sitting in a bent over position," or, as another witness said, "with his head bowed," perhaps indicating the attitude and posture of prayer. After prodding Keytowieack with a steel-tipped harpoon to no effect, Sala struck him on the left side of the head with the harpoon. Adlaykok, using Charlie Ouyerack's gun, then shot Keytowieack, first in the shoulder and then in the head, killing him.

About two weeks later, on 9 February, Charlie Ouyerack was again preaching the impending end of the world to a smaller group, consisting of about seven adults, at a camp on Tukarak Island. He declared "that he was Jesus and that all the Eskimo must be his followers for he was also God." When one of those present, Alec Keytowieack (whose name differs from the previous victim's in his given name "Alec"), did not accept Ouyerack's claim to be God—"I believe a little bit, but not it all"—he was denounced as a thief and a "Devil." Alec Keytowieack was shot and killed outside the igloo. Each of the three shots, two through his back and one through his head, was on a specific order by Charlie Ouyerack given to Quarack, Alec's father-in-law.

Most of those present "rejoiced at the death of the man who wouldn't believe Charley Ouyerack was Jesus." Even the dead man's wife, Quarack's daughter Sarah, admitted: "I was also glad a little bit." One man present, Moses, would not follow Ouyerack's order to shoot Alec Keytowieack: "I believed in Charlie but I did not want to kill a man and did not agree with shooting Key-towieack." Moses reported that after the shooting the others said, "We will sleep well tonight because he is dead." Peter Sala arrived after the shooting and at his suggestion the others covered Alec Keytowieack's body with rocks. The usual Inuit rite involving a proper burial cairn was not followed in this case; the stones were carelessly thrown over the body.

Peter Quarack, the man who shot his son-in-law Alec Key-towieack, told the coroner that he believed in Charlie Ouyerack because "I thought he would take me to God." Quarack also reported that "Charlie Ouyerack said Keytowieack was no good because he did not want God and Charlie was the big boss." Alec Keytowieack told Ouyerack that "he believed in God but not in Charlie being Jesus." Then, according to Quarack, "the two of them quarrelled over who was the biggest or best man in regard to the bible," a comment supporting the possibility of a shamanic contest between the two men, Charlie Ouyerack the messianic prophet and Keytowieack the Anglican catechist.

Peter Sala, in his statement about Sarah's death, agreed that her brother, Alec Apawkok, "said Sarah was no good, and she was like Satan." He continued, "I think I was crazy at that time. We all thought we had halos, Adleka [Adlaykok] family, Keytowieack family, Shoolukshuk family, Kugvik family, Apawkok family, Char-lie Ouyerack family. Charlie said he had the spirit of Jesus he made us believe him." The specific nature of Sala's last statement—"he had the spirit of Jesus"—contains an important qualification differ-ing from other testimony that Charlie Ouyerack claimed he actu-ally was Jesus. One witness, Inookpuk, said that "he believed Sala and Ouyerack had divine powers but there was a God in heaven as well" (*Montreal Gazette*). When defense counsel J. P. Madden asked what Jesus looked like, Charlie Ouyerack replied that "He looked like a person only he was brighter than the sun." Madden continued: "Where does he live?" Ouyerack answered, "I don't know where he lives," and in reply to further questioning said that he knew about hell but not heaven. Images of light and brightness appear frequently in these accounts, including phenomena in the skies like northern lights and shooting stars, the "haloes" referred to by Sala, and the conventional image of Jesus as "brighter than the sun" invoked by Ouyerack. In traditional Inuit religion the shaman appeared as a fiery presence, or shining with an inner light (Merkur 1985, 158-68).

Oddly enough the two white men on the Belchers, the HBC post manager Ernie Riddell and the clerk Lou Bradbury, knew nothing about the killings, though they lived only about ten kilometres away from the scene of the third death. On 12 March Riddell set off for Great Whale River with a dog team and Peter Sala as his guide (Price 1976, 45-46). Along the way Sala insisted repeatedly to the puzzled Riddell, "I'm a bad man." After their arrival at the Great Whale River post Sala told Harold Udgaarten, a longtime HBC employee of mixed Cree and European parentage (see Twomey 1982, 206 n. 5), about the three murders. At this news a telegram was sent immediately to the HBC headquarters in Winnipeg advising a police investigation. Two weeks later Peter Sala and Ernie Riddell returned to the Belchers accompanied by Rev. George L. Neilson, the Anglican missionary from Great Whale.

On arrival the party discovered that six more deaths had recently occurred, on 29 March, involving two women and four boys. Tragically, Peter Sala was directly connected to each one of the six victims: his son Alec (age 8); his adopted son Johnny (age 7); two nephews, Johnasie (age 6) and Moses (age 13); their mother, Kumudluk Sarah (age 32), who was Sala's widowed sister; and Maria Nukarak (age 55), the mother of Sala (Corporal W. G. Kerr, 26 April 1941). And the woman who was the instigator of this tragedy was Mina, the sister of Peter Sala. (Sala's sister, Mina, usually called "Mina, wife of Moses" in the reports, is distinct from Sala's wife, also named Mina.)

Mina, the wife of Moses, had been present with her husband at the previous murders, both on 26-27 January when Sarah and Keytowieack died and again with the smaller group on 9 February when Alec Keytowieack died. As Sala testified, "Mina believed very much in Charlie as Jesus and Charlie was using her as his wife." Ouyerack later confirmed this relationship with Mina. Just before noon on 29 March, while camped on Camsell Island, Mina "by threats and gesticulations" forced about a dozen others, mostly women and children, out on the sea ice. According to Inspector Martin's report, "She made the natives very frightened by dashing around and amongst them and calling that 'Jesus was coming' she made all of them take of [sic] their Parkhas and some their boots, including her husband Moses." Martin continues: "After she led them far out on the ice she took the pants of the children and prevented them from reaching or putting back on any of their clothes." A statement from Corporal Kerr's investigation, also written on 26 April, connects the divesting of clothing here with the previous destruction of a rifle and dogs: "Mina was actuated by her belief that Jesus was coming and it was necessary to meet him without the material things that constituted their garments."

Asked if his wife appeared normal before this incident Mina's husband Moses replied that "for some days before she appeared to think God was coming. Before that I think she was normal." Asked next whether she had been normal in her mind since the occurrence, Moses answered: "She has been improving every day and now appears to be over her belief of that time and is sorry for what she did." When Mina herself was asked by the police whether she was aware of her actions of 29 March, she replied: "I remember afterwards all that I said and did and was very sad." Mina was taken to two Toronto psychiatric institutions for observation where she was judged to be sane. But on her return to the Belchers for the trial she "was brought into court bound hand and foot and strapped to a stretcher, by several men. She raised quite a row about it all" (R. A. Olmstead, 11 October 1951). The coroner, Dr. T. J. Orford, testified that she was suffering from a "progressive dementia praecox." The jury immediately pronounced her unfit to stand trial.

When news of the murders reached the mainland—and eventually Ottawa—police held a brief investigation in April, followed by a coroner's inquest in May, and finally a murder trial held over two days in August 1941. The difficulties of conducting the investigations and trial were enormous, especially because most planes and pilots were committed to the war effort and sea travel was treacherous even in the summer. The judge (Charles P. Plaxton), crown counsel (Richard A. Olmstead), and defense counsel (J. P. Madden) came by ship to try the seven accused Inuit in a large white tent put up specially for the occasion. The jury consisted of six white men: two mining engineers from a prospecting party on the Belchers (M. E. Holtzman and Jack Rubie), two reporters (James McCook from the *Toronto Star* and William Kinmond from Canadian Press), one ship's engineer (Ed Cadney), and one fur trader (Ernest Riddell from the Hudson's Bay Company post on the Belchers). Three of the accused—Charlie Ouyerack, Peter Sala, and Adlaykok—were found guilty of manslaughter and sentenced; Quarack got a suspended sentence for manslaughter but was ordered to provide for the families of the three men sentenced; the rest—Alec Apawkok, Akeenik, and Mina—were either found not guilty or were considered unfit to stand trial.

Akeenik, the woman who clubbed Sarah to death with the rifle, was found not guilty on the grounds of temporary insanity, though no such provision actually existed in Canadian law. The option of manslaughter was not available in her case and the jury did not wish to convict her of murder, so they gave full weight to the testimony that "her action took place during a period of violent religious hallucinations" (Olmstead, 4). Though all four men could have been convicted of murder Justice Plaxton directed a verdict of manslaughter, citing a parallel case of homicide by an Indian involving "mistaken belief." The Indian had actually shot and killed a human being while (wrongly) believing his victim was an evil spirit or "Wendigo" who had assumed human form. Similarly, the three Inuit murder victims were killed on the basis of the "mistaken belief" that they were "Satanasee." In short, if you murder someone whom you genuinely though mistakenly believe to be the Devil you are guilty of the lesser charge of manslaughter.

While Charlie Ouyerack and Peter Sala received the harshest sentences (two years' imprisonment with hard labour), neither man directly caused anyone's death by means of gunfire or beating (though they ordered the killings). Quarack, however, who actually did kill his son-in-law with several gunshots, received a suspended sentence. While it is true that Ouyerack and Sala were central in the religious movement, one wonders if their more severe sentences were partially punishment for what non-natives took to be blasphemous claims to be Jesus and God. Their larger "crime," against the orthodoxy of Christian monotheism, may have rested on a misunderstanding. Peter Sala's testimony suggests that his actual theological "heresy" amounted only to a belief that he had divine powers; it appears, from his response to questions, that he did not believe himself actually to be God or to embody divinity. Perhaps these considerations seem irrelevant or at least a bit fanciful. Still, it is fair to say, judging from the reaction in Canadian newspapers in 1941, that the public was as much interested in the religious dimensions of the case, though understood at best partially and prejudiced by a restricted Christian point of view, as in its legal aspects.

THE CONTEMPORARY REACTION TO THE MURDERS

FOR CANADIAN JURISPRUDENCE the murder trial on the Belcher Islands raised perplexing issues. The difficulty and expense of conducting such a trial during wartime on a remote island in the midst of Hudson Bay echoes through the hundreds of pages of government documents housed in the National Archives of Canada. Why conduct this exercise involving imported jury members and translators, counsel for the crown and defense, and a judge, all accompanied by two newspaper reporters who ended up serving on the jury? A murder conviction carried with it the penalty of capital punishment, a result that struck everyone involved as a deplorable "solution" to the problem of the murders. Verdicts of manslaughter or insanity were therefore brought in.

The question of the appropriate punishment for these crimes was thoroughly debated, because imprisoning all the perpetrators would deprive the Belchers Inuit of some of their best hunters and food providers. Judge Plaxton's charge to the jury displays some of the worst features of patronizing colonialism. He commented that though "these Eskimos are in fact still at an early stage of evolution as human beings, ... the King's Writ reigns in these islands as our presence here attests" (Price 1976, 60). The legal aspects alone of this case deserve close analysis, especially in the light of recent discussions about culturally appropriate justice systems among Canadian native peoples. While the question today of televising murder trials is a contentious issue, John Grierson of the National Film Board sought and obtained permission to film the Belcher Islands murder trial on the understanding that "the film is for purposes of the archives and not for public distribution" (letter from W. Stuart Edwards, 7 August 1941). The filming was never done because of the costs and transportation difficulties.

Problems arise as well with respect to the non-native understanding of insanity as applied to the case, especially concerning

Mina. Under observation by psychiatrists in Toronto she was judged to be normal and "in fact found her way into the hearts of many of the people connected to this case." Two experienced Arctic missionaries, who regarded Mina as "undoubtedly of superior intelligence," were asked to visit her in the Toronto hospital and offer their assessment. They regarded it as "not only unwise, but practically impossible" to attempt an understanding of Mina's motives in the crimes: "From experience and from knowledge both of the native mind and language we judge that no direct questioning of this native in a foreign environment, while lacking sure knowledge of the real happenings in the native camp, could produce any concrete results." They recommended returning her to the Belchers and questioning her there "in the presence of other natives with knowledge of her past history" (letter from W. G. Walton and Maurice S. Flint to R. A. Gibson, 12 June 1941). Unfortunately, the courtroom trial staged on the Belcher Islands was no more appropriate a context for comprehending Mina's actions than a Toronto psychiatric hospital.

Richard A. Olmstead, the counsel for the crown, wrote a remarkable memorandum of nine pages to the deputy minister, Department of Justice (11 October 1941) in which he summarized in detail the events and subsequent legal proceedings, along the way making several recommendations. In the first of these Olmstead states: "I recommend and strongly urge that never again should the provisions of the Criminal Code be applied to the Eskimo. The cap of Canadian jurisprudence does not and cannot be made to fit the head of these primitive people" (8). In subsequent passionate paragraphs he considers various possibilities for providing services to the Belchers Inuit, including moving them all to the mainland "if the Government insists upon supervising their welfare." But instead of such an extreme measure Olmstead strongly opposed any interference with the Inuit. Finally he recommends that "these people [should] be left entirely to themselves so far as government intervention is concerned." With regard to religion he urges strongly "that unless and until some church considers it worthwhile to the Eskimo to place a missionary permanently on the islands, no sporadic attempts at religious instruction be made" (9). Olmstead's position of nonintervention reappears among others who considered the future of native-white relations in the north. Alan Sullivan concludes his semifictional retelling of the murders in the *Queen's Quarterly*: "To-day they ask little more than that they be left alone in the bleak wilderness they know so well. Why, then, should we violate the austere seclusion of these Spartan lives?" (1944, 28).

The general reaction of newspaper reporters to the Belcher Islands murders includes attempts to explain the religious background to the event, mostly with no consideration of traditional Inuit religion. In some accounts explanatory attempts are fraught with such phrases as "frenzy," "hysteria," or "mania," suggesting that religious zeal or excess was at fault. Alternatively, the problem is seen as a matter of too little Christianity among the Belchers Inuit, or Christianity little understood, or Christianity introduced without sufficient teaching and supervision. To paraphrase Pope's dictum, it seemed that a little religion was a dangerous thing. Of course, such views assume that before the appearance of Christianity the Belchers Inuit had no religion (cf. Gualtieri 1984).

A *Toronto Star* story is typical in oversimplifying religious issues for mass consumption, putting them in terms understandable by most Canadians: "The strange tale of the northlands started in 1924 when a missionary left on the Belcher Islands . . . a copy of the New Testament in Eskimo. It has taken them years to puzzle out the story of The Master. Much they did not understand" (26 July 1941). From here the article goes on to describe how the murders arose from a disagreement about the exact date and time of Jesus' Second Coming, presumably deriving its view of the dispute from the kind of predictive dating prevalent among millennial Christians in southern Canada. An earlier article that appeared before any of the investigations had been conducted portrayed a disagreement between two families, one of which said God could come any time—"next week or perhaps next year"—whereas the other family declared that God would not come soon and not for "many-times-many years." "When the argument became heated, blows were struck and two men and a woman of the family that didn't believe God was coming soon were killed" (*Toronto Star* 9 April 1941).

Many whites associated with the murder investigation and trial, whether police, coroner, judge, counsels, jury, or reporters, reminded other Canadians that the Inuit were a primitive people of a childlike mentality and outlook whose understanding of religion was but little developed because of inadequate teaching. Their suggested remedy lay in a few simple admonishments—issued after the trial by police, judge, or clergy—to the Inuit to revise their false religious views. Both reporters who had been jury members clearly pitched their newspaper stories to largely Christian readers. They tended to make the religious murders into a kind of morality play in which the Inuit catechist Keytowieack became the defender of true Christianity against pagan antagonists. For example, as James McCook wrote in a Canadian Press story: "Unsung hero of the Belcher Islands 'devil hunt' which resulted in nine deaths this year was the aging Keytowieack who stood true to the faith the missionaries taught even though it meant death..." (*Globe and Mail* 26 August 1941). William Kinmond, writing in the *Toronto Star*, took a similar line: "Although no missionary had visited the islands for 16 years, Keytowieack said the men claiming divine powers were wrong. But there was little he could do" (29 August 1941).

ANALYSIS

THE BELCHER ISLANDS MASSACRE has been reported and dealt with in various ways: popular magazine articles in *Life* and *Maclean's* (Callhoun 1941 and Phillips 1956); dozens of Canadian newspaper articles in 1941; a fictionalized version of the events imagined through the persona of Peter Sala in the *Queen's Quarterly* (Sullivan 1944); in several chapters of *The Howling Arctic*, a popular book of reminiscences of northern life by Ray Price (Price 1976); in an exhibition catalogue of Inuit carvings from the Belcher Islands (Winnipeg Art Gallery 1981); in an article in the *Beaver*, the magazine of the Hudson's Bay Company (Harrington 1981); as the inspiration for a short story (Kreiner 1983); and, in a dramatized episode of the CBC radio program *The Scales of Justice* ("God of the North" 1985). The available principal sources used by these accounts consist of trial transcripts, police reports, government documents, and interviews with whites associated with the events. Though none is lacking in sympathy, they are all by whites, representative of the law, the HBC, the church, and the arts. Some of these accounts are quite imaginative; others border on the sensational. None has footnotes or referencing of sources, making it difficult to assess their accuracy (or even follow their trail) without a complete examination of the voluminous files of the relevant archival material.

The present task is, for one thing, to try to find out just what kind of religious event this was. It has been called a Canadian instance of Jonestown in miniature ("God of the North" 1985). The Belcher Islands massacre took place during a harsh winter when food was scarce (Phillips 1956, 119). There had been only brief and sporadic contact with missionaries, though the Inuit had New Testaments and hymnals in Inuktitut. Anglican missionaries had been present at the nearest post on the mainland, Great Whale River, since late in the nineteenth century, though missionary visits to the Belchers were few. One victim of the killings, Keytowieack, was an Anglican lay reader or catechist who resisted the movement. Archibald Fleming, the Anglican bishop of the Arctic, told the *Toronto Star* that "it had been many years since there was a missionary on the Belchers who could help the Eskimos solve their theological difficulties" (9 April 1941). Fleming had himself tried to cross from the mainland (probably by boat, though it might have been by plane) three years earlier, but fog prevented him. Illness and weather kept Fleming from reaching the Belchers again by plane in 1942 (see Fleming 1965, 287).

The Belcher Islands murders are not precisely an instance of a cargo cult because goods or cargo come into the story only marginally. An RCMP inspector who had gone to the Belchers in 1919 on a previous murder investigation reported that the Inuit there were "the most destitute natives I have ever seen" (Price 1976, 53). The Belchers Inuit had then asked the police to approach the government with their request for a boat, tents, blankets, guns, ammunition, and fishing nets (ibid., 54). Nothing ever came of this request though the inspector urgently recommended granting it. While the request for supplies in 1919 and a missionary visit a few years later might have laid the ground work for a cargo cult, nothing in the Belchers violence is overtly directed against whites. Though, as we have seen, a Hudson's Bay Company outpost was established on the islands in the 1930s (see Twomey 1942, 191; cf. Price 1976, 54), the two whites who staffed it that winter knew nothing about the murders until weeks or even months after they occurred.

The two HBC employees, Riddell and Bradbury, were apprehensive after the initial police investigation because the Inuit knew they had summoned the RCMP (though, oddly, Riddell served on the jury without objection). According to one account, the Inuit had even discussed among themselves the possibility of killing the two whites or destroying their radio (Price 1976, 55-57). There is the suggestion that the Inuit decided not to harm the two whites because they got along well with them. Anyway, these considerations arose only after the murders had taken place and the police had arrived.

Perhaps the movement and killings were protest gestures against a dominant society before which the Inuit felt increasingly powerless. For instance, caribou had changed their migration patterns about fifty years earlier and had not been seen in the Belchers since. Previously plentiful furs became scarce and markets changed—white fox furs had dropped in value from about $40 in the 1920s to about $10. In the winter of 1941 the Qiqiktarmiut lacked the means to buy tea and tobacco, their usual luxuries. Perhaps it was these changes that made the Inuit more receptive in the first place to the teachings of the Anglican missionaries. As John Webster Grant says, natives accepted Christianity "when all the birds had fled," to quote Brébeuf's famous hymn—that is, when game became depleted, suggesting a failure of the natives' spiritual resources (Grant 1984).

Charlie Ouyerack may have been a shaman who had visionary experiences. He was weak and frail, as many shamans were, and therefore unsuited to hunting. Ouyerack was an angry man whose own father was murdered. According to one account he may have had some traits of whites, such as envy, untruthfulness, and covetousness (Phillips 1956, 23). He had studied the New Testament, envied the powers of Jesus, and finally imagined that he himself was Jesus. Ouyerack, who was twenty-seven years old, became angry with the forty-six-year-old Inuit catechist, Keytowieack, who was reading from the New Testament in Inuktitut. Ouyerack announced both that Jesus was coming and that he himself was Jesus. The next day when Peter Sala returned from a hunt the people were waiting for the arrival of God. They proclaimed that Sala was God, and Sala accepted this. These epithets may mean that in the figures of Ouyerack and Sala we have the figures of the prophet and messiah respectively.

The various accounts, as well as the circumstances, are confusing and inconsistent. The two Inuit men were upheld by some as Jesus and God, perhaps meaning only that they had divine powers, but people were also awaiting the appearance of God or of Jesus from the sky, suggesting a continuing belief in a "high God." An

RCMP report, however, makes this appropriate qualification, showing astute insight in a debate while others were content with sloppy generalizations: "Although these two were accepted as God and Jesus they, and the rest of the natives, still believed that there was a supreme God in heaven, to whom they would all go to after the world had come to an end. It would appear that Sala and Ouyerack had assumed the status of prophets with God-like powers" (Annual Report of "G" Division, RCMP, Ottawa for the Year ended March 31, 1942). The killing of Keytowieack, the lay reader, may have been partially directed against white influence. Catechists, "often chosen for their strong personalities, somewhat resembled new shamans with authority from whites" (Saladin d'Anglure 1984, 503). If Charlie Ouyerack were a shaman, he might have seen Keytowieack as a competing shaman.

The Belcher Islands massacre bears some general traits noted by Hultkrantz in his description of prophetic movements or messianic movements: "Wherever a tradition-bound culture has come into difficult straits, where there is open dissatisfaction with existing conditions, there seems to be seed for a messianic movement. The ecstatic visions of shamans or other clairvoyant persons release cherished dreams for the oppressed multitudes" (Hultkrantz 1979, 151). Further, the presence of Christian impulses strengthens religious expectations and demands, especially "messianism, a goal-oriented ethics, and an eschatological message." Peter Worsley claims that millennial cults generally occur among people living in "stateless" societies, lacking centralized political institutions, and living "in small, separate, narrow and isolated social units" (Worsley 1970, 235). Missing here is active opposition to whites or a desire to restore the old culture.

John Webster Grant sagely observes that it is "racial arrogance" to "assume that only Europeans could precipitate crises enough to call forth a prophetic tradition" (Grant 1980, 133). He continues: "Especially in the marginal economies of the north, a succession of hard winters, an epidemic affecting animal life, a failure of local leadership, or an unusual portent in the sky might have had this effect, especially if coupled with a perceived weakening of traditional religious sanctions" (ibid.). Most of these factors were present in the Belcher Islands at the time of the religious murders. The various accounts mention that Charlie Ouyerack and the others were impressed greatly by the presence of falling stars and northern lights at the time. During the height of the movement Charlie took another woman in the place of his wife; loosening of normal sexual conventions is a common aspect of apocalyptic movements.

The Belcher Islands massacre might be seen as a prophet movement with a visionary proclaiming the imminent transformation of the world. Though the Qiqiktarmiut burned their syllabic New Testaments as superfluous, destruction of property by fire is a frequent aspect of these movements. The Inuit also destroyed or discarded aspects of their native culture. They shot some of their sled dogs and removed their clothing (made of animal and bird skins) because they regarded them as unnecessary. The movement, then, is not consistently or exclusively directed against removing all traces of white influence from their society.

The movement began entirely through Charlie Ouyerack proclaiming that he was Jesus. According to one account he had made about thirty-five followers out of the 200 families of Inuit on the Belchers before the first murder took place (Calhoun 1941, 14). He especially admired Jesus' abilities to walk on water and raise the dead. It is widely accepted that "the authority of the shamans was menaced by the missionaries" until they were eventually baptized. However, along the way some shamans attempted "to integrate Christian elements with their shamanism." One shaman on the Belchers, according to an anthropologist, publicly dismissed his four spirit-helpers when he decided to become a Christian (Saladin d'Anglure 1984, 503). Several syncretistic religious movements occurred among the Inuit in northern Québec in the first half of the twentieth century. One on Ungava Bay is strikingly similar to what happened on the Belchers: "About 1920 at Payne some Inuit began to announce the end of the world; they killed all their dogs in order to follow biblical prescriptions. Jesus being about to arrive, everyone gathered to pray while awaiting him" (ibid.). At other places prophetic dreams took place or a dead person was resuscitated. In one prophet movement a woman who practised clairvoyant arts proclaimed Jesus' return, called for marriages, and rearranged existing couples. "Similar phenomena," according to Saladin d'Anglure, "occurred in nearly all the villages, especially between 1936 and 1950" (ibid., 504).

The Belcher Islands incident follows the pattern of other movements among the Inuit of Québec and Hudson Bay during the twentieth century, and is comparable to messianic movements among Canadian natives of the northwest as described by Grant. Further, the general description given by Worsley of millennial movements seems to fit as well. Worsley claims that the stimulus need not be something external to the society: often the "cutting edge has been directed not against foreigners or conquerors but towards members of other classes within the same society" (Worsley 1970, 239). Within Inuit social structures there are, as we shall see, grounds for this internal enmity too. Worsley says that "internal, not merely external, antagonisms can equally produce millenarism" (ibid.). Here, he continues, the evils of the world are blamed not on foreigners or the church but on the people themselves: "Their sins are the root of evil; salvation can only come about by the recognition of guilt and self-purification, not by war against the ungodly Establishment" (ibid., 240). Worsley cites examples of millennial movements in Central Africa where the activities of witches were regarded as the source of evil. Saladin d'Anglure contends that syncretistic religious movements among the Inuit, while accompanied by biblical features, "are only truly understandable in terms of shamanism and traditional beliefs about identity, reincarnation, and possession" (1984, 504).

Edmund Carpenter has described what he terms "witch-fear" among the Aivilik Inuit north of Hudson Bay in the 1930s and 1940s. There, following insecurity resulting from disease, depletion of game, hostility from other Inuit, an uncertain economy, and loss of traditional values, human agents rather than angry deities or malevolent ghosts were the source of misfortunes (Carpenter 1968, 56-57). What would previously have been a community problem became an interpersonal one. This might explain why in the three cases where Belchers Inuit were put to death when they opposed the movement each individual was regarded as "Satanasee," that is, the person was possessed by a spirit. In a memorandum to the deputy minister of Justice, the Crown counsel, R. A. Olmstead, points out that the murder of the teenaged Sarah was not "for something she had done or because of malice against her." Rather, states Olmstead, "its motive was to rid their camp of Satan which, according to their interpretation of the New Testament, they were in duty bound to do. Everyone was greatly pleased that Sarah had been killed and a celebration was held" (11 October 1941). The murder of those regarded as deviant was a tradition among the

Inuit; here those opposing the movement are deviant or representations of evil. It is possible they were regarded as witches, even
though, as among the Aivilik, magic was a thing of the past by this
date (see Merkur 1989). This explanation of "witch-fear" from an
anthropological perspective supports, while adding nothing substantial to, an interpretation from religious studies drawing on
Inuit shamanism and spirit possession.

Ironically, the way missionaries presented Christianity to the
Inuit may have encouraged the syncretistic religious movement
among the Qiqiktarmiut of the Belcher Islands in 1941. As Hugh
Brody points out, "Many missionaries, assisted by having learned
the hunters' languages, told people that what they believed was
true, but that the spirits central to shamanism constituted the devils in Christian theology." He adds: "Paradoxically this encouraged
some of the profound and lasting integration of Christian ideas
into existing spiritual systems" (1987, 207). Perhaps by turning the
Inuit animistic view of a world populated by many spirits into an
ultimate metaphysical dualism of good versus evil Christianity
raised the stakes in Inuit transactions with the supernatural.
Instead of being possessed by spirits (or, in Christianity, by devils
or demons) needing shamanic exorcism, now the individual incar-
nates or embodies Satanasee who must be destroyed.

Archibald Fleming, first Anglican bishop of the Arctic, tells
how in his travels among the Inuit of Baffin Island he learned to
present Christianity as fulfilment of what the Inuit already knew:
"We had worked on the principle that in all thought one must pass
from the known to the unknown, and we had not argued with the
Eskimo about their religious beliefs." Fleming says that the Inuit
position towards receiving Christianity was summed up one hunter
who said, "Our fathers told us many things both wise and good.
They did not lie to us but there were many things of which they
were ignorant. If you can tell us more we are willing to hear your
words" (Fleming 1965, 110). As a consequence of this Inuit openness, Fleming says he and other missionaries did not directly challenge the shamans or question their powers. Fleming understood
that the shaman operated when there was adversity, mediating
"between the people and the unseen powers that control the forces
of nature." While he professes "a profound regard" (155) for the
shamans, Fleming also distinguishes the goals of Inuit religion
("magic") from those of Christianity ("true religion"): "The pagan

is unhappy in the power of evil spirits and uses magic in an effort to control them, whereas true religion aims at union and communion with the Unseen" (154).

Perhaps, as Sam Gill says of the ghost dance movement of the late nineteenth century among Amerindian plains tribes (1982, 98-109), or as Charles Long says of cargo cultists generally, the Belcher Islands Inuit attempted in their syncretistic movement to bridge the old and the new. As Long suggests of the cargo cultists, they represent the task to be undertaken by many individuals today who criticize the present order, seek new meaning, and yet also try to establish continuity. They must, he affirms, live in two worlds at once, being "forced to come to terms with a world that is not insured to them through tradition." Through this experience the cargo cultist, perhaps like all of us, must attempt to create new human beings, "new in the sense that these persons will be neither mimics of the West nor persons who wish to go back to their old traditions" (Gerhart and Yu 1990, 213-14).

Arthur Twomey tells about Meeko, a Belchers Inuk piloting his boat in rough weather amidst rocky shoals. Twomey asked Meeko about the mixture of songs he was singing as he did so, some of them recognizable as Christian tunes while others were not. Meeko explained: "I sing hymns to the wind and the waves, for they know me always. I beg them to carry my prayers for me up to the white man's God, for I am too little an Eskimo to ask him all by myself" (Twomey 1942, 359). Quite naturally Meeko turned to his customary spirit helpers, thus affirming his continuity with the past, even as he acknowledged the power and potency—as well as the relative inaccessibility—of the "high god" of European Christians.

A PERSONAL EPILOGUE

ADDITIONAL FEATURES OF THE Belcher Islands massacre are either local in nature or not discussed or accounted for in the literature I have read, either on the murders themselves or in the theoretical accounts of parallel movements.

Charlie Ouyerack, a slight and delicate man to begin with, died of tuberculosis during the first year of his imprisonment at Moose Factory. Peter Sala finished his term there, but was forbidden to return to the Belchers. His sister, Mina, became an outcast from the community after the murders. Her husband, Moses, drowned in October 1943. An RCMP report from Port Harrison in 1953 recorded that "Peter and Mina Sala for the past few years have been wandering from one camp to another and have not found conditions to their liking." The RCMP had heard that they wanted to return to the Belchers. Later Peter Sala lived in exile on the mainland at Great Whale River, the nearest community to the Belchers, where I interviewed him in February 1982 (though not about the events of 1941). One writer, in a *Beaver* article on the Belcher Islands community of Sanikiluaq, says that Sala had visited there to see his eight grandchildren, the children of his son Markosee, "but the islanders did not encourage him to stay" (Harrington 1981, 13). In 1983, however, Peter Sala was at last allowed to return permanently to the Belchers to live with his grandchildren. In many ways Peter Sala's involvement in the murders is the most poignant.

As a leader and great hunter he had a high reputation, both among Inuit and whites. That position probably led to Charlie Ouyerack nominating him as God and to Sala's participation in the movement when others accepted that claim. Sala was already lamenting his role in the killings when he told Riddell en route to Great Whale that he was a "bad man." This acknowledgment came before the discovery of the murders, prior to his confession to Harold Udgaarten at the Great Whale post. Tragically, Sala discovered on his return to the Belchers that his own family members had died on the ice when his sister Mina summoned them to meet Jesus. Corporal W. G. Kerr reported concerning Sala during his imprisonment at Moose Factory: "He is unquestionably penitent of his misdeeds, and has stated that he was to blame for the plight of the other prisoners, not in the sense that he was the instigator of the crimes, but rather that, as a leader, he should have prevented them from committing them. His personal loss of Mother, Sister, and Children, no doubt lies heavy on his conscience. His manner is that of one who has incurred a penalty and is doing his utmost to pay it to the fullest extent" (19 May 1942).

Arthur Twomey praises Peter Sala in his account of a scientific expedition to the Belchers in 1938. He was adept with a kayak, a skilful hunter, and quickly learned how to use an outboard motor. Twomey records that at their first meeting Sala had just landed his kayak, and pulled out his bowler hat from beneath the deck to wear for the occasion (Twomey 1942). Perhaps this episode indicates Sala's desire for the perceived power and prestige of whites, as when Charlie Ouyerack wanted to be able to walk on the water like Jesus. This kind of emulation has its further religious aspects too.

In the present Anglican Church building at Great Whale River a mural behind the altar has the traditional New Testament scene of the Apostle Peter walking on the water to meet Jesus. This mural, however, has undergone an interesting indigenization as the biblical Peter is portrayed as an Inuk departing from a Peterhead boat containing both Inuit and Cree against the background landscape of Great Whale River itself (see James 1981b, 62 n. 5). The artists who rendered this scene of Peter walking on the water were reportedly in demand in the community to paint scenes of the Last Supper, with local Inuit portrayed as Jesus' disciples. In the early 1980s the Anglican priest was taking communion to Peter Sala in his house every month.

A Canadian Press story by James McCook tells how after the trial the Inuit returned to the courtroom tent "to sing hymns and listen with close attention to Rev. George Neilson, Anglican missionary from Great Whale River, as he spoke to them in Eskimo, explaining that Biblical teachings forbid the taking of human life and require obedience to our God" (*Globe and Mail* 25 August 1941). Even Corporal Kerr added his voice to those religious admonishments when he spoke to the Inuit prisoners at Moose Factory: "Through an Interpreter, I gave the Eskimos concerned a lecture on their future conduct. They were very definite in their rejoinder that all their previous concepts of religion were now a thing of the past and they regretted the 'Craziness' that they were foolish enough to allow to govern their actions on the Belcher Islands" (12 September 1942). Kerr also noted that the four Inuit prisoners at Moose attended services every evening and three times on Sunday "where the ministrations of the Rev. Gilbert Thompson should be given credit for giving them a religious outlook both tractable and tolerant and, in my opinion, has definitely offset the 'Hell and Brimstone' type of religion taught them by less experienced Missionaries further north" (29 August 1942). Kerr was not the only one among white observers and commentators who attributed the religious murders to "bad theology," though he suggests the bad theology might have derived from some whites, not Inuit distortions.[6]

FIG. 1. PETER SALA, GREAT WHALE RIVER, QUÉBEC, 1982

When I visited Peter Sala in his home he was in his early eighties. I have a photograph of him sitting there in his kitchen in Great
Whale River, Québec (Figure 1). He is wearing a blue tee-shirt,
possibly a souvenir of his recent visit to the Belchers because on
the front are the words "Sanikiluaq, N.W.T." Sanikiluaq is the main
settlement on the Belcher Islands. This inscription may show Peter
Sala's longings to return to his island home little more than one
hundred kilometres to the west in Hudson Bay. The same photograph shows two objects of Inuit art ("Inuit" in subject matter
even if the techniques derive from non-Inuit artistic modes). On
the kitchen wall hangs a red banner with a block print showing a
classic image of an Inuk woman with a child in the hood of her
amautik. Opposite is a twelve-month calendar with an illustration,
apparently of an Inuit family—a couple and two or three children—in an *umiak*. Between these two Inuit works, and just to the
right of Peter Sala's head, is a framed piece of conventional Christian (probably Roman Catholic) art depicting Joseph holding the
child Jesus in his arms. Both Joseph and Jesus have halos; the
Easter lilies in the picture are a traditional symbol of Joseph's
chastity. What Sala might have made of these pictures or why he

chose them for his wall is anyone's guess. How did a Roman Catholic picture come into the hands of this Anglican? What did he make of Joseph as the father of the infant Jesus? Did he think, as I did at first, that the depiction of Joseph and Jesus was instead of the adult Jesus cradling a child?

For anyone knowing Peter Sala's history this juxtaposition of pictorial images on his wall is immeasurably poignant. Here there is no Jesus portrayed as an Inuk, no reconciliation of native and Western worldviews, though they coexist side-by-side. The common theme in all three pictures is the portrayal of children in the affectionate company and care of adults. The two Inuit scenes are representations of traditional native life, not at all mythological in theme or content—they are "secular," not "religious." The religious picture is conventional Christian iconography. Perhaps Peter Sala, having paid a heavy price for attempting religious integration, has wisely chosen to separate, at least for public display on his kitchen wall, Christian theology and Inuit life.

In 1993, curious to know what might have become of Peter Sala, I used a phone number from a letter received several years earlier and phoned the school at Sanikiluaq on the Belchers. Yes, I was told by the person who answered, Peter Sala had returned to live on the Belchers, and he died there in 1990. One hopes that those last years back home provided him with some measure of peace and contentment, some reconciliation and respite after more than forty years in exile.

As René Girard has so ably argued, "Violence is the heart and secret soul of the sacred" (1977, 31). In Girard's terms, the disequilibrium experienced among the Belcher Islands Inuit in the winter of 1941 broke into their midst with the force of an unknown disease in a sacred and dehumanized form. The subsequent Inuit deaths were in a sense sacrificial killings, directed towards checking or countering the impersonal violence unleashed among them. Into this situation of "primitive" sacrificial killing came the Canadian government with its "civilized" apparatus of legal punishment to exact further reprisals and to strike the last blow in the effort to redress and end the previous violence. For the Inuit this remedy was the experience of a new form of sacralized violence, systemic, judicial, and total in its devastating effects.

NOTES

1 The worst example is "'Messiah' of the Ice-Fields" by Philip H. Godsell (*Winnipeg Free Press*, Magazine Section, 10 January 1942). Derogatory references to "voodoo killings," to an "avenging blood feud that's stained the ice-fields scarlet," to Inuit women as "dusky debutantes" and "broad-hipped," and to "the inability of Stone Age savages to distinguish between divinity and the black magic of their stone age gods" are typical. One Inuit man is "oily-faced," has "beady eyes," and wears a "dirty surplice." Two photographs accompanying this lamentable article, identified as being of Charlie Ouyerack and Mina, are actually file photos of other Inuit individuals.

2 See "Part II: The Belcher Islands" in Twomey 1942, 183-360. Part I of *Needle to the North*, about the expedition to discover a fresh-water seal in northern Québec, was revised and published in a new edition by the present author in 1982 (see Twomey 1982). Bernadette Driscoll provides a useful brief account of the Belcher Islands (Winnipeg Art Gallery 1981, 37-48).

3 In my 1982 interview with Peter Sala about the events set forth in *Needle to the North* he recalled the fear of the two white men when he piloted their boat. He also remembered the unpaid work he did for them, and how he pretended not to understand their requests. Later, in Inocdjouac, he avoided being seen by the whites to keep from being assigned more tasks. In particular he recollected the many heavy steel boxes he helped move about and in which the two scientists kept their samples of birds, plants, and animals for return to the Carnegie Museum.

4 I was unable to locate this statement, quoted in the CBC radio program "God of the North," in the transcript of the trial proceedings held in the National Archives of Canada. That record, however, appears to be incomplete—some pages are missing. Other such statements in "God of the North" that I have checked are accurate and reliable.

   Government documents related to the Belcher Islands murders are held in several large files of material at the National Archives of Canada in Ottawa. They contain numerous RCMP and coroner's reports, trial transcripts, newspaper clippings, and Justice Department memoranda. Precise reference is difficult except by author and date. While the newspaper's name and date is provided (and correspondingly cited in my own parenthetical references), no page reference is provided for news clippings.

5 This passage from Mark is quoted in reference to the falling star in the *Toronto Star* 26 April 1941.

6 Recently James Houston has given an unflattering portrayal of the unnamed Anglican missionary he met at Great Whale River in 1950.

The man is presumably George Neilson, especially since Houston says his appearance reminds him of "some distant Viking heritage" (Houston 1995, 43). When Houston mentions that he had read much about him in the papers in connection with the Belchers murders, the missionary claims that "the press made an awful hash of that," and offers to tell him the truth: "It wasn't my fault" (42). The only other white person at the post, the HBC trader, will not speak to the missionary (who, ironically, refers to the trader as "that stingy lout"). The missionary asks Houston to take along a gift on his behalf for a trader further north along the coast. At first he carefully selects six ptarmigan—"these did not seem to be the largest"—from "the waist-high pile" of a frozen store of "three or four hundred" birds, gifts from his parishioners. Though Houston explains that the plane is half empty and that he'll take along as many birds as he wants, the priest decides to reduce the gift to four ptarmigan: "Let's say two for Mr. Ross and two for Ralph, his clerk" (43).

Later Houston sums up another disparaging portrait of a second Anglican missionary with the comment: "It would be hard to say that I admired most of the missionaries I've known from my Arctic days" (ibid., 149). He defends the strength and persistency of shamanism among the Inuit and wonders why it should not coexist with Christianity.

CHAPTER 6

THEODICY AND THE SACRED:
A. M. KLEIN AND HUGH MACLENNAN

PARALLEL DISLOCATIONS

BEFORE CONSIDERING IN DETAIL how the sacred is dislocated—through the decentring of the Protestant voice in Canadian fiction—by undertaking a close reading of *The Watch that Ends the Night*, it might be worthwhile to examine the pattern more broadly and comparatively. The Protestant experience of the dislocation of the sacred has its parallels in other Western theistic traditions too. The problem of evil (especially as evident in undeserved suffering), launching the attempt at theodicy (the effort, that is, to vindicate divine justice), is perennially central to all religions, and not just monotheistic ones. The experience of unwarranted affliction, and the attending reconsideration of the role of divine providence, may first be examined in another novel, *The Second Scroll*, which bears remarkable similarities to MacLennan's, though originating from a prominent member of Montréal's Jewish literary community, A. M. Klein. As Michael Greenstein observes, thereby establishing its thematic relevance in several ways among the other works considered in this present book, *The Second Scroll* returns "to a religious past even as it progresses toward a secular future—a pattern followed by later Jewish-Canadian writers" (1989, 34).

Published in the same decade by authors residing in Montréal, Hugh MacLennan's *The Watch that Ends the Night* (1959) and A. M. Klein's *The Second Scroll* (1951) correspond at several points. Each novel is strongly autobiographical, resonant with experience from its author's life; each probes the devastating events of twentieth-century history from a midcentury vantage point;

Notes to Chapter 6 are on pp. 152-53.

launched by an experience of the dislocation of the sacred, each attempts a theodicy, raising questions about a providential God's role in the historical drama; each self-consciously breaks new fictional ground, using stylistic techniques appropriate to the demands of a new theme; each incorporates the epic quest of a messianic Ulyssean or Odyssean hero seen through the narrative eyes of his protégé; each attains its resolution by revelatory event, in part, the repetition of a biblical pattern with a final cosmogonic renewal—the stilling of chaos with the founding of a new world at the end.

Klein's novel, like MacLennan's, contains its apostrophes to Montréal. Each novel is rooted in its author's experience of living there as part of the Jewish immigrant enclave or the Scottish Presbyterian one. Both writers had in their previous work shown their awareness and concern for the French in Québec, and both would be disappointed that those sympathies appeared to some to be lacking in depth or subtlety. With the title of one of his novels MacLennan made famous the phrase "two solitudes" to describe the situation of French and English in Canada, whatever people felt he meant by it or however they misinterpreted it. (The quotation from Rilke establishes the conditions of love in separateness—the "two solitudes" might "protect and touch and greet each other"—rather than accepting the inevitability of their enmity due to difference.) And Klein, in his poems of Québécois life, *The Rocking Chair*, had shown poetically an empathetic understanding of francophone and habitant life in Québec. Their novels of the 1950s, though rooted in Montréal, open outwards to a wider world: in *The Watch that Ends the Night* to Ottawa and New Brunswick and, in Jerome's epic voyage, to a circumnavigation of the globe; in *The Second Scroll* as the pursuit of Melech takes the narrator to Rome, to Casablanca, and to Israel.

Beyond their Montréal origins and far-flung journeys *The Watch that Ends the Night* and *The Second Scroll* share other similarities too, mostly deriving from epic characteristics. Each has a larger-than-life hero of epic proportions viewed from the perspective of a narrator who is the hero's protégé and, in some respects, the hero's son. George Stewart describes Jerome Martell as like a father to him, whereas Klein's narrator at the end proudly "intoned the kaddish for my uncle who had had no son" (Klein 1951, 92). Each narrator has changing perceptions of the respective heroic figures, Melech and Jerome. Each hero disowns his childhood religion, and then recovers it at the end, though perhaps in new form, meanwhile either having become a Communist or seeming to have done so. Each hero, too, causes a disturbance or rebellion and is viewed as a healer, sage, or leader almost to the point of reverence. Each hero, for a time, is disavowed or disowned or reviled by the group from which he has come. Finally, in each case there is an apotheosis, when the narrator receives some message or wisdom from the heroic figure who then leaves him, more mature, to continue alone while the hero departs.

To consider MacLennan and Klein, these two Montréal authors, alongside each other, highlights similarities and differences, making the differences stand out even more because of the similarities. Born within a few years of each other (MacLennan in 1907 and Klein in 1909), longtime residents of the same city, both lecturers in McGill's Department of English (Klein in poetry in the late 1940s, MacLennan in prose from the early 1950s on), both winners of the Governor General's award in 1948 (Klein for *The Rocking Chair*, MacLennan for *The Precipice*), these two men bear comparison for other reasons than thematic similarities in their novels.

That there is no evidence of any influence or friendship between them—though each was a close friend of lawyer/poet F. R. Scott—shows how ethnicity and background created enduring insularity even among those sharing other (perhaps literary) commonalities. (Though on at least one occasion "creative ideas were exchanged" between the two authors, when MacLennan was working for the National Film Board in the summer of 1951 [see Cameron 1981, 247].[1])

MacLennan and Klein both imagined their respective Montréals into transformed heavenly Jerusalems beyond time and space. Each man transcended his religious background to attain a universal humanistic vision still continuous with that background. MacLennan the Presbyterian found an individual and personal resolution; Klein the Jew discovered a collective and corporate vision. Each grappled with evil and the meaning of history, attempted a theodicy, and then enacted a corresponding existential verification, as it were, of that literary resolution.

The Second Scroll as Theodicy

UNLIKE HUGH MACLENNAN, A. M. KLEIN confronts a problem not primarily personal and individual, but shared collec-
tively by all Jews, when he addresses the possible annihilation of
European Jewry by Hitler. Yet *The Second Scroll* is deeply rooted in
his own visit to Israel in the late 1940s and written, as Klein put it,
as "a record, a conspectus of my pilgrimage to the Holy Land." His
novel, though, quickly transcends personal travelogue, becoming
an "heirloom to attest to the fact that I had been of the generation
that had seen the Return." Klein becomes the epic voice singing the
tale of Jewry's rescue from Hitler in which he sums up the feeling,
"that even the most sceptical felt," that "something messianic, mil-
lenial, had occurred" (Mayne 1975, 12).[2]

The narrator's search for his uncle, Melech Davidson, is a messianic quest. The narrator follows his uncle to Rome (where
Melech had several meetings with a monsignor and wrote an appreciative philosophical essay on the Sistine Chapel paintings), to
Casablanca (where he organized a rebellion of the outcast Jews of
the mellah), finally to Israel (where Melech was shot from ambush
at Safed, his body soaked with gasoline and then burned).
Melech—"everywhere suspected, nowhere seen" by the narrator—
is a "messianic personality" whose martyred features are finally
unrecognizable. Klein intends to say that this messiah finally "is an
unidentifiable entity made up of the anonymous fractions of total
Jewry" (Mayne 1975, 13), or as he explained to Leon Edel, "the
Messiah is, or is of, or is in, the ubiquitous anonymity of universal
Jewry's all-inclusive generation, he is the resurgent creativity of the
incognitos of the folk" (Mayne 1975, 25).

At Melech's funeral the speakers eulogize him as "a kind of
mirror, an aspaklaria, of the events of our time" (Klein 1951, 92).
The narrator's messianic search has a parallel mission, and similar
fulfilment, in his assignment to translate the best of Israeli poetry.
He finds no "great creative feat" in any of the published poems he
reads; instead, he discovers the miracle of poetic creation evident
all around him in the "nameless authorship [that] flourished in the
streets," as the "Hebrew imagination" is shaped and manifest in
the "inspired metaphor" of various signs and advertisements (84).

Klein's task goes beyond "a joining of biography, autobiography, and history" to achieve an almost audacious and breathtaking
status as new scripture. Perhaps his breakdown is presaged here, or

a phenomenon parallel to Klein's overinterpretation of Joyce's *Ulysses* in which he was finding meanings within meanings. Similar to MacLennan, Klein seems to believe himself divinely inspired in the writing of his novel. To his Christian friend, A. J. M. Smith, he wrote: "As if by lucky accident, everything fell into a pattern, seemed to repeat the stations of your Messiah, seemed to make up a seconding of a testament already seconded." He continues: "I intended a book—an evangel grew under my hand" (Mayne 1975, 13). Klein is maintaining, then, not only the parallels to the Pentateuch explicit in his chapter titles ("Genesis," "Exodus," etc.), and amplified by the appended glosses ("since no Jew can conceive of a Pentateuch without commentary" [ibid., 25]), but parallels as well to the life of Jesus, and to that extent he claims to have written another New Testament, a gospel. Edel puts it well when he says that Klein wanted to show "the Messiah as the Jewish universality and within this, I suppose we might say, the universality of Christ" (ibid., 27).

The novel's narrator (and through him Klein as author) repeatedly proclaims the "one obsessive theme" of the miracle they witness. Even the journalist on the plane, "member of an assimilated Jewish family," who reminds the narrator that "the miracle of miracles for Christians . . . was the miracle of the Incarnation" (71), sees the establishment of Israel as "our version of the Incarnation" (73). Throughout the novel Melech's words are repeated: "When the years were ripened, and the years fulfilled, then was there fashioned Aught from Naught" (38; cf. 86). For Klein, there stands the miraculous fact that "over the abyss of recent history there had risen the new bright, shining microcosm of Israel" (39). Out of the furnace and its smoke comes a resurrected Jewry, just as Melech crawls from the mass grave at Kamenets (36).

But in the midst of the buoyancy and extravagant surplus of *The Second Scroll*, even without its author's claims for it in his exegesis, there is a kind of overreaching. What of, for example, Klein's insistence of divine purpose behind the Holocaust? At the end of the chapter entitled "Genesis" Melech is "enveloped by the great smoke that for the next six years kept billowing over the Jews of Europe—their cloud by day, their pillar of fire by night" (26). Providence is apparently at work even in the smoke and fire of the crematoria as the Jews are led, after their suffering during the Holocaust (comparable to Israel's forty years of purgative wandering in the desert), to the Promised Land.

Klein's theodicy here, proposing the emergence of good out of evil ("Aught from Naught"), extends further in "Gloss Hai" where in the poem entitled "Grace Before Poison" the poet thanks God for creating various fatal substances including nightshade, opium, hemlock, alcohol, and cocaine. Seeming to suggest that whatever is, is good, Klein's exuberant acceptance has about it the feel of something dangerous—as in the poems of *The Hitleriad*—some impulse or idea carried too far, to say nothing of what Leon Edel gently called the "ironic blasphemies" of the suggestion that he had produced a Pentateuch of his own. To propose that the founding of Israel in 1948 is somehow compensatory for the deaths of six million Jews during the Holocaust appears, perhaps especially from the vantage point of a half century after, audacious and overstated. To go even further and suggest that God was at work even in and through the atrocities as part of a providential plan, seems yet more preposterous (though some have claimed that strictly consistent adherence to Orthodox Judaism demands such a conclusion). M. W. Steinberg mentions various juxtapositions by Klein, all of which "clearly suggest a close relationship, a kinship of good and evil" (Klein 1951, xiv). Steinberg maintains that Klein's view understands "evil and death are not things in themselves; they have their place in God's scheme and therefore are not to be vilified or unduly lamented" (ibid., xv). Klein's optimism furnishes in *The Second Scroll* his version of a fictional "solution" to the problem of evil.

Klein's novel, written in the first blush of his enthusiasm at the founding of Israel, is his discovery of the renewal of faith and hope in that historical event. *The Second Scroll* stands in marked contrast to another literary account written as memoir of the Holocaust's meaning. Elie Wiesel, who maintained literary silence for ten years before writing his epochal work, *Night*, sees, like Klein, parallels in the Holocaust to biblical events. He, too, uses the images of cloud and fire to suggest that the Holocaust is a second Exodus in which the Diaspora Jews are led to the ovens. But unlike Klein, what Wiesel in youthful innocence mistakenly apprehended as messianic event turns out to be the unleashing of a monstrous evil, the emergence of the Kingdom of Night when the antimessiah took over the earth. Wiesel's insistent cry—"Where is God?"—receives no answer except silence and, with that, the implication that the providential deity of Jewish history has died, departed, or joined humanity in suffering.

For Wiesel the decisive parallel to Christianity in the Holocaust's meaning for Jews resides in the image of the crucifixion, so central, as Michael Brown has pointed out, in *Night* (Brown 1978, 476-88). Though he makes the death camps the Jewish equivalent of Calvary, and though he maintains that the Holocaust has a stature within Jewish history as sacred event, Wiesel stops far short of invoking any redemptive parallels of the kind Klein offers. The Holocaust may be an Exodus in reverse for Judaism, leading Jews to their deaths; its significance in Jewish history is unmatched since the first Exodus; its importance equals, for Jews, the significance of the crucifixion for Christians. Wiesel, though insistent on maintaining continuity with Judaism—lest Hitler, having failed in his project to kill all Jews, should have a posthumous victory by destroying their religion—proposes no explanation for the Holocaust, nothing to ameliorate the enormity of its evil, preferring the ambiguities of silence (with the tales emerging from that silence), and the persistence of questions to the too-easy answer or facile affirmation.

In his contribution to a panel on "Klein's Achievement" during a symposium in May of 1974 (though not subsequently published in the symposium proceedings), Irving Layton stated that A. M. Klein was not able to assimilate the meaning of the Holocaust and of evil in the twentieth century. Klein, Layton argued, could give us the poems of innocence, but not of experience. Finally, unable to face the conflicts within himself and the darkness of our time, he fell silent (an allusion to Klein's subsequent breakdown and the succeeding years of withdrawal and silence). Layton expressed his agreement with George Steiner's position as advanced in *Language and Silence*, that the only appropriate answer to the Holocaust is silence. Layton claimed that the problem of evil was something from which Klein averted his gaze, as he had earlier done in *The Hitleriad*. While Layton's position had its dissenters, notably M. W. Steinberg, and while characteristically overstated, it remains basically accurate.

The Watch that Ends the Night AND SELFHOOD

HUGH MACLENNAN SETS OUT IN DETAIL, and in several places, the story of his writing of *The Watch that Ends the Night*. He has told how over a period of eight years and with the writing of millions of words, he tried "to shape a new bottle for a new kind of wine" (MacLennan 1960, 39). During the 1950s MacLennan lived continuously with the consciousness of his wife's illness. Her rheumatic heart caused a series of embolisms, operations, debilitating reversals, and recoveries, until MacLennan saw them both experiencing an almost endless cycle of deaths and resurrections.[3] As he commented in a letter to John Gray after a trip to Scotland: "In the course of writing it I became a religious man, and the book is essentially religious in nature. One night in the Highlands its real theme came to me. It is contained in the verse of the 90th Psalm: 'Thou turnest man to destruction; and sayest, Return, ye children of men'" (see Cameron 1981, 286). Dorothy Duncan's death just after Easter 1957 finally released in him one last burst of creative energy in which he recast the entire novel. MacLennan reported that the effort almost killed him, but that he felt divinely inspired and guided in his writing. His letters to John Gray about *The Watch* suggest an author confident that his work is deeply significant, originating beyond himself—"I saw how I had been used by sources very mysterious" (ibid., 281)—and certain to have life and meaning for many years to come, whatever its critical reception.

MacLennan confronts not just the numbing question of natural evil, and the maldistribution of illness and death, as George Stewart wonders why Catherine should be condemned to an early death while thousands of others go free, but his narration poses the question of what meaning human life can have when it becomes a seemingly endless cycle of near-deaths and recoveries. George sees Catherine as a mouse being played with by a cat—"and the cat was God." The question of the goal and final purpose of life is posed with a particular insistency when each recovery, each resurrection from death, becomes simply a renewal of the struggle, another round in the match. The futility of being condemned to a seemingly endless cycle of repetitions without the telos of linearity is addressed when Stewart compares himself to Sisyphus, Camus' paradigm of the absurd hero.

During the decade of the 1950s it appears that MacLennan decided, as he later said to an interviewer in a film about his work, "to hell with the God of Calvinism"[4] (National Film Board 1982). And so MacLennan in *The Watch* discards one part of his Presbyterian upbringing—the idea of double predestination, that is, the election of some by God to salvation and of others to damnation. Even more significant is the apparent rejection of the notion of a particular providence by which a benevolent Protector-God super-intends the details of each life. Instead, MacLennan arrives at a psy-chological, perhaps Jungian, view of inner resolution through a reconciliation of opposites, of learning how to acquire and preserve individuality in the face of impersonal pressures that would make each self into an "Everyman." While MacLennan maintains he did not know of Jung at the time, it is no wonder that Robertson Davies, who was already an admirer of Jung, in his review in *Satur-day Night* so approved of *The Watch* (see Davies 1981, 213-16).

Rather than a drama of collective salvation enacted in a vicari-ous atonement for the sins of humanity, now the death and resur-rection of Jesus becomes a demonstration of how each individual can learn to live in the face of death, or die to self, to be reborn. The revelation at the end of *The Watch* is that life itself, whatever its duration, remains a gift to be accepted and enjoyed. As meagre as it may seem, that is the fictional "solution" apparently offered by the novel, though only at the individual and personal level, to the problem of theodicy. MacLennan turned at this point in his fic-tion to finding inner and spiritual solutions rather than social and political ones. In a survey of MacLennan's first five novels, Robert D. Chambers neglects this inward turn in *The Watch that Ends the Night*, stressing instead how character "is shaped not primarily by inner-directed impulses, but by the play and interplay of those his-toric forces which sweep across Canadian life" (Chambers 1967, 4).

In 1969 MacLennan, ever-conscious of the reception and interpretation of his work, wrote that what he had been trying to say in *The Watch that Ends the Night* "was that the decade of the 1950's was the visible proof of my generation's moral and intellec-tual bankruptcy" (MacLennan 1969, 31). In one aspect, then, his novel was an indictment of the "fake revolutionaries" of the 1930s who were convinced that "the combination of politics and technol-ogy is just what the Doctor of History ordered." But, says MacLennan, "the *papier-maché* intellectual armour I had picked up in the Thirties contained more built-in obsolescence than any shiny new model you see advertised on the TV screen" (ibid., 33). This obsolescence became so apparent to MacLennan in the 1950s, that during the last few months of writing *The Watch* he was like a snake shedding this intellectual skin of the Depression generation.

Yet the novel had a positive aspect too: "In *The Watch that Ends the Night* my intuitions were forcing me to utter something socially blasphemous in those years. They were asserting that God had not been outmoded by the Christian Church, Bertrand Russell, the social scientists and modern education" (ibid., 32). To put the case bluntly, *The Watch that Ends the Night* is about the recovery or discovery of a religious faith in the lives of its three main characters. Each of the three is struggling to find within the self a religious basis for coping with the Depression of the 1930s, the tumult of the Second World War, and the prosperity of the postwar 1950s.[5]

The Odysseus myth, the love triangle, and the flashback technique are skilfully harmonized and focussed on this perennial problem experienced in its modern context. The *Odyssey* undergoes a Christian metamorphosis as Jerome Martell (the returned wanderer) comes home. True to the Homeric archetype, he returns only to renew his wanderings, but this Odysseus does not expel the suitors of Penelope (that is, Catherine, Jerome's wife). Instead Jerome is the means by which Catherine's miraculous recovery from an embolism takes place. To George Stewart (the narrator and the man Catherine had married during Jerome's absence) he imparts the spiritual wisdom found during his journeys. Speaking of the *Odyssey*, David Grene has remarked that the domesticity and realism of the world to which Odysseus returns contrasts with the heroic and marvellous world of the wanderings from which he has come (Grene 1968, 47-68). Similarly, the reader of *The Watch* is less engaged by the exploits of the heroic Jerome than by George's effort to discover meaning in life when he realizes that his wife's rheumatic heart will certainly result in an early death for her.

For George, Jerome, and Catherine (each born at the turn of the century) there is a brief period during which conventional Christianity was adequate. Then the experience of the First World War (for Jerome) and of the Depression (for George) overwhelm their childhood creeds and the old, inherited forms of religion prove inadequate in this new age. Catherine, too, finds her faith eroded in the trying interim between the wars. She expresses her sense of the vacuum when God is absent: "We're not like the man who built his house on the sand. We're like the man who tore down all the walls of his house in November and then had to face the winter naked" (MacLennan 1958, 266). MacLennan sees the major problem of life in the 1930s as the collapse of the old order and the withdrawal of God. Under these conditions George finds himself left with no resources to draw upon: "This is what happens, I thought, when the leaders close their doors and the walls of custom collapse. This is what happens when people try to play a game making the rules as they go along. I saw Catherine, Jerome, myself and everyone I knew like lost shadows moving perilously over a crust covering a void" (283). As Jerome puts it: "A man must belong to something larger than himself. He must surrender it. God was so convenient for that purpose when people could believe in Him. He was so safe and so remote" (270-71).

George calls the politics of the 1930s the "neo-religious faith." It was, he says, a time when people made gods of political systems and caught politics as they had previously caught religion. From his narrative vantage point in 1951 George discovers that in the intervening two decades politics has ceased to be fundamental. A process of individualization has resulted in such insularity that although John Donne's famous words may have been true in the 1930s, each person in the 1950s is alone. George Stewart and his contemporaries are bound together by their anger during the 1930s, by their fear during the 1940s—when "the whole world went over a frontier"—and by nothing at all during the 1950s: "In the bleak years we at least were not alone. In these prosperous years we were. The gods, false or true, had vanished. The bell which only a few years ago had tolled for all, now tolled for each family in its prosperous solitude" (323).

This collective experience of a generation parallels the inner lives of Jerome, George, and Catherine. Each acknowledges the need to belong to something larger than the self, as Jerome put it. For a time there is an attempt to find that "something larger" in each other, in a triangular relationship with Jerome as George's "spiritual father," and with each of them loving Catherine. Finally, Jerome, as fatherless in reality as George is emotionally, pushes outside the triangle in his search for something greater. Declaring the need of humanity at large to be more important, he leaves his home and family to help in the Spanish cause against fascism. His departure has the effect of teaching Catherine that "human love isn't sufficient," so she learns how to paint, declaring that if she could paint it would not matter how she felt about anything. George, disillusioned in Jerome for leaving his responsibilities as husband and father, turns to Catherine and makes her, as he says, "my rock and salvation." When, two years later, news of Jerome's supposed death leaves George free to marry Catherine, he feels that all his dreams have been realized. Only when Jerome returns ten years later and Catherine suffers the near-fatal attack does George have this ground of his security shaken. The unresolved problems of the 1930s come rushing back in upon him.

MacLennan tells us that between 1951 and 1959 he wrote more than three million words before he produced his finished manuscript of 140,000 words. While this fact alone may be insignificant, he claims he was "learning how to shape a new bottle for a new kind of wine." MacLennan relates that in 1951 he was struck with the realization that the modern novel had failed to keep pace with our changing attitudes. Governed by dramatic requirements, the novel had tried to render human destiny, as found in the interplay between characters, into external actions. The educated public, however, informed by modern psychology, had realized that "the basic conflict was within the individual." Thus, MacLennan made a significant resolution: ". . . somehow I was going to write a book which would not depend upon character-in-action, but on spirit-in-action. The conflict here, the essential one, was between the human spirit of Everyman and Everyman's human condition" (MacLennan 1960b, 39).

The 1950s, then, emerge in MacLennan's scheme as the decade when there is, in a sense, nothing really significant to be done externally, in relation to one's environment. The relationships of the characters to their surroundings become less important than what is going on within each of them. Each character is bound to mortality by a merciless fate (the human condition), this fate being opposed by the life-force within (the human spirit).

The problem of theodicy in its classic form of reconciling God's benevolence and omnipotence is redefined. Now George Stewart searches for immortality in the midst of mortality, for the manner in which "all loving is a loving of life in the midst of death." George discovers what Amos Wilder has put so well, that "death is a catalyst of transcendence." Character-in-action, therefore, becomes spirit-in-action most clearly when Catherine almost dies and George states: "Now in her final phase what I used to think of as her character ceased to matter in Catherine; her character almost disappeared into her spirit" (323). The essential Catherine now seemed to George to be "like the container of a life-force resisting extinction."

THE EVERYMAN AND THE SELF

MACLENNAN SEEMS DELIBERATELY to have been vague concerning the nature of this "life-force" and it is difficult to decide precisely what he might mean by it. Elsewhere he calls it "spirit" and sometimes "soul." At the very least the problem of individual identity is clearly involved. When character ceases to be important, when the person becomes a container of the life-force, then the individual becomes Everyman. Yet, as MacLennan points out, "All of us is Everyman and this is intolerable unless each of us can also be I." When what we normally call our "character" is minimized then a crisis of identity occurs as character becomes so overwhelmed and even obliterated that only the spirit remains. Then a kind of death results, from which a new self is resurrected and an appropriate consciousness of what it means to be an individual.

The isolation of the self in the 1950s, then, precedes the removal of the last prop—the personality mistakenly believed to be the real self. Then there follows either a rebirth and the emergence of a new selfhood, or an annihilation which submerges the individual: the individual must be Everyman, but must also be an "I." The rebirth occurs when the life-force unites itself with the divine to assert itself against the fate that threatens it. Only then does a person discover immortality in the midst of mortality, accepting both death and life. The idea that the individual must come to recognize oneself both as self and Everyman is most clearly expressed by Jerome: "Each of us is everybody, really. What scares us is just that. We want so much to be ourselves, but the time comes when we find we're everybody, and everybody is afraid. That's when you must die within yourself" (366).

MacLennan does not really succeed in resolving this Everyman-self paradox, at least not in a way reducible to the logic of discursive prose. He sees it as simply one of several paired opposites that no writer can ever satisfactorily express. To see an effective resolution he says we have to turn to music: "One musical idea uttered in the minor in a certain tempo is surrender, despair and suicide. The same idea restated in the major with horns and woods becomes an exultant call to life. This, which is darkness, also is light. This, which is no, also is yes. This, which is hatred, also is love. This, which is fear, also is courage. This, which is defeat, also is victory" (344). In the first instance, then, the life-force creates.

Looked at again, it destroys the very self that it had created. Again, and it brings together these two contradictions in an act of re-creation that produces a harmony of opposites.

Although the nature of the inner conflict becomes clear only towards the end, this clue from the final chapters illuminates the entire novel. Thus, the quest of the 1930s is the quest of character-in-action which resolves external difficulties: Jerome goes to Spain; Catherine takes up painting; George marries Catherine. Although mature character may result, the inner spiritual conflict remains. The terror of the person as Everyman seeking a self is left unmitigated. MacLennan renders the quest of spirit-in-action by the archetypal symbol of the voyage, though perhaps unaware how his artistic imagination resolved contradictions that his narrator could not harmonize rationally.

Probably the most memorable episode in *The Watch that Ends the Night* is that beautifully evocative description of the ten-year-old Jerome fleeing from his mother's murderer in his tiny canoe down the New Brunswick river. Dorothy Farmiloe claims, with forgivable excess, that "Jerome's trip in the canoe is a Canadian counterpoint to Huck Finn's flight down the Mississippi on the raft and ought to occupy the same place in Canadian literature that Huck's holds in American" (Goetsch 1973, 149). She maintains that Jerome's childhood experience is "a mythologized version of the early years of this country" and that his canoe trip is reminiscent of the voyageurs, seen elsewhere by MacLennan as the true makers of Canada. I agree rather with Douglas Spettigue's view that this is a "personal canoe" (not a national one) in the rising sea of the subconscious or of fate. The quest is universal, not because Jerome is symbolic of our nation, but because he is Everyman seeking an identity (ibid., 159). The significance of the voyage as portraying the spiritual pilgrimage is a theme continuous throughout the novel.

The novel's initial flashback shows George just returned from a summer-long canoe trip through a part of the Great Lakes. What might have been his initiation into adulthood fails to bring him out of his adolescence. When he returns an overbearing aunt badgers his father into making George take another year of prep school instead of going to McGill with Catherine. Although Catherine urges George to assert himself—"Grow up and go," she tells him—he cannot. George cannot even consummate the love he feels for her when she offers herself sexually. Catherine got a sailboat that same summer, and she asks George to be her "crew," to come along and hold the jib sheet for her. George continues in this role, metaphorically speaking, for some years, rather than becoming "captain" of his own vessel.

Jerome, meanwhile, grew up, not on the outskirts of civilized Montréal, but in a lumber camp in the New Brunswick bush. His mother, whom later he could barely remember, was the camp cook, but of his father—"his unknown begetter"—he had no memory whatever. Two other men were significant in his early childhood. An old English sailor tried to make Jerome promise that "when he grew up he would take to the sea," while a French Canadian fashioned a miniature birchbark canoe for him, the craft Jerome uses to flee for his life. Thus prepared, Jerome launches his career as a seafaring adventurer. At this stage, not even knowing his last name, Jerome has no identity of his own and is Everyman. Striking differences emerge when Jerome's canoe trip is compared with George's: George is seventeen, Jerome is ten; George paddles with a group, Jerome is alone; George's trip is for pleasure, Jerome is fleeing for his life; George paddles from one lake into another, whereas Jerome paddles down a river to the sea. Furthermore, if the sea is the primitive, destructive force that threatens life and society, then George, who lives well inland, is far removed from that threat. Jerome, of course, grows up in the wilds only a few miles from the sea.

When the Martells adopt the runaway Jerome and take him to Halifax, they too help prepare him for the sea. Giles Martell tells Jerome about Halifax: "There are big ships and small ships and we'll teach you how to sail—a real boat and not one of those Indian canoes you saw on your river" (211). Sure enough, during his years in Halifax Jerome has his own sailboat. Moreover, twice during his youth he hired on to a schooner and went out with the fishing fleets to the Grand Banks.

During one of his summer holidays in the early 1930s George sailed to the West Indies on board a fruit ship. Later he was to discover that Jerome, at the same time, had rented a sixty-foot ketch for a month's cruising in the Caribbean "and if his money had not run out he would have taken the craft through the Panama Canal" (156). Again Jerome's voyage overshadows George's. George becomes Jerome's protégé, duplicating in miniature those actions

which Jerome performs on the grand scale. His emasculating
dependence on Catherine keeps him from attaining that creative
separation that Jerome achieved in childhood. Jerome becomes
master of his own fate and captain of his soul in a way that George
does not: whereas George crews or signs on as a hand on another's
craft, Jerome becomes captain of his own vessel.

One further pair of voyages assumes a large significance in the
development of George and Jerome. In 1939 Jerome departed for
Spain for the second time, beginning an absence that lasted until
1951. During this period of twelve years he escaped from Spain
into France, was imprisoned at Auschwitz, then became a doctor in
a Siberian town. Finally, he made his way to China and then to
Hong Kong. At last he returned to Montréal by way of Vancouver.
Jerome becomes an Odysseus who circumnavigates the globe on a
journey that begins and ends in Montréal.

At the same time—during the summer of 1939—George took
a job leading a tour to Russia. His observations of the situation in
Russia and Europe that fateful summer led to a series of radio
broadcasts. Thus, the summer tour became the stepping-stone to
George's first significant employment as a political commentator.
In a later (and typically introspective) glance at this trip, George
pinpoints it as the event that at last launched him into maturity
after a thirty-five-year childhood. For Jerome, already mature and
professionally successful, his odyssey is a spiritual pilgrimage.
Jerome discovered from a rabbi in the death camps how to lose his
life to himself, thus learning to live and also to die. Jerome then
imparts this spiritual secret to George, his protégé.

In the midst of all these other voyages, Jerome's flight by
canoe down the New Brunswick river becomes the central governing image of the novel. MacLennan uses it to point up the Everyman-self paradox, and to contrast external action in relation to the
social environment with the inner spiritual pilgrimage. Jerome tells
George the story in Part Five of the novel. Then, in Parts Six and
Seven, the picture of Jerome paddling down the river by night
flashes into George's consciousness during his narration. Indeed,
the image links together these last two parts of the novel as the
action shifts from the 1930s back to the 1950s again. Six times in
less than one hundred pages the vision recurs as George remembers
Jerome's story (see 271-72, 289, 315, 329, 343, and 367). At first, it
seems to mean no more to George than Jerome's quest for identity,

as the little canoe moves out onto the ocean and the storm rises. Then, in the 1950s, George realizes that Jerome is Everyman and "discovers in dismay that what he believed to be his identity is no more than a tiny canoe at the mercy of an ocean." Though for years the ocean may seem to "slumber beneath the tiny identity it received from the dark river," now the waters are rising: "The ocean rises, all frames disappear from around the pictures, there is no form, no sense, nothing but chaos in the darkness of the ocean storm. Little man, what now?" (345).

Jerome, fatherless and now motherless, has emerged from the birth canal of the river apparently to assume a new identity with his adoptive parents, the Martells. In reality he has emerged from the river only to find himself upon the sea, the universal mother and source of all life. In the cataclysm of the 1930s Jerome's identity is threatened again as the sea seeks to engulf him. As the frames disappear from around the pictures and the forms dissolve, Jerome (and the entire generation of which he is symbolic) experience "a reintegration into the formlessness of preexistence" (Eliade 1963, 188). As the darkness descends once more the sea reverts to its primeval state as primordial undifferentiated flux. There is always the possibility of storms, of rocks, of hurricanes, and of the ever-present Leviathan (the monster of the deep) lurking just below the surface. So then, the sea threatens identity with final extinction, while it retains the promise of regeneration and new life.

Chaos into Cosmos

As W.H. Auden has made plain in his book *The Enchafèd Flood*, the city is the symbolic opposite of the sea—it is the state of order as opposed to the state of disorder. In childhood Jerome dreamed of a white city on a hill overlooking the sea: "I used to dream that if I worked hard all my life, and tried hard all my life, maybe some day I'd be allowed within its gates" (245). When Jerome saw this city being besieged by the fascists he decided to go to Spain. Auden points out that when society is in peril then the ship becomes a metaphor for society: when Jerome sees his white city on the hill endangered then he takes to the sea. Spain during the Revolution becomes like Jerome's tiny canoe at the mercy of the ocean. Jerome's initial motivation for making the voyage arises out of his determination to do something about his

imperiled society. Here he exemplifies character-in-action, struggling against a hostile environment.

   There is another—more individualized—aspect of the symbol-
ization than the use of the ship as a metaphor for society. The voyage itself becomes a symbol. As Auden says: "The Christian
conception of time as a divine creation, to be accepted, and not, as
in Platonic and Stoic philosophy, ignored, made the journey or pilgrimage a natural symbol for the spiritual life" (Auden 1967, 8 n).
MacLennan uses the image of the sea to fuse these two ideas of the
ship as a metaphor for society in peril and of the sea voyage for the
spiritual pilgrimage. These two aspects of the symbolism are analogous, of course, to the Everyman-self distinction made earlier, and
also brought into harmony on Jerome's voyage. When Jerome sets
out it is because society is in danger and his character demands
some external action on his part to allay this danger. The symbol
becomes focused on this lone figure again in his tiny canoe seeking
identity while at the mercy of the boundless ocean. The lonely
canoeist is the struggle of spirit-in-action again. The Christian conception of time spoken of by Auden unifies these two ideas.

   Relating water symbolism to Eliade's "myth of the eternal
return" suggests an endless cyclical repetition of reintegration with
the formless, followed by regeneration. Once form is achieved
again, when separation from water occurs (every voyage has an end
after all), then "every 'form' loses its potentiality, falls under the
law of time and of life; it is limited, enters history, shares in the
universal law of change, decays" (Eliade 1963, 212). Jerome,
though involved in the historical events of his time, returns; yes,
and therefore seems to have escaped from his temporal subordina-
tion to a kind of timelessness. George, meanwhile, is only too
aware that for himself, and especially for Catherine, time is linear.
Catherine still lives under the sword of Damocles. Her third
embolism upon Jerome's return signals to her—and to George—
that the sword cannot forever remain in suspension.

   The title of MacLennan's novel is, of course, to be found in a
line of Isaac Watts' paraphrase of the Ninetieth Psalm: "A thousand
ages in thy sight / Are like an evening gone, / Short as the watch
that ends the night / Before the rising sun." The entire psalm,
referred to several times in the novel, is a meditation on the brevity
of life and the inevitability of death. Pessimism prevails throughout
as people are compared to grass that is fresh and new in the morn-

ing but withers and dies when evening comes. Yet towards the end the psalmist draws a lesson from this sense of life's transitory nature: "So teach us to number our days / that we may get a heart of wisdom" (Ps. 90:12).

Against this background the novel's title has significance at several levels within the story. First, on the obvious level, "the watch that ends the night" is the afternoon that Jerome spends watching over Catherine's unconscious form. When George goes to the hospital at supper time expecting to hear that Catherine has died, the nurse tells him instead, "Last night I had no hope, but now I do." A miraculous change has occurred: Jerome tells George that he felt death leave the room.

Second, "the watch" may be the long period of George's waiting for some change to occur in his wife. When the story begins it is early February and on the night of Jerome's return the temperature reaches twenty degrees below zero (Fahrenheit!). When Catherine's sudden change takes place the weather changes too. As George leaves the hospital the weather is warmer and he can hear the rivulets form the melting snow. Thus the long, cold night of winter ends and, as the taxi driver tells George, you can "smell the spring in the air."

At the most significant level, however, Jerome's absence from 1939 to 1951 is a twelve-year watch when time stops. Time is suspended during this period because Jerome is away and has not yet reentered history, so to speak. Additionally, it seemed to George that the years after the outbreak of the War until the 1950s did not really take place in time at all. Only after the decade of the 1950s has begun does life seem to pick up where it left off after the Depression. The day after Jerome's return George has a conversation with a friend who asks, "Do you ever have the feeling that time stopped in 1939? . . . We were alive before then, weren't we?" (100).

When George married Catherine in 1941 they embarked on ten years of happiness when they shut out from their minds the sword hanging over Catherine. As George remarks, "Happiness annihilates time." Jerome's return starts the clock ticking again and all the unresolved problems from the 1930s return with him. Therefore, the night of "the watch that ends the night" here is the Depression and the prelude to the Second World War. This "dark night of the soul" is not over for George until Jerome returns from his twelve-year watch in 1951.

Here George comes to a new understanding of life's brevity:

It is of no importance that God appears indifferent to justice as men understand it. He gave life. He gave it. Life for a year, a month, a day or an hour is still a gift. The warmth of the sun or the caress of the air, the sight of a flower or a cloud on the wind, the possibility even for one day more to see things grow—the human bondage is also the human liberty. (344)

This realization, then, is George's realization of his createdness that Nathan Scott says comes to the person who lives in the presence of death: "the very contingency of his existence, as it is disclosed in the awareness that he must die, tells him that the origin and meaning of his life are not wholly immanent within himself: he did not create himself: life itself is received, it is a gift" (Scott 1966, 26). When George Stewart understands time as *kairos* and not as mere chronicity he understands too that life depends on God's grace. He is no longer troubled with his original problem of theodicy; he stops wondering why Catherine is condemned to a short life "among hundreds of thousands of others who went free."

Jerome's journey, then, assumes a transitional function between the 1930s when external action mattered most and the 1950s when the essential conflict was within the individual. What begins as a voyage with the ship as society in peril becomes a spiritual pilgrimage. Jerome's return signifies the victory of the solitary regenerated self over that sea of collective humanity threatening to submerge it. What enables this self to face death squarely is a true apprehension of the nature of time. George and Catherine learn to live under the sword of Damocles that hangs over Catherine's head: "What if the ocean of time overwhelmed her? It overwhelms us all" (373).

In the end this ocean is transformed in George's mind, though not as in the eschatological vision of the Book of Revelation where there is "no more sea." The sea, nonetheless, is no longer a sea of darkness and chaos, but a sea of light. MacLennan expresses this transformation of the dark watery chaos when he quotes two verses from Genesis: "And the earth was without form, and void; and darkness was upon the face of the deep. And the Spirit of God moved upon the face of the waters. And God said, Let there be light: and there was light" (Gen. 1:2-3; cf. 343).

The divine act of creation is repeated in George's life and consciousness; the sea too is transformed. The birth of the new human being is a symbolic reenactment of the birth of the world (Eliade). The light that empties the ocean of its terror also transforms the imperiled city, so that George looking down upon Montréal from a hospital window sees it as a sea of light. George comprehends this light, then, as ordering the cosmos and as ordering his immediate surroundings. He also sees it in the faces of Jerome and Catherine. He achieves his own spiritual maturity when he discovers the same light within himself too. Catherine's face displays what George can only describe as "the joy of the Lord" and, he says, "I knew its light would remain with me."

MacLennan views his first four novels as essentially optimistic. Once he discarded the intellectual skin of the 1930s, he says the result was that his next two novels, *The Watch that Ends the Night* and *The Return of the Sphinx*, were tragic. The significance of this remark is difficult to grasp, for the aesthetic shaping force containing that tragic vision (to use Murray Krieger's phraseology) relieves the tragedy, making it a vehicle for affirmation. Perhaps MacLennan's understanding of *The Watch* as tragic becomes clear when we remember that it was originally entitled *Requiem*: "Requiem for one I loved who had died [that is, his wife, Dorothy, who shared Catherine's illness and her passion for painting], but also more: requiem for the idealists of the Thirties who had meant so well, tried so hard and gone so wrong" (MacLennan 1969, 31).

The unrelieved adversity continues to reside in the chaos that MacLennan observes in the social scene, though in this chaos he sees a possibility for the individual to encounter the sacred in a form of transcendence: "It . . . fills me with awe and wonder to know that . . . the species to which I belong is stubbornly, blindly determined to remain human" (ibid.). George Stewart's conclusion may be his author's too: "Here, I found at last, is the nature of the final human struggle. Within, not without. Without there is nothing to be done. But within" (343).

Because MacLennan's account of things lacks any final prescription for society, or even an affirmation of the individual's context in human solidarity, he termed *The Watch that Ends the Night* "tragic." While the requiem for Dorothy Duncan is transfigured into a new apprehension of the sacred, the requiem for the 1930s generation—who "had meant so well, tried so hard and gone so wrong"—presents itself, in Joseph McLelland's words, more as threnody—or lament—than as theodicy (1994). MacLennan rejects John Donne's concept of the individual as a piece of the continent to the extent that William New has claimed that for MacLennan the individual remains an island, "but an island in position, as it were, as a part of an archipelago; the experience of the one is the experience of all, and each part functions both as an entirety for all and as an entirety in itself" (New 1966, 32-33). Whether the self's recognition of its identity as Everyman is satisfactory, it is the only solution MacLennan offers for the community of the individual with others. In this respect he persists as a "Protestant" novelist for whom the sacred is encountered in the relationship of the solitary individual with some form of transcendence.

NOTES

1 Elspeth Cameron, though she knows of no other contact between the two men, believes it probable that "Klein's and MacLennan's *ideas* on religion would have been passed *verbally*." She writes: "Scott was given to frequent informal parties—often involving reading poems etc.—and even if Klein were at some of these and MacLennan at others, the circle of people is so small that surely Klein's ideas would have been familiar to MacLennan and vice versa. In person, my guess would be that they would have been too alike temperamentally (somewhat remote emotionally) to have become very friendly. But this is idle speculation . . ." (personal communication, 6 March 1992).

2 Klein's words in this paragraph are from a letter to A. J. M. Smith, 18 September 1951 (see "Some Letters of A. M. Klein to A. J. M. Smith, 1941-1951" in Mayne 1975, 12). I disagree somewhat with Rachel Feldhay Brenner's attribution of "humanism" to Klein, whose supernaturalism could be seen in some sense as anti-humanistic. At least, the faith Klein puts in humanity is ill-founded when, like Melech, he established his own central premise of "the divinity of humanity" (Brenner 1989, 51). Brenner argues that not even the Holocaust could "destroy Klein's hopeful creed." Yes, but the incompatibility of creed and event destroyed Klein (see Brenner 1989; cf. Brenner 1990 where she outlines how Richler dissociates himself from Klein's project of humankind's moral reeducation).

3 The details of Dorothy Duncan's illness are found in the essay "Victory," written c. 1960 (Cameron 1978, 177-83). MacLennan concludes his tribute: "Through this experience became manifest some of those

mysterious things spoken of in the last chapters of St. John's Gospel, and I knew they were true" (ibid., 183).

4 Even a decade later MacLennan could still express a darkly Calvinistic view of the divine judgment in history: "What is happening everywhere today is being caused not only by the chaotic terror that assails men without either purpose or religion; it is happening also by the active working of what our ancestors called the Divine in human affairs. A subsequent phrase of mine, not really optimistic in any sense I can accept tranquilly, is 'I believe in God—and that is what scares me'" (personal communication, 15 October 1969).

5 Barbara Pell finds in *The Watch* a "new vision of God" by MacLennan in which "God is no longer a Person with an objective reality independent of man's perception of Him." She claims that it is difficult to portray in fiction "a relationship with this transcendent, impersonal deity" (1991, 48).

CHAPTER 7

LOVE AND THE SACRED: THE AMBIGUITIES OF MORLEY CALLAGHAN'S *Such Is My Beloved*

CALLAGHAN'S "CERTAIN PERCEPTIONS"

S OMEONE, ALLUDING TO THE TITLE of a book by William Emp-
son, once remarked that in this century there are as many types
of ambiguity as there once were deadly sins. And Allan Bloom, in
his indictment of American moral relativism in *The Closing of the
American Mind*, said that the comparative simplicities of falling in
love had been supplanted on college campuses by the inherently
problematical phenomenon of "having a relationship." Even before
postmodernism further complicated such ambiguities as love Morley Callaghan was illuminating its obscurities and making more
nebulous its received certainties. Callaghan's own position on this
inherent ambiguity of the human situation needs clarification. It is
time to reassess and specify some mooring points of Callaghan's
view of life, especially his Catholic and neothomist outlook. Once
an assumed mainstay of Callaghan criticism, his theological views
have never been as deeply investigated nor as fully supported as
they might have been. A consideration of *Such Is My Beloved*,
Callaghan's best-known novel, elucidates these bases of his
thought, illustrating as well its relationship to the biblical tradition
exemplified in the Song of Songs.

In the 1960s a critical consensus prevailed about Morley
Callaghan's "certain perceptions about human life" to which he
claimed a writer inevitably returns (Weaver 1962, 134). Such commentators as F. W. Watt, Desmond Pacey, and Victor Hoar agreed
that Callaghan's fiction until the end of the 1920s had shown the
strong influence of naturalism or determinism (see Watt 1959,

Notes to Chapter 7 are on p. 170.

Pacey 1965, and Hoar 1969). Whether attributed to the influence
of Hemingway (with whom he had a friendship in the 1920s) or to
the impact of the social sciences or to the Freudian or Marxist
account of the individual's place in society, Callaghan's earliest
work portrayed people at the mercy of forces larger than themselves. Yet there was also agreement that by the time of *Such Is My
Beloved* Callaghan "gave up," as Pacey put it, "the negative futility
that marked the early novels . . . and concentrated upon the spiritual lives of his characters rather than upon their physical
appetites" (Pacey 1965, 691).

Watt and Pacey contended that Callaghan turned to individualism or personalism or Christian humanism. As Hugo McPherson
maintained, Callaghan "became, in short, a religious writer" (Conron 1975, 60) who explored the relation between two worlds, one
empirical and the other spiritual. In this vein Pacey claimed that in
Callaghan the individual soul is defeated or destroyed on earth, but
achieves a triumph not of this world. As Jacques Maritain, whose
thought was highly regarded by Callaghan, wrote, society is indi-
rectly subordinate "to the perfect fulfilment of the person and his
supra-temporal aspirations." Each person transcends the common
good of society: "A single human soul is more worth than the
whole universe of bodies and material goods. There is nothing
above the human soul except God" (Maritain 1944, 11).

By the late 1970s, however, others began to question this earlier consensus. D. J. Dooley found other evidence in the novels of
the 1930s that mitigated this theme of the individual against society. Turning to *The Loved and the Lost* (1951), Dooley maintained
that Callaghan had written "a very paradoxical novel," leaving us
"reflecting on questions rather than answers" (Dooley 1979, 77).
Larry McDonald went further. He argued that "Callaghan criticism is mired in the slough of Christian personalism" (Staines
1981, 77), rejecting the dualistic metaphysic that he said many
critics had foisted on his work. From a close examination of
Callaghan's earliest fiction, McDonald discovered an emphasis on
the fulfilment of human potential developed in and through time,
not on Christian redemption: "there are no values or visitations of
grace from outside of time" (ibid., 84). For Callaghan, human
nature is monistic—in his view of life there is "no such thing as an
opposition between the spiritual and the carnal" (ibid., 83).

The remaining critical agreement includes recognition of Callaghan's novels of the 1930s as his finest achievement. Among them *Such Is My Beloved* (to cite the jacket copy of the 1989 New Canadian Library edition) "is widely considered Callaghan's finest novel." Commentators and critics also generally agreed that with his novel of 1934 Callaghan's fiction changed, usually attributed to the influence of Jacques Maritain, who was teaching in Toronto then (see Kernan 1975, 88-89). In 1951 Callaghan remembered his excitement about Maritain's presence at Toronto's Medieval Institute almost two decades earlier: "I went around saying, 'Jacques Maritain is in town,' with a beaming smile" (Callaghan 1951, 17). Callaghan, only recently returned from Paris, was dismayed that his enthusiasm was largely unshared in Toronto: "Maritain was a world figure everywhere but in my home town" (ibid., 18). Callaghan had learned of course that the mind and spirit of Thomas Aquinas had shaped the thinking of Joyce and Dante. Still, he was keen to discover more about the neglected thirteenth century, almost obscured in Ontario education by claims made about the Renaissance.

The terms of Callaghan's admiration for Maritain are lavish and unrestrained. He claimed that Maritain's presence had put the Medieval Institute "on the world stage intellectually," citing T. S. Eliot's comment that Maritain was "one of the great intellectual forces in Europe" (ibid., 17). The dedication of *Such Is My Beloved* states in simple homage: "To those times with M. in the winter of 1933." And, until the new edition of 1989 dropped it, the New Canadian Library paperback supplied the clue for M's identity by printing on the back cover Maritain's comment: "I have been profoundly touched by the absolute sincerity of this very moving book." The French philosopher apparently held the Canadian writer in equal esteem. These two men, and a few others (in particular, Manny Chapman, a Jewish convert to Catholicism), met frequently during 1933 to eat, drink wine, and socialize at the Callaghan apartment on Avenue Road.[1]

THE TWO CONFLICTING REALMS

IN HIS MEMOIR *That Summer in Paris*, famous for its descriptions of Fitzgerald and Hemingway in Paris in 1929 (and especially for Callaghan's "boxing match" with the latter), Callaghan comments that "Christian artists were finding new dignity and spiritual adventure in the neo-Thomism of Jacques Maritain." He may have had in mind Maritain's *Art and Scholasticism*, originally published in Paris in 1920.[2] He continues: "My own problem was to relate a Christian enlightenment to some timeless process of becoming" (Callaghan 1963, 94), perhaps suggesting his (at least intellectual) attempt to reconcile dualities, especially the temporal and the eternal. Whether Callaghan as a man wrestled with opposing dualisms, or having wrestled with them, resolved them, his fiction implies an author who deals with opposition and conflict. His novels do not present a monistic view of a harmonious human nature.

Though the implied author may view this conflict ironically, Father Stephen Dowling in *Such Is My Beloved* attempts to integrate eternity and time, the church and the world, the divine and the human. His failure to achieve reconciliation on earth may be an otherworldly triumph, however ironically portrayed by the impersonal narrator. Even without making any assertion about whether Callaghan as author believes in an ultimate metaphysical dualism, McPherson's judgment is too stark: "Thus though Father Dowling has failed by all temporal standards in his quest, he has, in the best sense of the Christian faith, triumphed" (in Conron 1975, 67). Something troubling and problematic remains in a view that dictates the continuation and opposition of two realms, unable finally to be harmonized.

George Woodcock remarked that "a whole essay could be written on the significance of the cathedrals which appear at crucial points in every novel that Callaghan wrote" (1976, 75). He went on to say that the "ambiguous symbolism of the Cathedral, particularly in *Such Is My Beloved*, extends this dichotomy [between moral man and immoral society] into the world of religion" (ibid., 82). A part—though not the "whole"—of this present essay examines Father Dowling's changing view of the Cathedral in the novel as indicator of his changing attitude towards the church in the world, and its relation to the transcendent.

In the terminology of H. Richard Niebuhr from his classic book *Christ and Culture*, the idealistic Father Dowling at first occupies the position of the "cultural" or "synthesist" Christian. He sees no opposition between Christ and Culture, no strain or tension between God and the world. One great virtue of Niebuhr's typology lies in its offering a range of possibilities between the extremes of monism and dualism. His "Christ of Culture" position (that of the "cultural" Christian) presents Christian life as simply the highest expression of life in culture; in the "Christ Above Culture" (or "synthesist") type God orders both the natural and the supernatural realms into a harmonious hierarchical structure. Niebuhr describes Aquinas as "probably the greatest of all the synthesists in Christian history" (Niebuhr 1956, 128), while claiming that the neothomist synthesis sought by Leo XIII and others "is not the synthesis of Christ with present culture, but the re-establishment of the philosophy and institutions of another culture" (ibid., 139). This, he declares, is Christianity "of the cultural sort," while the synthetic answer is absent from modern culture because of the prevailing understanding both of Christ and of culture.

At the novel's outset Dowling returns to the rectory from a pastoral visit. He is planning the next Sunday's sermon, "another powerful discourse on the building of a society on Christian principles" (Callaghan 1934, 4). Dowling smiles to himself as he sees the crowds coming out of the theatres. He turns the corner "mechanically," not bothering looking up to see the Cathedral spire, taking for granted the place of his church within society. The Cathedral, both unimpressive to visitors and unknown to most inhabitants, is undistinguished in relation to its surroundings—"it was really a Protestant city."[3] The parish has become poor, while the church "had been in that neighbourhood for so long it now just seemed a part of an old city block" (37). From his perspective the church is part of the city, neither conflicting with it nor separate from it.

When Dowling returns to his room after first meeting the prostitutes, Midge and Ronnie, he continues to think of these "two girls in my own parish and in a hotel I could almost see from my window" (7). When he thrusts his face against the windowpane to see "the place where he knew the hotel was," his vision is obscured by "the water that had streamed down the window." Later, returning home from the hotel, Dowling sees the Cathedral and spire, "hemmed in closely by office buildings and warehouses and always dirtied by city soot, and with the roof now covered by snow and moonlight shining on the white slope" (15). His reaction to this juxtaposition of the church with the other city buildings is a feeling of "fresh full contentment."

Some days later, after Dowling's second visit, one of the prostitutes, Midge, looks out through the frosted glass of her hotel window after midnight, thinking of the priest. His domain remains inaccessible to her: "The church was just on the other side of the block. But no matter how she strained her neck she could not see the spire" (30). Midge, who chased away a college boy after his request to dance for him, thinks her action would please Dowling, making it "more likely that he would give her money the next time he came to the hotel" (30). She lacks his sense of the connection between the church and the rest of the world, while he misses the implications of giving money to a prostitute.

On the next visit Dowling, with twelve dollars borrowed from his Marxist friend, Charlie Stewart, hurries along the street, engrossed in a prayer of thanks as he goes: "as he looked up eagerly at the stars he passed right by the Cathedral and kept on going around the block to the hotel" (45). Dowling slips the money under a cloth on the dresser, "with a strangely diffident apologetic nod" (47), and alone in the room with Midge, falls asleep with her. Though the reader knows Midge is lying on the bed, hoping that Dowling will "come over here and sit beside me," it is uncertain where he ends up after leaving his chair to put the money on the dresser. Callaghan leaves us in doubt whether he joins Midge on the bed or returns to his chair.

At confession a university student who fears the loss of his faith tells Dowling that he twice had been to a neighbourhood prostitute. Father Dowling thinks about "how united was all the life of his congregation, students, the mothers and fathers of students, prostitutes, priests, the rich and the poor who passed girls on the street and desired them" (76). He goes on to attribute a purpose to the lives of the girls, in a typically naïve (or outrageously sexist) justification, because "it was certainly better for that boy to have been with Ronnie or Midge than some pure young girl" (77). In the spring Dowling is full of fond thoughts as he makes his way from his house to the hotel: "He felt he would rather be here in the city and at the Cathedral than any place else on earth, for here he was at home in the midst of his own people" (58). Father Dowling's attempt to carry out this integration of his church with the prostitutes' lives, uniting the whole of his parish, brings a collision with his bishop. In misguided enthusiasm Dowling hopes by taking Midge and Ronnie to the Robisons' house to enlist his wealthy parishioners' sympathy for them and raise their prospects. The fiasco ends with angry words, bringing Dowling's recognition of the incommensurability of the social and economic (and spiritual too) worlds of the Robisons and the prostitutes. His disillusionment with these parishioners, until now taken as exemplary Christians, causes a revised attitude to the church evident in his changed reaction to the Cathedral's spire. As the priest walks away from the Robisons' house "his anger and disgust alternated so sharply that he did not realize he was back at the Cathedral till he looked up and saw the spire and saw, too, the cross at the peak thrust up against the stars and felt no sudden affection but just a cool disgust, as if the church no longer belonged to him" (94).

Back in his room Dowling looks out at the city's buildings and crowds, thinking of Midge and Ronnie. The chapter ends: "He felt full of love for them and sometimes he looked up at the stars" (96). By now, in Niebuhrian terms, Dowling has moved away from his earlier "cultural" or "synthetic" Christianity with its uncomplicated relationship between church and world. He approximates the more radical dualist position, comparable to Niebuhr's "Christ Against Culture" type with its clear tension between God and world leading to withdrawal from ungodly culture. Earlier, the church, situated comfortably into the city with the office buildings, signifies the redeeming presence of God in a world seen as potentially sacred in all its aspects.

Initially Dowling had no need to look beyond the world for the location of the sacred. He assumes that the church spire is a temporal symbol of the sacred, integrated into the cityscape amid the surrounding warehouses and office buildings. Later he sees the Cathedral as solely part of the temporal realm, separate from the eternal. Now Dowling searches beyond the temporal for the location of the sacred, most often finding sacrality in the stars. For Dowling the stars symbolize, as they commonly do in mythology and folklore universally, the spirit and the eternal, or human souls.

THE SONG OF SONGS: LOVE AND THE SACRED

WHETHER READ STRAIGHTFORWARDLY as an instance of the pre-1960s genre "Catholic novel," even when that means "informed by Catholic sensibility or vision which is not easily restated in terms of doctrine" (Gerhart 1990, 188), or as an ironic depiction (perhaps reminiscent of Kafka or Camus) of the impossibilities of conventional religious faith in the twentieth century, still *Such Is My Beloved* shows a collision between two realms rather than a monistic vision. For the contemporary reader the novel may principally exemplify Herman Melville's dictum that anyone who tries to apply literally the teachings of the New Testament ends up in jail or in the psychiatric hospital. Or, as Callaghan says of his work in general, *Such Is My Beloved* may be read as an investigation of the plight of innocence, the partial subject of a talk with Robert Weaver where he declares his long-term fascination with the subject. Callaghan tells Weaver that "there's a very thin borderline between innocence and crime" because both the saint and the great criminal share "a monstrous egotism." He continues: "The saint pits himself against the whole world . . . which he calls, of course, usually the work of Satan. But the great criminal also puts himself against the world and the laws of society" (Weaver 1962, 135).[4]

Callaghan makes a similar comment about his oeuvre in a television program: "The whole point of all my work, in a sense, has been a kind of rejection of the conception of innocence" (cited in Harcourt and Price 1971). He also characterizes the importance of love in his fiction: "All [my] stories are love stories—short stories or novels, they deal with some aspect of love, or the failure of love—I suppose mainly about the failure of love." In *Such Is My Beloved* Callaghan moves the priest's initial concern for the prostitutes' salvation into another realm where their love becomes the sacred value to preserve in a hostile environment. To examine the Song of Songs from the Hebrew Scriptures, whether used by the author as an epigraph for the novel, by the protagonist as a text for a sermon, or by a commentator as a heuristic device for interpretation, is instructive and illuminating. The role and interpretation of that pagan love hymn in the biblical canon parallels the problems presented by Callaghan's novel. The possibility of making human love the location of the sacred—and, therefore, the possibility of sacralizing human love—is at issue in both cases.

After Midge and Ronnie have been run out of town, and Easter passes, Dowling withdraws increasingly into an interior world. As he meditates on love, planning his commentary on the Song of Songs, "he heard the noises from people moving in the house, but these sounds now did not interest him at all" (139). Dowling wears an "expression of detached sadness" during a visit from Charlie Stewart; his eyes are dulled with "detached, depressed, heavy stillness" (140-41). His disengagement from society is complete when he goes to the psychiatric hospital by the lake. There the patients sit in the sun as if they were guests at a garden party waiting to be served, a bitter parody of the pastoral imagery of the Song of Songs where the garden is a refuge from the world. At the hospital, held "by an absolute stillness within him" (142), Dowling continues to pray in this idyllic setting as he looks at "the new ploughed land" and the "rich brown fertile soil." Unable to affect their material condition, Dowling concludes by offering his insanity as a sacrifice for the prostitutes' souls. In the novel's concluding lines three stars appear above the water: "His love seemed suddenly to be as steadfast as those stars, as wide as the water, and still flowing within him like the cold smooth waves still rolling on the shore" (144).

Callaghan's epigraph for his novel is the Song of Songs 8:7: "Many waters cannot quench love, neither can the floods drown it: if a man would give all the substance of his house for love, it [i.e., he] would utterly be contemned [i.e., despised]." Francis Landy comments that this verse, especially its latter half, is "ironic": "In the eyes of the world, to give one's entire fortune for love is folly; from the perspective of the Song, in which riches are ultimately worthless, it is folly" (Landy 1987, 318). The double meaning here is, first, that the world regards the lover as a fool to abandon wealth for the sake of love. Second, the rich person cannot purchase love or, as the Beatles' song put it, "Can't Buy Me Love." From the perspective of the wealthy Robisons, Father Dowling is a delusional fool who throws everything away for the sake of a couple of prostitutes. In the view of his bishop, fearing scandal as he is about to launch (with compounded incongruity), a "Charity Drive," Dowling's course of action is inexpedient. For Dowling, who finds love manifest in the concreteness of relationships, materialism is more spiritually imperilling than prostitution: "All around us there are all kinds of people prostituting their souls and their principles for money" (132).

The title, *Such Is My Beloved*, comes from the book in the Hebrew Scriptures known as the Song of Solomon, the Song of Songs, or the Canticle of Canticles. The Douay translation of the last verse of the fifth chapter has the words "Such Is My beloved" (whereas the King James and Revised Standard versions have "This is my beloved"). Both epigraph and title explicitly connect the novel with the Scriptures, a connection not much examined by critics. Given these two quotations from the same biblical book, additional thematic connections, and Dowling's use of the book, the relations between Callaghan's novel and the Song of Songs need attention.

The phrase "such is my beloved" occurs in the Song at the end of a chapter where a bride describes her Beloved to a group of bystanders. She tells them, in a catalogue of his physical features ranging from head to toe, about his hair, his complexion, his eyes, his cheeks, his lips, his hands, his belly, and his legs. She concludes: "His conversation is sweetness itself, he is altogether loveable. Such Is my beloved, such is my friend, O daughters of Jerusalem" (5:16). Since here a woman speaks these words about a man she loves, probably they describe best Midge's attitude towards Stephen Dowling.

Like the woman of the Song of Songs, Midge (whose name means "gnat" or, more positively, "tiny person") is referred to several times in the novel as "dark": she is "the little, dark one with the round brown eyes" (9); she is "the little dark girl" (13); and as Dowling depicts her to Charlie's girlfriend, Pauline, Midge is "dark with brown eyes" (55). Like the woman in the Song of Songs who is "dark and comely" (1:5), and therefore probably from the country, Midge is an outsider in Toronto. Her darkness is the antithesis of the conventional fair beauty of the city. A commentator on the Song explains: "In the Pastoral, courtly tradition, darkness of skin is ambivalent, while the conventional beauty is fair. . . . A white complexion is delicate, unspoilt; and readily merges with the symbolism of whiteness as purity." This difference in complexion becomes an index of moral virtue: "The unspoilt, delicate girl is virginal, carefully raised within society to await her husband. The dark girl . . . is available, and consequently less idealised and more enticing" (Landy 1983, 144).

The conventional beauty of the city is perhaps represented by James Robison's "two fine daughters" (39), or, even more, by his wife, who contrasts dramatically with Midge and Ronnie when Dowling takes the two women to the Robison home. Mrs. Robison has "slender white hands," "beautiful white streaks in her hair," and skin that is "soft and pink" (90). By contrast, Midge is a working-class woman from Montréal, one of a dozen children, and of French-Canadian background. She is also a prostitute and not the wife of a prominent lawyer.

Like the bride in the Song of Songs, Midge catalogues her "Beloved's" features, recalling Dowling's face, hair, lips, and hands, while she sits in her prison cell following her arrest: "And at last there floated into her thoughts the face of Father Dowling. She liked to think of his face now, his thick hair, and the gentleness in his smile. She began, too, to think of his big, soft strong hands as if they might hold her and strengthen her even as these thoughts were strengthening her" (112).

Callaghan's title "such is my beloved" echoes the New Testament pronouncement at Jesus' baptism in the Jordan River: "This is my beloved son, in whom I am well pleased" (Mt. 3:17).[5] Father Dowling may be like Jesus, presiding at a "last supper" of wine and sandwiches the night before Robison (Judas) betrays Midge and Ronnie to the bishop (Pilate). The title phrase may also imply that Dowling is Christlike in his befriending two prostitutes for whom he sacrifices himself. Bishop Foley comes close to stumbling on the nature and origins of Dowling's love for the two women. After his interview with Father Dowling Bishop Foley feels that the priest's love for them became "too concrete." While musing about this, and searching for "the conception expressed in the image," he seeks a suitable abstraction by which to grasp the problem: "From the word to the flesh, the word made flesh, from the general to the particular, the word made flesh, no, no, nonsense" (135). The bishop almost concludes that his priest's love for the two prostitutes is like God's love for all humanity, particularized in the Word become flesh described in the opening of the Fourth Gospel. In backing away he negates this conclusion, effectively denying the very good news he is supposed to uphold and proclaim.

In a CBC television program (mentioned above) Callaghan expresses his own doubts about whether you "can love generally, without loving concretely." Maritain describes what he terms theocentric humanism as "the humanism of the Incarnation" (Maritain 1938). Quoting from his own earlier work Maritain continues to the effect that the saint cherishes other creatures "as loved by God, and made by Him as fair and worthy of our love. For to love a being in and for God is not to treat them as a mere means or a mere occasion for loving God, but to love and cherish their being as an end, because it *merits* love . . ." (*The Degrees of Knowledge* [1937], cited in Maritain 1938, 65).

Throughout the novel Father Dowling becomes increasingly an apologist for the sacredness of love, especially through his own meditation and preaching on the Song of Songs. Early in the novel he believed that "his feeling for the girls was so intense it must surely partake of the nature of the divine love" (16), an instance of his dangerous naïveté. Perhaps he is only confusing erotic intensity with religious devotion; perhaps he is sacralizing human love; or, perhaps Dowling recognizes that he cannot love the two women merely instrumentally—that love must be end and not means. In his endeavour to love Midge and Ronnie "for themselves," as he puts it, Dowling is an example of incarnational humanism. After the collision with his bishop and parishioners that kind of love becomes a transcendent value.

While reading his Bible Dowling "understood some of the secret rich feeling of this love song, sung so marvellously that it transcended human love and become divine" (78). When he preaches on the Song he makes it a song "of a love that all people ought to have for one another" (78). At the close of the sermon he quotes the same words inscribed at the outset of the novel: "Many waters cannot quench love, neither can the floods drown it." Awaiting his bishop's decision about the discipline to be imposed on him, Dowling decides to write a commentary on the Song of Songs with the purpose of showing "how human love may transcend all earthly things" (139). At the end, as he watches "the soft rise and enormous flow toward him" of the waves of the lake, one assumes that his own love has not been quenched, however broken and disordered his mind might be.

Even in the brief concluding chapter, after Dowling realizes and accepts his "insanity," he still hopes for periods of clarity so that he can go on with his commentary on the Song of Songs. The psychiatric hospital is situated in a pastoral environment outside the city by the lake, next to fields of "new ploughed land" with "rich brown fertile soil, heavy and dark and moist" (142). With his seclusion Dowling has moved, like the lovers in the Song of Songs, from the city to the countryside (see Song of Songs 2:8, 5:1, and 6:2). The hospital is situated amid vistas of "a wide lawn with new green spring grass" the patients talk and bow to one other "as if it was a great garden party to which they had all been invited" (141). Dowling interacts little with the other patients; mostly he is "held there by an absolute stillness within him," though "aroused a little" by the blue waters and rolling waves of the lake (142).

Francis Landy writes perceptively about what he terms "the process of fusion and differentiation" in the Song of Songs. He describes the theme of the Song as "the paradise that only exists in the world through being inaccessible to it, or is only accessible outside its limits, through imaginative transcendence" (272). As he points out—and Callaghan's theme of the power of love bears similarities—love is as strong as death, but love is also like death, threatening dissolution and desolation. The psychological, spiritual, or amorous union the priest achieves with the two women leads to exile, both for him and for them. When Dowling is forced to obey the bishop his reason disintegrates. Sent away from the church and the city—those two communities he sought to unite and serve—Dowling experiences the inaccessibility of his previously known world. At that point of differentiation, as Landy would have it, Dowling achieves through imaginative transcendence a fusion with Midge and Ronnie, the objects of his love.

CONCLUSION: INCARNATIONAL HUMANISM

THREE MONTHS BEFORE HIS DEATH St. Thomas Aquinas had a powerfully transformative experience, resulting in his abandoning the writing of his great *Summa*: "Such things have been revealed to me that everything I have written seems to me rubbish" (Maritain 1931, 26). At times Aquinas was dazed, and was generally unable to teach or write. He may have suffered a nervous breakdown, a stroke, or exhaustion. It may have been that he experienced, either as cause or result of his physical condition, a mystical experience. During his final two weeks, with his death near, Thomas was asked by those around him for a memorial, perhaps some statement to preserve his memory. Accordingly, he dictated to the monks at Fossanova a brief commentary on the Song of Songs (ibid., 27; cf. Weisheipl 1974, 326). Though this deathbed commentary has not survived, Aquinas' most influential biographer describes this poignant account of its origins, in part derived from William of Tocco, as "a persistent view" (Weisheipl 1974, 326).

Stephen B. Boyd has connected Thomas's "preoccupation with the erotic imagery of the Song" with his "disillusionment with his intellectual work." Aquinas had previously "believed that the repression of sexual energy/passion was necessary to vitalize one's intellectual life." But the culmination, a vision of God that infused him with erotic passion, Boyd suggests, was "a glimpse of a different kind of sexuality and its possibility to enrich life and draw one

to God" (Boyd 1990, 8). Other recent commentators on the relationship between sex and religion have gone further. James B.
Nelson (1988), drawing on Paul Ricoeur, argues that we are now
experiencing a renewed sense of the spiritual power of sexual
expression. No longer is the sacred to be thought of as something
transcending sexuality. Instead there is, exactly as Father Dowling's
incarnational humanism would have it, the possibility for human
love to become divine love—for human love to be the location of
the sacred. As Nelson states, "in the depths of friendship with
another human being, I literally do experience the friendship of
God." More emphatically, he declares that this experience, not just
analogous to an experience of God, or even embodying divine
love," *is* God" (1988, 66).

The situation of Thomas's last days, especially as elaborated in
Boyd's interpretation of it, is strikingly close to Stephen Dowling's
at the end of *Such Is My Beloved*. Both men experience the
tremendous power of the sacred, the transcendent force of love, to
overturn their taken-for-granted worlds, leading them to abandon
their lives as previously lived and known. Whatever else he might
have gained from Jacques Maritain's neothomism, Morley
Callaghan through their friendship probably was prompted
towards imagining fictional parallels to the life of Thomas. After
all, Maritain had published his biography of Thomas in Paris in
1930 (Maritain 1930), just three years before his time in Toronto,
with the translation into English following in 1931 (Maritain 1931).
Maritain's book has the same details of Aquinas's last days as
appear in Weisheipl's authoritative biography (see Maritain 1931,
26-27). Given the frequency of their meetings and the interest
Callaghan showed in Maritain's ideas, Aquinas' life and thought
would have been a likely topic of conversation between them.

While Maritain's influence was widely accepted in Callaghan
criticism a generation ago, recent commentators have not much
heeded the direct impact of Maritain's ideas on Callaghan or his
specific borrowings from Maritain's work.[6] Yet the two men obviously had shared interests in the perils and possibilities of sainthood, a frequent subject in Maritain's writing. Callaghan amply
proves his abilities both to use the thought of someone like the
Catholic philosopher Maritain and to project himself imaginatively
into the mind of a saint or an innocent. In *Such Is My Beloved* (and
in *A Time for Judas* too) Callaghan sheds new light on an ancient

biblical text with the illuminations of a modern author's imaginative reflections. *Such Is My Beloved*, now more than a half-century old, takes on fresh meaning when interpreted in light of contemporary scholarship on the Song of Songs, on the life of Aquinas, and on the relationship between human sexuality and spirituality.

Finally, attempts to disengage Callaghan's literary imagination from the basic tenets of an essentially Catholic and neothomist outlook, nourished in particular by Jacques Maritain's influence, are misguided. Further, ignoring Callaghan's probing reflections on biblical materials (judging from the authority of the Song of Songs for *Such Is My Beloved*) overlooks these important resources for his fiction. Callaghan avoids both a dichotomous split of two conflicting realms into an absolute dualism and the complete merging of these two domains into one. His fictional worldview in *Such Is My Beloved* cannot finally be identified exclusively with either Niebuhr's "Christ Against Culture" position nor his "Christ Of Culture" position. The profane and the sacred, the temporal and the eternal, the carnal and the spiritual are neither completely separated nor totally collapsed. They are not combined into a monism of either radical immanence or total transcendence.

Somewhere in the ambiguous territory between these extremities Morley Callaghan stakes out the possibility of an incarnational humanism envisaging a more sophisticated and redemptive relationship between the two realms. The location of the sacred for Callaghan is neither "here" nor "there," neither "above" nor "below." Nathan Scott speaks of the Eucharist as illuminating "the essential genius of the sacramental principle, namely, its power to break down all partitions between the sacred and the quotidian." The sacramental imagination, says Scott, "is not concerned with any special world of sacred things that is conceived to stand over against the commonplace and the everyday; on the contrary, it has a lively vision of the sacredness of the commonplace" (1971, 51). For Morley Callaghan's Father Dowling the commonplace becomes the uncertain ground and ambiguous source of the sacred. For him human love becomes everything; when the basis and source of sacrality for Dowling is shaken and threatened he does not betray his shared experience with Midge and Ronnie of the sacred. Even in the midst of doubt to the point of insanity Dowling will not deny the realities of what he shared with two prostitutes. He persists in his conviction that these two ordinary human beings matter, that he will not abandon them for worldly principles of expedience nor retreat from them to the consolations of supernatural theism.

NOTES

1 I am indebted to Professor Gary Boire of Wilfrid Laurier University, author of a biography of Callaghan (Boire 1995), for generously sharing information about Callaghan's Catholicism, his relationship with Maritain, and the Toronto background to Callaghan's fiction.

2 The revival of Thomism began in 1879 with an encyclical by Pope Leo XIII. In 1914, with the approval of Pope Pius X, twenty-four propositions were published embodying the essential points of Thomas's philosophy, including characterizations of the immortal soul as capable of existing apart from the body and as the source of life and perfection (see *Encyclopedia of Philosophy*, 8:114).

3 This "Protestant city" of the novel is of course recognizable as Toronto, though Callaghan nowhere explicitly states it. Possibly the Roman Catholic Cathedral of the story is modelled on St. Michael's while the psychiatric hospital by the lake is based on an institution located west of Toronto on Lakeshore Boulevard. One of the assessors for *Canadian Literature* when this essay was submitted there in manuscript form suggested—though I think these possibilities less likely—St. Basil's Church on Clover Hill and the psychiatric hospital in Whitby, Ontario, as the originals for Callaghan's novel.

4 Jacques Maritain writes: "The saints always amaze us. Their virtues are freer than those of a merely virtuous man. Now and again, in circumstances outwardly alike, they act quite differently from the way in which a merely virtuous man acts. . . . They have their own kind of mean, their own kinds of standards. But they are valid only for each one of them" (Maritain 1966, 55).

5 Though echoing more directly the Song of Songs 5:5, the baptismal pronouncement is usually taken as a quotation of (or at least an allusion to) Isaiah 42:1, "Behold my servant whom I uphold; mine elect in whom my spirit delighteth," and/or Isaiah 49:3, "Thou art my servant, O Israel, in whom I will be glorified." The prophetic books of the Hebrew Scriptures, rather than the Song of Songs, are considered more likely (because more authoritative) source material for the author of the First Gospel. It is only through a later process of allegorization that the Beloved of the Song is seen to stand for Christ as bridegroom of the Church.

6 Though see the interview with Callaghan found in Cohen 1975, also the general discussion in Pell 1983, and the consideration of *They Shall Inherit the Earth* in O'Connor 1981.

CHAPTER 8

SACRED PASSAGES: NATIVE SYMBOLS IN ATWOOD AND ENGEL

THE FEMALE INITIATION PATTERN

THE OBVIOUS THEMATIC LINKS between Margaret Atwood's *Surfacing* and Marian Engel's *Bear*[1] have been remarked upon casually though explicitly by Northrop Frye, George Woodcock, and others (Frye 1982, 69; Woodcock, in Staines 1977, 95). Margery Fee offers these two novels by Atwood and Engel, along with a dozen more works, as examples of a narrative movement in which a white protagonist, confused about the past, achieves a resolution "through a relationship with an object, image, plant, animal or person associated with Native people" (in King et al. 1987, 16). Fee cites a comment from the chapter in *Survival* entitled "First People" where Atwood finds the writer taking a similar view both of nature and of natives: "an imported whiteman looks at a form of natural or native life alien to himself and appropriates it for symbolic purposes" (Atwood 1972, 91). The native thus becomes a psychic projection, says Atwood, of something the white Canadian either fears (violence or depravity) or wishes (lost instincts or moral values). My task here is to examine the appropriation by Margaret Atwood and Marian Engel of native symbolic forms, with some attempt to assess whether they have misappropriated them.

First, what are the large-scale similarities to be found in *Surfacing* and *Bear*? Each novel features an adult female protagonist, carrying the legacy of the failures of professional and personal life in an urban milieu, seeking regeneration in the northern wilderness of the Canadian Shield. A woman goes to an island home (whose very insularity suggests liminality), in some respects, though more explicitly so in Atwood, an attempt to return to an Edenic child-

---

Notes to Chapter 8 are on p. 187.

171

hood past before the complications of adult life. Their contact with nature is achieved in a rite of passage derived from native sources. The result is personal renewal, the prelude to a return to urban life that is the final stage in a three-part process of separation, liminality, and reaggregation (van Gennep 1960; cf. Turner 1977).[2]

In answer to a question put by a hitchhiking sailor, one of John Updike's stories concludes: "We in America need ceremonies, is I suppose, sailor, the point of what I have written" (Updike 1963). Updike's own fictional practice exemplifies how narrative form replicates certain life patterns, providing in its repetitions and parallels the paradigms of recurrent forms of human endeavour. Given our ceremonial insufficiency, our ritual impoverishment, there is no form or words for burying a dead cat, trading in an old car, celebrating the birth of a baby, or even saying goodbye to a dying parent. Contemporary women experience a much greater deficiency. They lack even the male rites, debased as they might be, for adolescent or other forms of initiation.

A part of what Atwood and Engel have accomplished is to show this inadequacy, this absence of any ritual form, for the transformation of a failed adult woman in the contemporary world. Clearly, male rituals will not do—indeed, a part of the privation experienced by women may be precisely the failure of attempts to adapt themselves to male-defined roles. The search for an appropriate model must be focussed elsewhere. As an oft-repeated generalization has it, the male initiation will typically go along a path involving differentiation, whereas its female counterpart will entail a contrasting integration of self with another: "Boys define their male gender identity principally through separation and individuation, whereas girls define theirs through attachment and identification" (Nelson 1988, 39).

Both Atwood's nameless narrator and Engel's Lou integrate themselves with the natural world, the initiation also involving a symbolic act of sexual union with another. Further, each follows something like the path outlined by Carol Christ in an essay on the female spiritual quest. Carol Christ discovers in Doris Lessing's *The Four-Gated City* a pattern in which a modern woman begins with an inadequate image of the self ("the experience of nothingness"); then, she proceeds to a vision of transcendence, learning from motherhood and from another woman; finally, she explores an extra-ordinary reality to become a seer and prophet who understands self and world (Christ 1979, 238). In Atwood and Engel this general pattern gets its specificity from native initiatory rites, themselves typical of the widespread phenomenon of initiation (see Guédon 1983, 91-111; VanSpanckeren 1988, 183-204; Pratt 1981, 139-57).

According to Mircea Eliade's survey of the "mysteries of initiation," the symbolic pattern of death and rebirth emerges as central and pervasive. The common features evident in such rites of passage begin with the neophyte's separation from the family and seclusion in the forest where a hut symbolizes the maternal womb. There the neophyte awaits the new day, undergoing ordeals and tortures at the hands of the mythic ancestors representative of initiatory death and prelude to a second birth—in short, reliving the cosmology. The final feature, says Eliade, "which appears in a great many initiations, and not always in the most primitive societies," is the injunction to kill a man. Manhood involves imitation of the behaviour of the god who has killed the neophyte during the initiation. In military societies and for the warrior-hero in particular the initiate proves his new status by killing (Eliade 1967, 197-200; cf. Utley et al. 1971, 135-37).[3]

Though there exists less detailed knowledge of them, in female initiations the pattern is largely similar in its early phases. With young women, as with young men, segregation occurs from family and community. Usually taking place at first menstruation, the adolescent female is isolated in a special hut in the bush. Both male and female initiatory rites, then, involve a deathlike ordeal taking place in a cosmic context and eventuating in a metamorphosis to a new mode of being. However, in the female initiation divergence from the male pattern takes place because of the woman's role with respect to fertility and giving birth, a secret realm unparalleled in male experience and, as Eliade terms it, "the revelation of the feminine sacredness." Early in his *Myths, Dreams, and Mysteries* and referring to the responsibility inherent in cannibalism for the continuation of vegetative life, Mircea Eliade quotes an Abyssinian song: "She who has not yet given birth, let her give birth; he who has not yet killed, let him kill!" (ibid., 46-47). This startling typifying injunction, comments Eliade, illustrates how "the two sexes are condemned each to accept its destiny" (ibid., 47). Ruth Underhill, describing the nature of "Woman Power" among North American Indians, says that a menstruating woman is the vessel of a supernatural power that allows her to give birth: "This power is so different from man's power to hunt and kill that the two must be kept apart" (Underhill 1965, 51). In some cultures, especially during the childbearing years, a woman must not touch hunting weapons, while, correspondingly, a male presence is widely regarded as unlucky at childbirth. How these two powers are kept apart may be seen in various tribal practices in native North America, ranging from puberty seclusion for young women during their first menstruation to the way in which male hunters on their return to camp transfer an animal's corpse to women to be turned into food (Cruikshank 1979, 14-15; Tanner 1979, 77-81, 153-55, 179).

The conductor Walter Damrosch remarked of Aaron Copland's first work, *Symphony for Organ and Orchestra*: "If he can write like that at 23, in 5 years he'll be ready to commit murder!"[4] Even granted that Damrosch might have had in mind the particularly dissonant qualities of the work, the comment implies a progression of musical genius from creativity to killing. As oversimplified and objectionable as it may be, frequently the quintessential male activity is characterized as one form or another of "killing," whether in literal terms of taking human or animal life or extended metaphorically, as Atwood's *Surfacing* does, to include other activities as well. Even allowing for the secrecy surrounding women's mysteries, the fact is that they have not been hallowed in story and legend to the same extent as have men's. One way of looking at the narrator of *Surfacing* and Lou in *Bear* is to see them as failed adult women in flight from a male-defined world to seek a new life, but lacking in their culture the paradigms for their search. Perhaps because our culture depreciates or neglects female initiation in adolescence, an adult woman who has lived according to a male script turns elsewhere for the rites to lead her into a new mode of being. In Canadian literature the lifeways of native peoples frequently provide such a possibility.

ATWOOD's *Surfacing*

THE INITIATION OF ATWOOD's nameless narrator in *Surfacing* takes place in the last third of the novel, chapters 17 to 27. It consists principally, during the opening phase in chapters 17 to 20, of her receiving two "gifts" from her deceased parents. The first gift, from her father, is the ability to acknowledge the truth about herself and her past. The shock of seeing his drowned body under-water as she dives looking for submerged rock paintings gives access to the truth underlying such fabrications as a drowned brother, a failed marriage and divorce, and a baby left behind in the city: all these stories were manufactured to cover up the painful fact of the abortion. Her second gift is a drawing the narrator had made as a child, a kind of pictograph of her own making preserved by her mother. Her reading of its meaning constitutes a challenge to confront evil and power, to commit herself responsibly to life. The immediate reaction to these legacies is to leave an offering of clothing by the cliff where she experienced the underwater vision and to copulate with Joe in ritual atonement for the aborted fetus. According to Carol Christ's scheme, all the various elements of madness, motherhood, and prophetic vision occur here.

Anyone studious of Atwood's background, revealed in inter-view, essay, and film, can probably identify the setting of *Surfacing* as an island on Lake Kipawa, site of her parents' cabin (see Miner 1975; Atwood 1987b; National Film Board 1984). Further, she has acknowledged her reliance upon Selwyn Dewdney's *Indian Rock Paintings of the Great Lakes* for much of the detail appearing in the novel about native pictographs (Dewdney 1967). And, as Dewd-ney's book indicates, Lake Kipawa is the location of some Algonkian pictographs whose position he provides. What begins as a scientific curiosity about the rock paintings on the part of the narrator's botanist father develops into experiential encounter—on his part, though proleptic of his daughter's later involvement—with the sacrality inherent in the sites where the paintings are found. Thematically the pictographs link with the narrator's frus-trated attempt as artist to render the illustrations required by her publisher. What she cannot produce to order (illustrations for a book of Québec folk tales in sanitized English translation with an eye on American and British markets) comes unbidden as revela-tory vision during her psychic immersion into the depths. As she comments: "The Indians did not own salvation but they had once known where it lived and their signs marked the sacred places, the places where you could learn the truth" (155).

The next major stage of the initiation, in chapters 21 to 27, is her separation from her three companions, the subsequent seclu-sion on the island, and the almost literal reenactment of an Amerindian vision quest culminating in successive visions of her dead parents in animal form, her mother as a blue jay and her father as a wolf. The narrator's integration with the natural world ("I am the thing in which the trees and animals move and grow, I am a place" [195]) comes after her refusal of language, human habitation, food from tins, clothing, and all the rest of the accoutrements of civilized life in response to taboos and rules that allow her to "approach the condition they themselves have entered" (194). Having placed her feet into the prints taken to be her father's footprints, and "find[ing] that they are my own" (201), the narrator returns to ordinary life and to herself—"they have gone finally, back into the earth, the air, the water, wherever they were when I summoned them" (202). A Winnebago initiation ritual has the neophyte "killed," then spending a night in the great grandmother's lodge. In the morning the neophyte finds four "footprints of light," "the footprints of those who have passed into life again." The neophyte, upon stepping into these footprints, also gains a new and renewed life (Harding 1956, 5). Like the Ojibwa, the Winnebago Indians belong to the Algonkian linguistic group and are one of the culture groups of the Eastern Woodlands.

Basil Johnston, an Ojibwa teacher and ethnologist, has set forth in two related volumes, *Ojibway Heritage* and *Ojibway Ceremonies*, his people's religion, myths, legends, and rituals. The geographic range of the southeastern branch of the Ojibwe (or Anishnaabeg, to use the term many Ojibwe speakers prefer) includes Johnston's home reserve of Parry Island and much of present-day central and southern Ontario. Their territory also extends east across the Ottawa River into the province of Québec, including Lake Kipawa, the setting of *Surfacing*.

In *Ojibway Heritage* Johnston describes "the attainment of womanhood" as the "most singular event" in a girl's life and "the greatest of gifts." At the time of initial menstruation the girl was separated from the village for a week ("so unique and personal was the gift of life-giving"), fasting in isolation, visited only by her mother or grandmother, to receive "the gift of Kitche Manitou" (Johnston 1976, 124). Johnston continues: "There was to be no distraction; hence no food; there was to be no interference; hence no visitors. And because the gift was intended for women alone, there were to be no men. The gift was denied to men ever to remain a mystery, sealed and closed" (ibid.). At the end of the vigil the child had been transformed into a woman: "She was now able to conceive and give birth; she possessed a gift she had not possessed before. Ready and changed, the girl was returned to her home and village by her mother where a feast awaited" (ibid., 125).

Though I have already referred to the narrator of *Surfacing* as performing "the almost literal reenactment of an Amerindian vision quest," perhaps the differences between "almost" and "total" should be commented on. First, the narrator is a failed adult woman, probably in her twenties, living in the city, and of European ancestry. She is not a twelve-year-old Ojibwa girl at the onset of initial menstruation. Further, her connection to the land is only partial at best, the result of her parents' seasonal alteration between city and bush. She has been forced to acknowledge her connection with the "killers" who are desecrating the landscape, cutting down trees, damming the lake, flooding the shoreline, killing animals, and sometimes submerging sacred sites where pictographs had existed. Even her father is one of them, a supposed "botanist" whose real work, in a moment of bitter realization, she sees as that of the "surveyor" who helped the process by making maps. Finally, *Surfacing*'s narrator has in her own terms misused her original and unrecognized "gift" of fertility. She passed from girlhood to womanhood without ceremony in an unmediated and unritualized fashion; then she "conceived"; then she aborted the fetus.

In some important respects, then, her reenactment of the vision quest cannot be a simple repetition of a rite for which she has been prepared by her cultural background, her ethnicity, or her own life experiences. A kind of purification and atonement is first necessary for her. Even then, there is no mother present to help and guide and visit her during her ordeal or to return her to the village once it is over. Her dead mother has entered another time, what native people might call the "Land of Souls." Among the Ojibwa, ghosts sometimes become intermediaries for prayers addressed to higher supernatural beings. On occasion the ghosts of ancestors might themselves bestow blessings or function as personal guardian spirits (see Hultkrantz 1981, 102-103). These additional complications and differences make simple "reenactment" impossible. Something like a complex adaptation is necessary, though the Amerindian rites provide for the narrator a model for what she finally has to attain, if not exactly by this means then by something similar.

The narrator has made the perilous shamanic journey to the land of the dead and back again. The insights she carries with her are imparted with an extremity of compression in a few pages in the book's final two chapters. To some extent the criticism of some feminist commentators that Atwood's narrator's wilderness quest does not get tested in the lab of urban experience has its validity. Even more to the point is the view that this individual spiritual transformation lacks a communal dimension. Here the vision quest of the narrator of *Surfacing* differs most markedly from the Amerindian model. Entirely absent is the supportive structure of family (except in the visionary appearances of her deceased parents), tribe, or village. Her reaggregation is not to a close-knit community but to the privatized anonymity of contemporary life.

Atwood's narrator knows that she cannot stay in the bush, that her place is in the city. The gods that were manifest in her wilderness transformation have receded, probably never to appear again (as she acknowledges). She accepts the limitations of language, the responsible exercise of power, the refusal to be a victim, the probable failures of love. Her integration of head and body, of logic and feeling, has healed her inner division and made her whole. She accepts her own capacity for evil, rather than imputing it entirely to "killers" (whether males or Americans). She accepts her role as a giver of life—"to prefer life, I owe them that"—to give birth and to be a nurturer, in a sacrificial world where all the negativities of dissection, separation, reason, and technology have been so evident to her. The narrator ritually fulfils the aims of the female initiation into the destiny to give birth.

ENGEL'S *Bear*

To the south across Georgian Bay's North Channel from the island on which Colonel Cary's Pennarth is situated is the town of Gore Bay on Manitoulin Island. Marian Engel's heroine, Lou, crossed Manitoulin Island on her way from Tobermory to Espanola, though she did not have time to stop at Gore Bay. She missed, then, the chance to visit town's museum, located in a building that once had been in part a jail and where, occupying one cell is all the malevolent looking equipment of a bygone dentist. In another room a bed is made up with old-fashioned covers and complete with a pair of embroidered pillowcases. One pillow reads: "I slept and dreamt that life was beauty." The embroidery on the other pillowcase completes the motto: "I woke and found that it was duty." The same kind of stern puritanical waking reality is expressed more simply on the famous quilt belonging to Pierre Elliott Trudeau and displayed at one time at Ottawa's National Gallery: "Reason over Passion." Lou comes to grip with the relationship between reason and passion, beauty and duty, life and art during her northern summer, after emerging from her subterranean life in the city.

Alec Lucas describes how nature writing fuses factual content about the natural world and the human imaginative and emotional response to nature (1983, 543-47). For more than a century Canadian nature writing displayed various strategies in the attempt to fit the natural and the human together, whether drawing upon earlier hierarchical assumptions about nature's subservience to human purposes, to a modern conservation ethic ascribing independent value to the nonhuman world, or finally to a contemporary view that sees nature as wise, revelatory, and containing within itself the fundamental clues to all existence, including human existence. Somewhere along this continuum of possibilities between a dominated nature and a numinous, revelatory nature lies a view of the natural world as having spiritual value—and its own wisdom— capable of being a repository of values for humans yet retaining its independence from the human world, perhaps allowing for some kind of peaceful coexistence of people and animals, the human and the nonhuman (see chap. 3 above).

The epigraph to *Bear*, from Kenneth Clark's *Landscape into Art*, is wonderfully suggestive as a clue to how the novel sees the imagination interacting with nature: "facts become art through love," it begins. This quotation shows the balance to be achieved by the protagonist, Lou, in her transformation from the underground, colourless, mole-like existence of her winter self with its weekly copulations with her boss ("the Director") to a passionate engagement with the animal world in which Lou, for a time, surrenders her caution, her puritanical strictures, and almost her reason. In this respect Lou is the spiritual sister of *Surfacing*'s narrator, who also makes a leap from a cerebral life without feeling to complete immersion in the natural world that effectively puts her in touch with the embodied aspects of existence. Like Atwood's narrator, Engel's protagonist must return to some midpoint of sanity in which the initiation into nature remains a continuing corrective that balances the intellectual and rational excesses of the earlier life. Each journey displays a distinctively feminist pattern of retreat from a male-defined world of rationality and culture to the healing insights of nature, imparting self-discovery.

Lou's profession is that of bibliographer and cataloguer—"she ordered the fragments of other lives" (Engel 1977, 92). She had left journalism after trespassing in an interview into the private life of one of her subjects, next choosing archival work because it was "the least parasitic of the narrative historical occupations" (101). Cataloguing Colonel Cary's library at Pennarth was to be an exercise for her in narrative history, in the hope that "research would reveal enough to provide her subject with a character" (5) and that his library would at least reveal enough "to develop the dim negative of that region's history" (5). Instead Lou discovers that "Colonel Cary was surely one of the great irrelevancies of Canadian history" (93), unconnected to anything. Cary's library is no more than a conventional nineteenth-century gentleman's library of British books. Lou works her way through them "methodically, because passion is not the medium of bibliography" and because she "did not believe in non-rational processes" (77). The upshot of Lou's attempt through cataloguing the library to transmute these facts into art is a failure.

After listening to Homer's story of the last Colonel Cary, a woman, Lou has a crisis of faith and conscience, questioning herself and her task. For Lou realizes that her own attempt to build a beautiful structure or to plumb a secret through her file cards would never amount to "anything as revealing and vivid as Homer's story, or as relevant" (93; see 40). When dispassionate bibliographer meets local storyteller the truths of anecdotal narration surpass historical facticity. The true pioneer most relevant to the region is the third "colonel," the least colonial colonel, the woman who skinned and tanned the lynx, not the first and most colonial colonel with his imported books.

The facts that Lou invests with love, raising them to the level of art, are the slips that fall from the books with Cary's lore about bears inscribed on them. As she reads and absorbs the zoological and mythological facts about bears, Lou begins to visualize the bear she is tending at Pennarth in the terms of this lore. Perhaps the "light" that zoology and mythology sheds upon "her" bear is that very "all embracing love [that] is expressed by light" to which Kenneth Clark avers. Perhaps it is here that passion begins to supplant reason, the beauties of mythology to transcend the duties of bibliographer. Lou begins to disown her inadequate life among facts, as defined by her bibliographer's task, aware now of its irrelevance to her personal task. She turns to a new branch of narrative history, that of personal quest or inner journey, where her guides are the truths of myth, not file cards. Lou has left behind "the imperious business of imposing narrative order on a structure devised internally and personally by a mind her numbers would teach her to discover" (40).

Lou's presentiments of rebirth and transformation begin to find fulfilment in her encounter with the bear. But Lou has been swept too far into the realm of myth, forgetting Homer's caution to remember that he is a "wild critter." She anthropomorphizes the bear—"she had discovered she could paint any face on him that she wanted" (78)—attributing to him a whole range of human emotions, seeing him variously as pet, companion, friend, lover, child, god. Sometimes he is "a cross between a king and a woodchuck" (58); then, he is "solid as a sofa, domestic, a rug of a bear," but someone still that she is moved to kneel beside (76). At the end the bear transcends history to become, in terms reminiscent of Faulkner, "an enormous, living creature larger and older and wiser than time" (140), though finally he recedes to the appearance of "a fat, dignified old woman" (164).

Lou's fullest fantasy, though, is her imagining that the relationship with the bear will culminate in sexual intercourse with him (not just lingual, but penile). At last Lou comes to several resolutions: "she knew now that she loved him" (137); "she felt sometimes he was God" (139); and, "she now lived intensely and entirely for the bear" (141). After an initial attempt to mount the bear and have him penetrate her, her guilt drives her to seek out Homer, both because "the quality of her love was different now" and "because she had gone too far with him. There was something aggressive in her that always went too far" (143). Yet it seems she has still not fully learned the lesson; the initiation is still not complete. When Lou presents herself on all fours in response to the bear's erection, he swipes her back with his claws. This painful gesture wounds her, but also makes her "at last clean," "clean and simple and proud" (162). This "claw that healed guilt" (166) completes the sought-for transformation, though at once in a way more painful and more healing than Lou anticipated. The clawing of her back appears to be several things: a rebuke for having to do with a bear, or at least for violating a taboo in that relationship; an atonement for her own past, especially for allowing herself to be objectified in the sexual relationship with the Director of the Institute; and, it is the restoration of Lou to herself (and metaphorically, to the status of virgin), after another instance of her having gone too far.

In the Athapaskan story of "The Girl and the Grizzly" the woman who (unwittingly) marries the bear is instructed not to look if she wakes up first in the morning. When she violates the instruction her bear-husband rebukes her: "Now you know." He apparently also strikes her, for the next words are: "But her mind is still fixed from that slap" (see McClellan 1970; cf. Cruikshank 1979). Marian Engel relates how during writing *Bear* she met the Haida artist, Bill Reid. On his advice she read Marius Barbeau's *The Bear Princess* and added another half-page to her manuscript: "And that's all the content that was needed to make the whole thing fall together" (Klein 1985, 28). Though I cannot find this additional half-page with Mouse Woman's comment about shooting the bear, this interview shows Engel's collaboration with a native person.

In one light Lou's expectation of a literal copulation with the bear may be the consequence of her mythomania, of making too drastic a swing from methodical bibliographer to the passionate lover of a bear. In another respect, it could be literal-minded interpretation of the slips of bear-lore to the extent that she anticipates sexual union with him, and even offspring by him—"there was something in her that went too far." As with *Surfacing*'s narrator, Lou has passed from one extreme of order, boundaries, and separation to the other extreme of complete breakdown of categories and the merging of self and other. She has, temporarily, left the human world for the animal world; she has, forgetful that she is not an Amerindian, tried to become "the girl who married the bear," as the widespread native mythology has it.

At the end of *The Symbolism of Evil*, in a chapter entitled "Conclusion: The Symbol Gives Rise to Thought," Paul Ricoeur, in terms that have become well known in discussions of hermeneutics, asks how to restore a myth as symbol without dissolving it into explanation (1969, 347-57). When no "primitive naïveté" is possible, when the immediacy of belief is lost irretrievably, it is through interpretation and criticism, says Ricoeur, that we can hear again. His version of the hermeneutical circle—"We must understand in order to believe, but we must believe in order to understand"—provides a way out for Lou, a means of balancing bibliographer and lover, of reason and passion, duty and beauty. Lou cannot become a bear; she cannot become an Indian; in the north, she cannot ever be more than a visitor or tourist. She cannot surrender her beginning point of departure. But she can aim at, and indeed achieve, a second naïveté in which the ancient symbols have power to transform and affect her without requiring that she surrender her own vantage point. Something like that is what Lou has, when on her return to the urban south she sees, amid the stars overhead, "the Great Bear and his thirty-seven thousand virgins," keeping her company. The Kiowa story of Tsoai relates how a boy turns into a bear and then chases his seven sisters, who run to escape him. Climbing upon a stump, they are elevated to the sky beyond his reach and become the stars of the Big Dipper (Ursa Major) (Momaday 1990).

Conclusion

A statement from George Grant's *Technology and Empire* has been quoted, given an almost canonical status in effect, by both Northrop Frye and Margaret Atwood (see chap. 3 above): "When we go into the Rockies we may have the sense that gods are there. But if so, they cannot manifest themselves to us as ours. They are the gods of another race, and we cannot know them because of what we are, and what we did" (Frye 1977, 28; Atwood 1972, 90.) In an interview about *Surfacing* in which she terms Christianity "imported religion," Margaret Atwood declares: "The authentic religion has been destroyed; you have to discover it in some other way" (Ingersoll 1990, 19).

Native religious traditions represent for her the means by which Canada's first peoples made contact with the gods intrinsic to this country, what non-natives have to recover or return to by another means. As Northrop Frye comments, referring to a poem by John Newlove: "The Indians symbolize a primitive mythological imagination which is being reborn in us: in other words, white Canadians, in their imaginations, are no longer immigrants but are becoming indigenous, recreating the kind of attitudes appropriate to people who really belong here" (Frye 1977, 40). The qualifying phrase "in their imaginations" seems to me to be crucial here. James Raffan, on the other hand, goes too far when he states, "There is a chance, I dare say, that one need not be an aboriginal to be native to a place, to have a sense of nativity related to a particular place" (Raffan 1990, viii). The notion of "nativity" as Raffan develops it is dangerously close to usurping what it is to be a native in the sense of being a "native person."

In the summer of 1980 James Raffan and five friends (including Gail Simmons, his future wife) canoed through the Northwest Territories, covering 800 kilometres in seven weeks. They began at Munn Lake, about 250 kilometres northeast of Yellowknife, then made their way northward along the dried-up Back and the rapid-filled Burnside Rivers, crossing two heights of land until finally reaching Bathurst Inlet on Coronation Gulf, just above the Arctic Circle. In a wonderfully evocative and thoughtfully reflective book Raffan describes that trip in both its literal and mythic dimensions.

James Raffan draws on such recent thinkers about nature and the impact of geography on human beings as Yi-Fu Tuan, Barry Lopez, Aldo Leopold, and Bruce Chatwin. He also draws on the exploration journals of John Franklin, Samuel Hearne, and Knud Rasmussen. He refers to northern historians and to other accounts of canoe trips. Some of the notions advanced some time ago by Glenn Gould about music being derived from the land are usefully employed here, with the suggestion that this may be a "journey in six/eight time," combining thereby the cyclical succession of days and tasks with the journey's linearity, and finally freed from its location in time and space, taking on the mythic qualities of an imaginative voyage. Through the lens of this particular trip in 1980 Raffan looks back at earlier trips and to the origins of his own interests in canoe trips from his childhood in southern Ontario and to summers spent at camp. The result is a distillation of a wealth of experience, sifted, held up to the light, turned over and examined again.

The idea of belonging to the land in a special way, particularly as experienced and focussed on a canoe trip, is here termed nativity, that is, "a meshing of the human spirit and the spirit of the land, which may well be the essence of being native to a place." Among other possibilities Raffan suggests the possible retirement of such stereotypes as the white as rapist of the land opposing the native person as its noble steward. All this gets us too quickly into theoretical white water, needing some further preliminary survey to spy out some lurking obstacles.

The term "nativity" is inherently problematical, besides its primary religious association with church festivals celebrating the births of Jesus, the Virgin Mary, or John the Baptist. For the belonging to the land that is indigenousness derives, etymologically and also legally and politically, from being born in that place. Oddly, Raffan wants to pry loose "nativity" from any connection with birth, suggesting instead that it comes from "sustained encounter with the land," and "not from the colour of one's skin or necessarily from one's cultural heritage": one can therefore experience "nativity" without being a native person.

In a sense anyone born in Canada is a "native person." We all sing that Canada is "our home and native land." And Lynn Johnston, cartoonist of *For Better or For Worse* fame, is described on the cover of the American edition of one of her books as "a native Canadian," though she probably has no Indian, Métis, or Inuit ancestry. While we might sympathize with someone wanting to say that belonging to the land can be experienced by someone who, while perhaps born in Canada, is not an aboriginal person, some other term than "nativity" ought to be used for that experience. This metaphoric borrowing careens perilously close to the brink of the kinds of cultural theft that natives so often and rightly complain of. How, for instance, do land claims get settled if the "nativity" of being an aboriginal person confers no more indigenousness than someone who "senses" belonging to a place while on a canoe trip (or while prospecting, lumbering, or building dams for that matter)? When the native people of the Mackenzie River Valley told Justice Tom Berger "the land is our mother" or "the land is our blood," that unique expression of "nativity" should be respected, not borrowed or usurped.

Surfacing and *Bear* also get us into the complexities of cultural appropriation or borrowing. They both skate close to the thin ice of the charge that white writers, when they make their stories out of the myths, symbols, or legends of native peoples, or when their characters purport to speak with native voices, quickly slip from cultural appropriation to misappropriation (usually a polite term for robbery). Some have charged that such borrowing lies on a continuum with other acts of white thievery, beginning with natives' land and extending to their children, religion, and language. Anne Cameron's retelling of the stories she says that she heard from Nootka women in *Daughters of Copper Woman* has raised serious questions about appropriation in her case.

In the 1990s in Canada a controversy arose after it was proposed that no grant support be given to writers who appropriated the voices and stories of others (not only of cultural minorities but of women too). This move was vigorously opposed by various Canadian writers who argued that it is in the very nature of literary art to speak with another voice or to see with eyes other than one's own. Native author and scholar Thomas King acknowledges that many non-natives through whose eyes natives have been viewed are sympathetic. "What," he asks, "do we do with writers who are not Native by birth but whose experience and knowledge may make them more perceptive writers and commentators than many writers who are Native by birth" (King 1990, xi).

Probably we ought to recognize what Atwood and Engel have *not* done in the novels under review here. They have not attempted to speak with native voices (or, if so, in the case of Engel, only in the most minor way). And they have not attempted to render a native narrative viewpoint. Their two heroines remain resolutely white and only in their liminal condition do they actually—and temporarily—experience the power of the native symbolic form. In some respects both texts implicitly recognize that there are limits—established both by an aware sensitivity and by one's own socialization—to the appropriation of another culture. There may be some parallels in E. F. Schumacher, whose *Small Is Beautiful* included a chapter on "Buddhist Ethics." Later Schumacher explained why next time he would use the resources of Roman Catholicism to make the same kind of case: he thought a person, in terms of religion at least, should "stay at home" (Fager 1977, 325-28). Schumacher said that if he had written on Christian economics no one would have listened, and that he first had to overcome his own "anti-Christian trauma." He discovered Gandhi's advice to his Christian friends from the West: "Stay at home!"

In some respects the wilderness sojourns of Atwood's narrator and Engel's Lou represent an undoing of the conquering relation to place characteristic of colonialism. Their journeys to the other world leave no mark upon it; the only thing they take away is a personal transformation. Both women know they are not natives, and both also know that a sustained access to the gods they have temporarily encountered in the wilderness must be discovered in another way.

NOTES

1 Atwood, *Surfacing* (1987a), and Engel, *Bear* (1977). References to *Surfacing* and to *Bear* are to the paperback editions and hereafter are cited parenthetically in the text. References for *Surfacing* are to the fourteenth printing (February 1987); earlier printings have different pagination.

2 At the conclusion of an earlier essay on *Surfacing* I commented: "In *Surfacing* the 'jail-break' and 'recreation' to which Atwood looks at the end of *Survival* has occurred. In Marian Engel's *Bear*, Lou, the questing female protagonist, is taken a little further from the scene of her island transformation along the road that leads back to the city" (James 1981a, 174-81). Due to the extensive critical commentary extant on *Surfacing* I have here avoided the kind of detailed close reading available elsewhere, or in my own earlier essay.

3 While no one seems to have done so, the application of the full pattern to Faulkner's novel reveals a failed initiation. Ike McCaslin, who has been ritually prepared not only to kill the bear but to slay Sam Fathers, cannot do either, his role being usurped by the half-wit Boon. His tragedy is exemplified in a gesture of relinquishment, the refusal of the inheritance of the land, culminating in his being childless ("uncle to half a county and still father to none"). In the terms suggested by Eliade and others on the respective "destiny" of the sexes to kill and give birth, Ike's failure to fulfil the terms of his initiation leads to his wife's refusal of sexual relations with him.

4 In the course of writing I heard this comment of Damrosch quoted on CBC radio. Cf. *The Concise Oxford Dictionary of Music*, ed. Michael Kennedy, 3rd ed. (London: Oxford University Press, 1980), 147.

CHAPTER 9

NORDICITY AND THE SACRED: THE JOURNEYS OF THOMAS YORK AND ARITHA VAN HERK

A PENDULUM CLOCK BROUGHT from the equator to a northern country will run fast. Arctic rivers cut deepest into their right banks, and hunters lost in the north woods unconsciously veer to the right as the earth turns beneath their feet. And in the north the dangerous storms from the west often begin with an east wind. All of these things are related to the Coriolus, the reeling gyroscopic effect of the earth's spin that creates wind and flow of weather, the countering backwashes and eddies of storms.

— E. Annie Proulx, *The Shipping News*

THE FUGITIVE

TOM YORK'S DEATH IN A CAR ACCIDENT early in January 1988 occurred twenty-five years after his first entry into Canada. Late in December 1962 York, with his wife Lynn, "fled precipitately, and with as little forethought as any fugitive" (York 1978a, 16) from his graduate studies at North Carolina's Duke University and from his draft board in Little Rock, Arkansas. His arrival in Canada made him, in those days before the Vietnam War was to bring many more, one of the earliest of the draft evaders to come north and cross the border. York's flight to Canada, even more than an evasion of the draft, was a search for God. He describes himself as having been impelled by a "woodward urge" (12, 19). The story of that flight and that search amid the flight is told in his spiritual autobiography, *And Sleep in the Woods: The Story of One Man's Spiritual Quest* (1978a).

Notes to Chapter 9 are on p. 212.

And Sleep in the Woods stands as the most articulate, stylistically gifted, and honest account we have, contextualized in a Canadian setting, of a classic conversion to Christianity. York's
autobiography has its place in a tradition of conversion narratives
beginning with Paul's on the Damascus Road, continuing through
Augustine's *Confessions* and Bunyan's *Pilgrim's Progress*, and
extending in the twentieth century to C. S. Lewis's *Surprised by
Joy*. York tells how with his wife Lynn he spent two winters in the
bush, first in New Brunswick and then in Ontario, until finally his
conversion took place. He finishes with an account of how then he
went back to face trial in Little Rock in 1973. He was convicted at
the first trial but later acquitted on appeal, meanwhile having again
become a fugitive.

After his conversion York entered Emmanuel College at the
University of Toronto, and was ordained in 1967 as a United
Church minister, eventually serving pastorates in British Columbia
(the Queen Charlotte Islands, Bella Bella, and Whistler and Pem-
berton), Yellowknife, and Toronto. York returned to Tulane University in New Orleans in the 1970s for a few years, finished an
M.A., and worked towards his doctorate. He finally received his
Ph.D. in literature in 1982 with a dissertation on Malcolm Lowry.
While working as a minister, and before his death, he also was able
to write and publish, besides the autobiography, four novels: *We,
The Wilderness* (1973), based on his experience with the Indians of
the west coast; *Snowman* (1976), adapted from the life of the leg-
endary northern adventurer John Hornby; *The Musk Ox Passion*
(1978b), winner of an award for the Best Comic Novel of 1978,
about an odyssey to pick qiviut (the soft underhair of the musk
ox); and *Trapper* (1981), the best of the fictional treatments of
Albert Johnson, "the Mad Trapper of Rat River," one of Canada's
most celebrated fugitives. With the setting of his posthumously
published novel, *Desireless* (1989), York returned (as he himself
regularly did) to the south and specifically to New Orleans.

York drew parallels between his own life and the heroic figures
he wrote about. In Yellowknife in the early 1970s he learned from
talking to old-timers that John Hornby and Albert Johnson "were
two northern characters through whom I might come to terms
with the Arctic" (1981, xi). He compares his paranoia with Johnson's during the time of his skirmishes with the FBI in those years:
"As the FBI pursued me from the Mexican to the Canadian border,

and raided the places where I hid, Albert Johnson became my conscious and visceral model" (ibid.). In 1978 York retraced the hazardous route of Johnson's flight from the point of his arrival in Fort McPherson to the site of his death. Then, "with the external imprint of the land, and the internal memory of having been pursued" (ibid., xii), York underwent a two-year siege in a room while he wrote *Trapper*, an account with factual names, dates, and places, but fictional characters—"I had ghosts of my own to exorcise" (ibid.).

Tom York constantly ranged between—seeking to reconcile and hold in tension—various contradictions and opposites: city and bush, activity and passivity, domesticity and wanderlust, war and peace, flesh and spirit. He canoed, lifted weights, ran, worked out, and built cabins in the woods; he also sheltered refugees and homeless students, preached and prayed, loved and struggled. He was deeply religious, yet committed to the secular. Tom York was active in several organizations of authors, including the Writers' Union of Canada and PEN. From 1985 until his death in 1988 he was chaplain at St. Paul's United College, University of Waterloo.

Faithful to friends, but divided in his allegiances, York once described himself as "ambiguous, not ambivalent." He depicted himself as torn between two spirit principles: the "light, dry, cold male spirit" of the North and the "dark, warm, wet Mother Earth" of the South. He would have agreed with Graham Greene on the "virtue of disloyalty": "If you have to earn a living . . . and the price they make you pay is loyalty, be a double agent—and never let either of the two sides know your real name" ("Under the Garden," quoted in Stratford 1973, 581). Greene maintained that whereas "loyalty confines you to accepted opinions," and prohibits a sympathetic comprehension of others, "disloyalty encourages you to roam through any human mind: it gives the novelist an extra dimension of understanding" (in Stratford 1973, 609). Partially as the price of this kind of "disloyalty" York fought many battles, from major ones with the United States government to minor skirmishes with a United Church presbytery, while seeking peace and justice.

In a lecture at Queen's University in 1980 Tom York spoke of modern life as seen typically in literature from a "post-mortem" perspective—that is, as if from beyond death. He bore an acute consciousness of the existential and international darkness of our age. In a sermon in 1986 he described the human situation as one of living "in the meantime," during which we are "captives of an

unruly present, herded by events toward an uncertain future."
While his dark vision of things tended to exclude any cheap and
facile optimism, he also lived in hope rather than despair. Even during the personal "in the meantime" periods of one's life he urged
involvement and engagement, confident of a redemptive dimension
to such moments in our history and in individual lives, aware that
the time is seldom "right," confident that "God is in the details,"
as he was fond of saying. His choice in the early 1960s was to come
to Canada: "I have been living in the meantime ever since. Now
when I meet veterans of that tragic war, we recognize each other as
fellow travellers who spent a decade of their lives dealing with
events that overtook us" (Baccalaureate Sermon, Queen's University, 9 March 1986).

With the poet Theodore Roethke, Tom York affirmed that he
learned where he had to go only in the act of going. He always
seemed to be going somewhere. Whether running or seeking, he
was always going somewhere and learning along the way. Passionate
and active, Tom York was, like Pastor André Trocmé of Le Cham-
bon, *un violent vaincu par Dieu* (a violent man conquered by God).
Aware of death, and it seems increasingly of his own mortality, in
one of his last published pieces, York tells of Trapper Ray ("He was
either drunk or crazy, in fact he was a little of both"), who planned
to run the suicidal rapids of the Liard River's Grand Canyon before
they were dammed. The river that had been Trapper Ray's home
would become a swamp. York wonders: "Why not go out with one
last gesture of defiance?" (York 1986, 147). York's own life ended
suddenly and violently while returning to his northern spiritual
adopted home from the southern home that was the matrix of his
early life. He would have preferred to have died on the Liard River
than on Route 66.

THE SPIRITUAL QUEST

"NOT ALL JOURNEYS HAVE PRECISELY the same symbolic
intentions: some are carefully planned journeys; in others
the hero does not even know he is on a journey; sometimes the
reader does not know it either." With that, one critic (Vogel 1974,
185) introduces his attempt to provide a lexicon of journey literature, differentiating six various kinds of literary journeys—journey,
wandering, quest, pilgrimage, odyssey, and going-forth. A quest,

according to Vogel, requires "an original sense of mission" shared among author, reader, and hero, and though a definite goal may be absent, the protagonist will know on arrival that the goal has been attained, because the stages along the way have been predestined (ibid., 186). A wandering hero does not know the meaning of the journey; a pilgrimage has a definite goal; and, an odyssey lacks a spiritual or moral mission. Where does the flight of the fugitive fit into this scheme? York's mission in *And Sleep in the Woods* is at the outset a negative one, to flee, though his exodus is not exclusively a flight from the Little Rock draft board. When his ailing father, during a last visit that turns out to be their farewell, accuses him of being afraid of two years in the army, twenty-two-year-old Tom replies that "it's not just that." He explains: "It's that I can see the end here, before I've even begun. . . . There's a prefab pattern that I can't see myself fitting into—it's not the South, it's just me—that I'd sooner commit suicide than conform to" (12).

But at least the South's "prefab pattern" includes the possibilities of security afforded to him (and perhaps even more necessary, as his father reminds him, for his wife) by jobs and money, food and shelter, and family connections. But negative images of threat and engulfment are put forth in the autobiography's early chapters as well. The miasmic swamp is nicknamed, in terms reminiscent of Bunyan and Pogo, "Great Dismal" by Tom and Lynn. With its frogs, snakes, and turtles this massive and forbidding swamp near their rented house on a disused North Carolina cotton plantation is envisaged by Tom as "stretching southward as far as I could imagine" (8). A bloody community hog-slaughter with its "drawing and pressing and turning inside out and then stuffing of long strings of guts involved in the making of chitterlings" both evokes the Prodigal Son and presages the coming massacre in Asia. As York puts it, "Behind us was the feeding trough, which we associated with slaughter; ahead, the land of struggle and freedom, land without fences, land of snow" (17).

Tom and Lynn's precipitous nonstop flight ("mad and violent and driven") in their truck from North Carolina takes them to the Canadian border at Fort Erie, where they enter as landed immigrants. As they drive on towards Ottawa the "vague haze of trees on the horizon were a hand in the webwork of spirit beckoning us on," like a "dark angel's wing," like a lure "of country, and beyond that more country, and, beyond that, wilderness" (17). After an interlude of a few weeks in Ottawa, the Yorks arrange to spend the rest of the winter in New Brunswick's Gaspé woods where even in March the snow is still six feet deep and the temperature twenty below. The train stops at Bartibog Station between Moncton and Newcastle to deposit them near their borrowed cabin. En route York supplies a picaresque appendix in response to a Selective Service request for his "Mailing Address." With a map of Canada borrowed from the porter York provides this fantastic explanation of his inability to provide a stable address:

> For the next 4 or 5 years I will be living a nomadic life along the following route: from within 75 miles of Bathurst, New Brunswick, on a line with Cape Breton Is., northeast across the Gulf of Saint Lawrence by coracle and overland through Newfoundland, then north along the Labrador Highlands to Hudson Strait, and across to Baffin Is. (which by snowshoe will take about 2 years) to Pond Inlet and across to Devon and Ellesmere Islands, from thence to Lands End and the start of the Polar Cap, where I will either die or return. (20)

If the precipitous flight from the South and the draft board was the negative impetus for the emigration from the States, the spiritual quest, though it may have a sense of preordination or compulsion about it, at this point lacks a mission as well as a goal: "How could we know what it was we searched for until it had been found? Or how could we say what the quest was until it was behind us?" (28). The "we" here must be either rhetorical or an unconscious sexism because it is not at all clear that Lynn shares her husband's "woodward urge"—the quest is his, not hers. In this first phase, as he embarks on long solitary snowshoe journeys in the woods, York withdraws from relationships, "where an excess of energy is squandered" (45). His search is for "something I had not found, without which life was not worth the living" (46). York's reflection here has an Augustinian ring as he retrospectively locates God's prevenient grace in this preliminary phase of withdrawal: "And God, whether He put that desire in my mind, or whether He is mind itself, saw fit to fulfil in us and for us ... the promise proclaimed by the prophet" (46). York here refers to Ezekiel 34, the source of his autobiography's title, the promise of peace and blessing "so that they may dwell securely in the wilderness and sleep in the woods."

Tom York, it becomes clear, is not what James Olney (1972) terms a "simplex" autobiographer who distances the former from the present self, or tries to escape the limits of subjectivity, attempting no criticism of the assumed narrative stance adopted in the autobiography. In such instances, as Roy Pascal (1960) puts it, "the author fails to distance himself from himself." But Tom York is, rather, a "duplex" autobiographer who adopts a position in relation to the narrative stance being taken in the autobiography itself. He subjects himself to self-criticism, recognizing the effects on Lynn of his "single-minded pursuit" while he is engaged in learning Greek and Hebrew so he can read the Bible so he can read *Paradise Lost*. While Tom turns inwards Lynn moves outwards, undertaking various attempts to meet other people—by getting up to greet the 4 a.m. passing train, by befriending the section-men staying in a bunkhouse nearby, and by intercepting the reclusive shell-shocked priest who, apart from a filthy old trapper, was Bartibog Station's only other resident. York recognizes, as autobiographer duplex, something during his writing not apparent to him earlier: "And, now I think on it, it was I, your husband, and not Father Murdock, a stranger, who refused to let you come into his heart and who wanted to be left alone" (37).

This instance, related to York's general consciousness of how his spiritual quest affected his wife, is one of many occasions where he addresses his wife directly as "you." He regularly uses "we" (and "our") in places where the first-person plural pronoun could be a reference to "the two of us" (that is, "Lynn and I") rather than to "you and I." But early in the narration, referring to their rented house in North Carolina, he states, "You found it, Lynn" (6). The direct address to his wife becomes, in its cumulative significance, not just a matter of asides: in effect, she becomes the confidante and recipient, the implied reader and armchair companion, for his narrative. By contrast, Augustine apostrophizes God throughout his *Confessions*, and not only in the scriptural quotations that frequent his work—"You are great, Lord, and highly to be praised" (Augustine 3). Augustine also credits God in a personal way for particular gifts or accomplishments within his life—"I myself acquired this power of speech with the intelligence which you gave me, my God" (ibid., 10).

What is the significance, in the narration of a spiritual quest, of referring to God in the third person while addressing Lynn as "you," of shifting the implied auditor from God to spouse, from the vertical to the horizontal dimension? It may be, of course, in part a recognition that God is other people, a relocation of the sacred from eternity to the human. York still seems to retain, throughout *And Sleep in the Woods*, his Barthian conviction of God as transcendent, as Wholly Other. The clue, I think, lies in the difficulties and tensions in the narrative's contemporary vantage point—Toronto in the late 1970s—from which York looks back to his spiritual quest and the beginnings of his marriage to Lynn.

The autobiography opens in the present (perhaps 1978) with Tom awaiting Lynn and the children outside a suburban Toronto mall. Then, like Bunyan in *The Pilgrim's Progress* or Chaucer in *The Parlement of Foules*, he falls into a dream as he walks into a picture in the mall's art gallery and finds himself at the beginning of the narrative itself. In his "Author's Note" York writes, "I began with a dream, and awoke to a nightmare. I set out to chronicle a sleep in the woods, and found myself battling a dragon" (x). The "nightmare" and "dragon" refer to his battle with the draft board and law courts with which the narrative ends, in 1972, before the narrator awakes and walks out of the painting to rejoin his family. This "Author's Note" concludes with York's comment that "I have long since awakened from that dream I once had, while asleep and at peace in the woods, of a nation not imprisoned, and a house not divided" (x). While the dream of a "house not divided" may refer to Tom's relationship with his Arkansas parents, especially his father, more likely the allusion is to his more proximate family, his wife Lynn and their children. The final pages support this possibility as York, echoing the opening lines of *The Parlement of Foules*, acknowledges his "belated awareness" that "the craft too long in the time too short at the cost too high was love" (219). At the end realizing that, beyond knowledge and faith and hope, "only love, then, and only that which taught love was worth learning" (220), Tom uncharacteristically takes Lynn's hand.

And Sleep in the Woods may be an "apology" in two senses. First, in the sense of John Henry Cardinal Newman's *Apologia pro Vita Sua* and as religious autobiography, it is obviously a defense and justification of his motives and convictions as York traces the course of his conversion. *And Sleep in the Woods* is an apology in a second, more popular, sense. In ordinary language an apology is an expression of regret. Here the subtext of the narrative is not an apologia addressed to God but an apology addressed to Lynn as Tom surveys their early life together trying to discover what went awry. The intention at this level is the effort to comprehend the origins of the differences that became evident in Toronto during the late 1970s. Most explicitly—though awkwardly—this level of intentionality finds expression in the initial paragraph of each of chapters 8 and 9 where York first praises his wife for suffering poverty and hardship for the sake of love (49) and then boasts of her trustworthiness (56-57).

In its depiction of the role of women *And Sleep in the Woods* exhibits the typical lamentable problems evident in many portrayals of the male spiritual quest. Paul's misogyny (especially evident in some of the Epistles), Augustine's abandoning his mistress, Bunyan's Christian leaving his wife and children behind to seek the Heavenly City, Lewis's refusal to include his relationship with Mrs. Moore as relevant to his spiritual life story—all these precedents are consonant with York's dragging Lynn along on his flight to Canada and to the woods, and then separating himself from her as he single-mindedly pursues his own vision.[1] Perhaps the worst example of this spiritual tyranny occurs when, during their second year in Canada, he imposes celibacy on Lynn "for virtually four years," the consequence of a "twisted" reading of Malachi 2:15—"Let none deal treacherously against the wife of his youth" (see 153; cf. 174).[2]

Their first Canadian winter ends in May with a trip by Lynn to the outside. On return she announces to Tom her enrolment in teachers' college in Kingston: "I'd like for us to go together; but if you won't, I'm going anyway, and I'll come back for you in the fall" (64). Tom decides to go. Once there he insists on living out of the back of their truck in a farmer's field rather than taking a room in town (a further hardship for Lynn in the midst of her studies). Apart from that, and continuing his reading (which now includes the Upanishads), and doing volunteer work in the Prison for Women, he discovers a religious difference between himself and his wife. Walking through the farmer's field he tells her that ironwood trees and big boulders suggest God to him, to which Lynn replies that she "would rather find God in the field of ripe oats or the cows" (77). York defines this as his first discovery that his own sense of the sacred has to do with "only the most immovable rocks and the most durable trees," a view Lynn terms "grumpy and stern" (77-78). He calls hers "superficial" and wishes she would change.

The distance between them grows when Lynn tells him she has taken a teaching job in Barrie. Tom sees this as a sabotage of the quest "on which we'd [sic] only got started" (78). But he combs the concession roads in the area surrounding Barrie, "driving wildly down side road after side road searching for a concession block secluded enough on which to build a shack." York is convinced "that the journey psychological would begin when the journey geographical ended, and that to make oneself receptive to any signals from on high one had to place himself as far from all distractions as he could" (84-85). In October 1963 York begins to build his cabin deep in the woods, a mile from the nearest road, preparing his house for the winter—"my wood shrine" in a "dark cedar grove." For it was there, York declares, that "I was finally to determine for myself whether or not the words of the biblical Prophets had any power, the promises of the Apostles any substance, the meditative method of the sages any value—in short, whether or not the classical religious quest, entailing withdrawal from society, restraint of the senses, and concentration of the mind, still had, as according to Paul, Augustine, and Luther it once had, power to save" (85-86).

The delay of winter gives York a chance to complete his cabin in the midst of a grove of cedars. There in this "holy grove" the cabin faces what York refers to several times as a gigantic "princess pine," its crown forty feet higher than any of its neighbours, beneath which York prayed each morning.[3] He wanted to see this tree covered with snow and, in fact, the anticipated arrival of snow became associated by York "with the bestowal of light from above" (99). In December, after the snow came, and then deepened, Lynn departed, first to move to a room in town closer to her school, and then to fly home to North Carolina for Christmas. The path from the cabin through the woods to the road had become nearly impassable. Though York simplifies his life to the point where he lived like a mystic, "only God and me," he realizes too that he had not put Christ into this religious quest. He had become locked in a dualism, the dichotomy of subject and object, an "I-Thou impasse" as he terms it. He became increasingly tangled in his own methodology and spirituality, lacking humility.

The release from this self-absorption comes with the chance arrival of an angel disguised as a hunter who tells him that Lynn is his first responsibility and who suggests that he consider becoming a minister. As a result Tom realizes the importance of his becoming other-directed. He realizes too that as a consequence of his flight from "the dark warm wet mother-earth, toward the light dry cold father-spirit" (113) he had rejected the possibility of the sufficiency of nature for himself. Nothing less than "pure mind" would satisfy him. Yet also he has encountered a kind of stasis in his efforts to scourge God into being ("since God could not be coerced"). York comprehends that he has reached the same point as Augustine and Luther and others "whose yearning to merge with God was also a desire to make themselves godlike" (113). He identifies this yearning, whatever its possible source—whether fear of death, relationships, or the body—as finally deriving from a principle antagonistic to life.

The resolution of York's spiritual quest comes on 30 January when he has a vision of Jesus, gouging out the old wood from a dead tree (interpreted by York as the world). Then, in this vision, Jesus draws himself into the tree's trunk until lost from sight, and invites York to join him. York's experience of complete freedom then harmonizes his vision and its resolution with other spiritual quests: "There was no compulsion, no constraint, no command; merely example and invitation—to enter the dead trunk of the world, as He had done" (117). In its lack of compulsion the invitation York receives bears similarities to C. S. Lewis's moment of choice, to "open the door or keep it shut," offered to him as he rode on the upper level of a bus. In Lewis's case "neither choice was presented as a duty; no threat or promise was attached to either. . . . I was moved by no desires or fears" (Lewis 1959, 179). Whereas Lewis's conversion develops in successive stages occurring over several years (his decision to "open the door" is followed by the acceptance of theism, and finally of Christianity), York's conversion has effectively been completed at this point: "The quest was ended, all passion spent" (118).

Typical of many conversions in which conflict builds and intensifies during the preceding stages of frenzied activity, almost to the point of being unbearable, the actual resolution is for York a point of quiet and stillness. But often, immediately following this conversion experience, the conflict resumes and the struggle ensues, frequently in similar terms. At least now York has achieved a focus because he has attained union with God.[4] The next phase is to be his "gradual withdrawal from the woods and spirited return to the world" with the concern "that others come to know Christ" (121). But York's basic personality has not changed: "I was an eccentric—part nature mystic, part zealot—whose rustic habits and rank smell and sheer intensity put people off" (121-22).

Although York's conversion takes place at the midpoint of his narrative, on pages 117-18 in this book of 222 pages, the pace and direction of the story changes dramatically once the quest has ended. In the following brief chapter of ten pages, for instance, he covers the intervening months from January to June 1964 when he and Lynn begin their first employment with the United Church. If anything, his treatment of Lynn becomes worse as Tom demands, now that he has attained his own quest, that she quit her teaching job, begin meditating as he had done, and "save what's left of her soul" (as he wrote home in a letter to his father). York's father summoned his energies—he was to die a month later—for a last letter expressing his outrage at Tom's treatment of Lynn: "By what right allwise or otherwise do you presume to play God with the lives of other people? And since when do the spiritual attainments of life require that one quit work?" (123). While the senior York could accept Tom dragging himself into privation, he felt strongly that "to drag others with you does not seem to me anything more than selfish" (124).

York does not return to Little Rock for his father's funeral (though Lynn does) because he wants to avoid being apprehended for draft evasion. His mother told him that the FBI had been to her house. The agonies of this gulf between Tom and his dying father do not seem to affect Tom as much as a reader might think they should. Perhaps his grief is overwhelmed by his continuing zeal, as indeed it turns out his sexual energies were, as everything is now directed towards the vocation to become a minister. The efforts previously spent on the now completed spiritual quest are chan-nelled towards a new mission—"Having made my own peace with God, I was ready to act as an agent" (130). As winter passes into spring, Lynn travels on weekends from her rented room in Barrie to join Tom, though sometimes he walks the thirty kilometres so they can go to church together. Some of Tom's excess of vigour goes into making maple syrup in March, but mostly the remainder of that winter and spring are an interlude preceding the move to North Whitby "for the most energetic, charismatic, zealously prosecuted survey ever launched (under the auspices of the United Church of Canada, at least) on a sleepy suburb" (131).

For this project, and the move necessary to accomplish it, Tom makes Lynn give up her teaching job before the end of the school year (as he had in North Carolina when they fled the States in midyear). Forcing her to break her teaching contract a second time remained, understandably, a sore point for a long time (141). But Lynn is more social and less a hermit than Tom and she throws herself into the survey work with him. The whole business is plotted and strategized (and written about) as if it were a military assault on the unsuspecting townspeople, probably deriving from Tom's graduate studies in military history. Together they canvass the growing suburb of North Whitby to determine if there is enough population and enough interest to found a new church there. As much as anything their own enthusiasm in their door-to-door visits creates the movement that begins with a Bible study and rotating house-church meetings and that eventually grows over a period of two years into a full-fledged church. York's account of that summer and the two succeeding years (while he was a United Church theological student at the University of Toronto) is full of warmth and humour as the couple draws people together into a community.

Though fired by their enthusiasm and passionate innocence, having anything regularly to do with a church is a new experience for both Tom and Lynn: "All we knew was that the woods were behind us, the world was before us, around us in unseen communion the martyrs and saints of all ages urging us on to augment their number with sentient creatures, living souls" (142). So unaccustomed to an experience of church are the Yorks that they have to spend hours learning hymns together, Lynn playing the piano. Their energetic and intimate engagements with the people they encounter stand in sharp contrast to the relative somnolence of the downtown Whitby church whose conservative and bureaucratic minister is Tom's supervisor. His first public reading of scripture in that church, for which Tom practises by the hour in both Hebrew and English, becomes an oratorical performance before a congregation in part made up of outpatients from the Whitby Psychiatric Hospital—"It was said of John Wesley that 'he set himself on fire and let the people watch him burn.' Thus I did that Sunday morning" (154).

One attractive feature of this early ministry—probably accounting for its appeal to unchurched, to disaffected, indifferent, and lapsed Christians, and to evangelicals alike—is the emphasis the Yorks put on love rather than sin. Open and friendly, at door after door Tom and Lynn would introduce themselves—"We're from the church"—and go on to gather information about the residents, their ages, their affiliation, and so on. Occasionally they were invited in and friendship followed: "We told her we'd come from the woods and that I'd had a vision of Jesus; told it as briefly and nonchalantly as that, sitting in her living room" (144). Amid other spiritual autobiographies York's is refreshing, not only for its stylistic qualities, descriptive powers, psychological insight, and intelligence, but as well for its originality and the absence of any post facto imposition of a formulaic scheme. While Tom York's spiritual quest conforms to and is intelligible within a narrative genre relating a conversion, it is marked by its own unique characteristics too. The complete lack of any emphasis on sin, conviction, and repentance is one of its originalities and strengths. As York puts it, "We ourselves had no awareness of sin, and why should one condemn in another what he does not feel in himself?" (149-50). Two of the Yorks' charges were "Mr. and Mrs. Nude Ontario" who kept foisting their nudist camp photos on them, only to be disconcerted when they were not offended. Practising celibacy, and as "nature mystic" and "anchoress" respectively, Tom and Lynn were self-disciplined and ascetic. But, as York expresses it, "if for the sake of the Gospel we were intolerant with ourselves, we were to that degree tolerant of others" (150).

Of course, gradually organization replaced spontaneity and enthusiasm, the evangelicals split from the liberals, and politics replaced prayer. In two years the movement initiated by the Yorks had in effect been succeeded by a new "garden-variety" middle-class United Church. York felt that his messages had moved away from their early focus on the "simple truths" of Jesus and his teachings to "the harsher demands" of Bernard of Clairvaux, Francis of Assisi, and Martin Luther. There began to be talk about replacing Tom with an ordained United Church minister. In effect the narrative of Tom York's spiritual life ends at the conclusion of the two years in Whitby. In a chapter entitled "A Decimation of Easters" he catalogues nine Easters, from 1964 to 1972, and how he spent them, arrayed with images of context and of the surrounding cast. Beginning with the first at the cabin in the woods near Barrie, York continues through three more in southern Ontario (two of them in Whitby), goes on to the next three spent in different parts of British Columbia, and ends with those of 1971 and 1972 in the Arctic. The tenth, Easter of 1973, is missing—"the terminal Easter was lost" (177).

The recovery of that apparently "lost" Easter takes place as York faces trial in October 1973 in Little Rock, Arkansas, where York had voluntarily surrendered in August. There in the court-room he recalls his anonymous return to Little Rock the previous Easter after seventy-two hours of travelling on buses south from Yellowknife. To escape detection he stayed briefly at the "Y" on the visit, not even contacting his mother. A Presbyterian minister whose service he attended refused to pass a message to York's mother, ordering him to leave town immediately—"Ah never saw you, heah?" (203). In effect York's initial return to and immediate departure from Little Rock took place so abruptly and quickly it is "as though Easter hadn't happened" (204). Why did York decide to return to Little Rock to stand trial for failing to report for induc-tion and for failing to keep them informed of his address? In his view Little Rock was the single place on earth "where, in order to understand fully, you needed to be understood" (206). In this respect *And Sleep in the Woods* understood as apologia stands as York's defense and explanation of his decision to leave the United States in 1962. The autobiography sets forth York's reaction to being summoned for service in the United States Armed Forces. The reader becomes judge and jury, asked to decide whether his flight to the north was evasion of the draft or spiritual quest.

The entire concluding chapter ("The Dragon at Bay") is cast, so York once told me, in the manner of Faulkner's *As I Lay Dying*. The account of his return to Little Rock also derives stylistically from Faulkner, with its sentences that fill a paragraph and its para-graphs that occupy pages. The indictment of the American South—indeed, of the whole of the United States—for its corruption is there too. The depiction of the trial itself mixes transcript material with York's own thoughts. York explains that he never used an alias, never concealed his address, and never refused to tell anyone where he was. The jury nonetheless brings in a guilty verdict, endorsed by the judge: "It seems fairly clear that the defendant, whatever his motives, went to Canada and remained there for the purpose of evading service under the Selective Service Act" (211).

York emphasizes that he did not go north to avoid military service but rather because of an "internal compulsion": "I felt compelled to go to the bush. I didn't know why" (195). York comes to understand this inadvertent "draft evasion" as having less to do with avoidance of military service than a prideful refusal, inherited through his mother from her father, to take seriously any human authority (including the authority of the military and of the state). From his Grandfather Byrd Tom York also inherits such a passion "entangled with the South" and such a "fury in our veins" of "cypress roots and black women and buzz saws and whips and horses" that he had to go North, "to the hibernating, purifying snow," to escape (197).

The judge refuses to grant amnesty, though the draft law had by this time changed, and sentences York to three years' imprisonment, believing that the sentence should exceed the two years of military service he had avoided. Then York makes a defiant and passionate speech before leaving the courtroom. After he inveighs against the trial and verdict and sentence then he, in his turn, finds the state guilty and sentences its citizens to imprisonment: "It's not me who's been on trial here today, it's the system. I would not go to war for such a system. I would not willingly return to live under such a system. And do you tell me that I should go to prison for a system I repudiate?" (218). A brief concluding note tells the reader that Tom York's appeal to the U.S. Appellate Court was granted in April of 1974.

On his first trip south to Little Rock in 1973, at Easter, Tom York considered the possibility, while he was in Memphis, of turning around and heading back to Canada, in effect reversing his three-day bus trip in favour of northward flight again: "From Memphis to St. Louis, to Chicago, transfer there to Minneapolis, through customs . . . and on to Winnipeg, then Edmonton, and finally Yellowknife—the end of the road, the gate to the North, the treeline of sanity" (189). Fifteen years later Tom York died in the initial stages of this northward route, as he travelled back to Canada by car in the first few days of January 1988. After a Christmas visit to his mother in Little Rock, driving north (within a month of being twenty-five years after that first precipitous northward flight), between St. Louis and Chicago and before turning eastwards towards Ontario, he was killed when his car was struck from behind by a truck.

THE RETURN TO THE SOUTH IN *Desireless*

"I AM A DECEASED WRITER NOT IN THE SENSE of one who has written and is now deceased, but in the sense of one who has died and is now writing." Tom York, in an article on Malcolm Lowry's "post-mortem point of view" (York 1983), quoted this statement from *Epitaph of a Small Winner* by the nineteenth-century Brazilian novelist, Machado de Assis. In his last, posthumous novel, *Desireless*, York himself is a deceased writer in some sense intermediate between these two meanings of the term. Because his death came after he completed its writing, but before the novel's publication, we have the illusion of a deceased writer still writing. It is tempting to search for encoded messages from beyond the grave.

But the real post-mortem point of view in *Desireless* comes from the dead and dying protagonist, James Antoine Girard, who has already "died" twice at the novel's opening and finally completes the task by the novel's conclusion. Girard's initial "death" was a botched suicide attempt from a bridge; his second, the result of a more prolonged electroshock therapy: "Having died once, and after that the treatment, his only desire this time around was to die desireless" (20). The eventual post-mortem on Jimmy Girard's death, the culmination of three days of wandering his old haunts in New Orleans, is conducted by a playwright and a doctor discussing the circumstances of Girard's end.

Like the southward bus trip at the end of *And Sleep in the Woods* and the airplane's arrival at Little Rock in York's unpublished story "Reunion," *Desireless* also opens with a return to the South, though with a sense of seediness and indeterminacy: "It wasn't clear where the bus was going. Looming out of the dark and reeling past were dirty stucco houses, bungalows with peeling paint, boats for rent, an isthmus of trees against a desolation of water, a lacing of bridges, causeways, railroad bridges, shipyards" (3). Girard has returned home to New Orleans, "The Big Easy"—"cesspool, sumphole, miasmal swamp that it was"—not, as he says, to resist it, but to flow along with whatever else is flowing "down the river of regret, through the delta of desire, to the gulf of oblivion" (19). He is trying to forget his former wife, Lee Anne, and trying to avoid alcohol. He is unsuccessful on both counts. Instead, he drifts along oblivious to any imperatives or demands, has a few casual sexual engagements, witnesses a few violent deaths, and sells his former black girlfriend, Val, into slavery (or is it escape?) to a sleazy purveyor of pornographic snuff films.

So sordid and bleak is the novel's initial section, "The Landscape of Desire," that it seems to lack any controlling moral viewpoint. When reading this first part of *Desireless* in manuscript before its publication I found it emotionally impossible to go on any further, not even for the sake of my friendship with the author (who understood and did not press when I offered evasions to his gentle queries). I should have persisted. For in the second and third parts of the novel, "Girard Loses His Way" and "Homewood," Girard's background, conveyed through flashbacks recounting his past and upbringing and marriage, make his present, his return to New Orleans, his desire to achieve Desirelessness, understandable. He gradually becomes a character to care about, if not identify with. A lot stands in the way of a reader's total acceptance of Girard's way of seeing things.

Readers of York's first four novels will find much of the terrain familiar in *Desireless*, in spite of his forsaking a setting in northern Canada, where the "light, dry, cold male spirit" principle prevails, for southern Louisiana, domain of "dark, warm, wet Mother Earth." The literary landscape is characterized by many of the same unreconciled contraries, by a fugitive hero on the run who, like Albert Johnson in *Trapper*, remains a puzzle and enigma to onlookers, by the same thematic blend of the comic, the violent, the dark and brooding, and the spiritual, and by the same conjunction of eros and thanatos. Similarly, the return to the south in *And Sleep in the Woods* is in part the fulfilment of York's spiritual quest, born out of a desire to confront the problem and give an account of himself in the place of his origins and youth. There the southern earth-mother principle is a temptation to indolence and sloth and ease and comfort, though southern fecundity also represents a disguised threat of female engulfment in forgetfulness of principles of justice. In *Desireless* the return is not so much that of the prodigal to his home, or of the defendant to face the court; here, the fertile has been negatively transformed into an inverted world of waste and decay. The earth-mother has become spider-woman. The place of return is a place from which there is no escape.

That the presiding female spirit principle in the south gets rendered negatively means that the misogynistic vision complained of in York's previous works is in *Desireless*, if anything, even more evident. For Girard's underlying difficulty seems to be his entrapment by a succession of three female keepers—his mother, his wife, and his sister. As in Nikos Kazantzakis' *Last Temptation of Christ* or Ken Kesey's *One Flew Over the Cuckoo's Nest*, the fatal lure is domesticity, the greatest barrier to male self-fulfilment is engulfing female power.

Catherine Bush, reviewing *Desireless* in the *Globe and Mail*, puts it well: "At moments it reads like an obsessive road trip confined to one city, as Girard roams the streets, relentlessly remapping his life." In the fourth and last section, "Death in Desire," James Girard achieves his transcendence in death, as did Albert Johnson in *Trapper*. Here Girard, making his way through a flood-ravaged New Orleans, returns to places to which he had already returned, attempts to undo what he had already done, and undergoes his final passion. The conclusion is gripping, powerful, and moving, immensely contrasting with the lassitude pervading the novel's opening pages. Desirelessness, then, becomes not a state of apathy, but more a Buddhistic elevation beyond craving and its attendant sorrows.

"No End to This Road": Aritha van Herk

Tom York's *Desireless* is set in New Orleans, on the Mississippi Delta, the swamp and sump and outflow of the waste of the United States, and the last stop for Jimmy Girard. Aritha van Herk's *No Fixed Address* features a female fugitive who flees first west and then north. At the end of her westward flight, on Vancouver Island, she reaches the ocean: "This is the edge; not end but edge, the border, the brink, the selvage of the world. She can no longer go west. She is going north now but that will end soon; she has retraced her steps into this ultimate impasse and reached not frontier but ocean, inevitable water" (291). In *No Fixed Address* van Herk takes a female hero on the road, giving her an itch for mobility and a yearning to travel normally reserved for the male quest.

Chapter 4 above raised the question of the applicability of the quest pattern, examined there in terms of the canoe trip, to the experience of women. There was evidence that the quest, especially as employed in certain kinds of initiatory rites, could become a trial by ordeal for developing traditional masculine values. The male quest has been integrally a part of literature since the *Odyssey* and *Gilgamesh*. Aritha van Herk told an interviewer that the traditional regions of women, that is, home and family, are distinct from "the quintessentially male regions of fiction which have been the great theatres of the world" (quoted in Goldman 1993, 24). She says that "men always write about war and peace and action and heroes" (ibid.). Joseph Campbell's "monomyth" of this quest details how such a hero ventures forth from home, has adventures, wins a victory, and returns (usually changed or with new insights) to the point of departure.

Clearly males have traditionally been the ones to go questing, while women have had to be content with staying home and "nesting." Or if the female hero has gone on a quest, the result has not always been a happy one (consider *Fanny Hill* or *Sister Carrie*). Perhaps the warning is that terrible things can happen to women who venture forth. But in our age increased mobility and the changed role of women in society has meant new possibilities. Tom Robbins' novel, *Even Cowgirls Get the Blues*, portrays the adventures of a woman, Sissy Hankshaw, blessed with outsized thumbs, making for a prodigiously successful hitchhiker. In Canadian literature, one thinks of the quests of such characters as the hero of *Surfacing*, Morag Gunn in *The Diviners*, and Marian Engel's Lou in *Bear* in which the external journey, even if it does not achieve a definable goal, is matched by some form of inner development. Such stories as these usually involve a return either to "home" or to a place of beginnings.

In Aritha van Herk's second novel, *No Fixed Address* (1986), the protagonist is a travelling sales representative. Her name is Arachne ("spider"). Her mother gets the name from a friend who explains, "Spiders are rogues. They eat each other when there's nothing else to catch" (83). Arachne is a rogue who catches men when she is on the road. She travels in a vintage, eye-catching, and well-restored 1959 black Mercedes that she inherited as a teenager. Arachne loves her Mercedes instrumentally, not for its own sake; it is not the car she loves, but driving: "She is infatuated not with machines but with motion, the illusion that she is going somewhere, getting away" (68). She sells lingerie, specifically panties for Ladies' Comfort of Winnipeg. Arachne however wears no underwear—her personal line is not "Ladies' Comfort" but her own freedom.

Her car stocked with samples, Arachne sets forth from her base in Calgary (the central point towards which her spiral net converges) and drives from one small western town to another, cajoling owners of general stores and managers of variety and department stores to stock her lines. She is good at it, wins an award, and likes her work, though after several years feels the need to keep herself amused. But these prairie towns are important chiefly because they provide the reason for travel. She loves "the pace and seduction of journey, the multifarious seduction of movement" (164). Arachne epitomizes the classic model of the travelling sales representative, "a rep who makes traveling her life, not like the new ones who want to work six or seven hours and return home at night to suburban houses and spouses" (214). There is purity and single-mindedness in her objective of travelling for its own sake without goal or purpose—"Arachne travels to travel." Yet each day's travel to three or four or six towns brings her to a destination, and that is a problem: "Her only paradox is arriving somewhere, her only solution is to leave for somewhere else" (164).

On the road Arachne is constantly on the lookout for a likely man to pick up (it is this that, presumably, makes hers "an amorous adventure"), not because she is questing for a partner; her preference is for the one-night stand with a stranger. Arachne, "faithful to only her body," wants pleasure instead of obligations: "There is something square and direct about fucking for its own sake, no other considerations: wifely or husbandly duty, buying, selling, payoff, gratitude" (220). Back in Calgary the home fires are kept burning in a role reversal by her perfectly faithful, unbelievably patient, loving, and understanding housemate, Thomas, a cartographer who works for the Geodetic Survey. He is, as one would expect in one "so impossibly good," orderly, preferring the fixities and certainties of his maps to her penchant for wanderings. His maps specify and define the landscape over which she roams freely. He is the one who has chosen the china and who polishes the floors in the Calgary home she keeps returning to. While Arachne is "not unkind" to Thomas, she is, with his knowledge, "consistently unfaithful." He understands and accepts her infidelity, for "she is also unwilling to engage in the polite rituals that are expected when a woman is connected to a man" (62).

Arachne will not be confined, the point of her refusal to wear underwear. Her refusal is personal, not political. While on one hand women's underwear can be seen as symbolic of imprisonment and bondage, Arachne does not see the liberation of her sisters as her particular task. She has no hesitation in selling what her friend Thena sees as the instruments of other women's bondage to men, fashion, and convention. Arachne wants freedom for herself, not the fashionable woman's shape "inevitably controlled by a supporting apparatus underneath" (9). Her incompetent parents—they were not neglectful, just ignorant—and her streetwise upbringing in Vancouver's East End made her into a tough teenage gang leader (her gang is the Black Widows). This background makes her unable to fit the conventional expectations and aspirations of North American women.

Arachne is a likeable solid woman—bold, brassy, belligerent. Finally her own footloose nature drives her away from anything that might anchor her. In her travels she meets, beside Thomas, two other friends. One is her confidante, Thena: "For what is a traveler without a confidante? Every adventuress requires a teller of her tale, an armchair companion to complete the eventualities" (146). The same question gets asked a little later and the response is that "it is impossible to fictionalize a life without someone to oversee the journey" (154). The other friend is a fellow rogue in the form of a nonagenarian Serb, Josef, imprisoned by his daughter. When Arachne liberates Josef and takes him on the road with her, she ends up being charged with kidnapping. Though Thomas posts bail for her Arachne takes off, becomes a fugitive. While on the run, having kidnapped Josef and abandoned Thomas, she ends up robbing another man and killing yet another. Here and for the remainder of her adventures the career of Arachne parallels that of the heroines in Ridley Scott's 1991 film, *Thelma and Louise*. There two female fugitives transform the classic Hollywood road movie about two buddies becoming outlaws into a story about sisterhood. For Thelma and Louise, though, there is no turning back and no rescue: they drive their T-bird over the edge of the Grand Canyon into oblivion.

Like Huck Finn, Arachne ends by lighting out for the territory ahead, heading first west to the extremities of Vancouver Island, and then returning to the mainland and veering north. But she becomes, at the end, more like Thelma and Louise when she eventually she drives right off the map and disappears. The narrator whose italicized voice retraced Arachne's last trip concludes her story, what is termed the narrative of "one of her lives": "*Now the road begins to frighten you. There is nothing anymore, no promise of a town or a place. You are heading for the Mackenzie Mountains that separate the Yukon and the Northwest Territories; and if you reach them, you'll be nowhere . . ."* (317).

If for Tom York the north represents the male spirit principle differentiated from the mother-earth principle of the American South, for van Herk it stands for a different possibility. According to Marlene Goldman, van Herk may be searching for the possibilities of an ungendered terrain because "the western literary tradition is a thoroughly male terrain" (ibid., 21). She quotes van Herk's statement that the art that defined the west is masculine. If the western landscape has already been artistically mapped from a male perspective, then the north represents a kind of untrammelled potentiality for a woman writer (and for her picaresque questing hero): "With its emphasis on the north as anonymous territory, *No Fixed Address* develops a link between the unmapped northern landscape and the cognitive space where women can plot radical alternatives to traditional representations of female identity" (Goldman 1993, 30).

At the end of Thomas York's *Trapper*, the fugitive Albert Johnson has finally been tracked down, shot, and killed. The "Epilogue" has Johnson—like Callaghan's Dowling in the company of Midge and Ronnie and like Engel's Lou—undergo a stellar transmutation. He takes his place in the brightest constellation, having become "the blue-white star below the belt and below the Great Nebula" looking down on his pursuers. This star (or Johnson as this star) at the foot of the Hunter, becomes model, challenge, and aspiration "whenever anyone breaks free of himself and the herd and look[s] up at the night sky in winter" (York 1981, 417). Van Herk's Arachne belongs in this fugitive company of fierce spirits seeking freedom who transcend themselves, leave the rest of the herd behind, and at the end of the road find themselves nowhere, off the map, and out of this world.

How then is the sacred to be located in van Herk's and York's fiction? The answer hinted at in these contemporary (even postmodern) portrayals of characters who go to the very edge and then beyond it is that at the extremities of what can be mapped—and beyond them—lies transcendence. As Joseph Campbell puts it, though our senses are enclosed in time and space, and our minds in thought categories, "the ultimate thing (which is no thing) that we are trying to get in touch with is not so enclosed" (1988, 62). With Arachne, who through the narrative ministrations of her confidante becomes a legend, or with Albert Johnson, who takes on an otherworldly posthumous existence as a guiding star, it is almost as if we return to the older supernatural verities of a transcendence beyond the earth and beyond the boundaries of the temporal life.

NOTES

1 Corresponding narratives of a woman's conversion prior to the twentieth century are infrequent, less well known, or just now being explored. But Theresa of Avila's *The Interior Castle* employs alternative images of the religious life, stressing integration and relationship rather than separation and individuation in distinction from what may be the basically male pattern of the road or journey. Once again the problem (see chap. 4 and below in the present chapter) is raised of the applicability of the male quest pattern to female experience or the necessity of women developing their own narrative patterns (see chap. 8).

2 The Roman Catholic Jerusalem Bible translation seems to make this verse into an anticontraceptive injunction: "Did he not create a single being that has flesh and the breath of life? And what is this single being destined for? God-given offspring. Be careful for your own life, therefore, and do not break faith with the wife of your youth." The RSV takes these words more as a warning against adultery—"do not be faithless ... for I hate divorce." In the RSV God desires "Godly offspring," presumably meaning spiritual children rather than the Jerusalem Bible's "God-given offspring," apparently enjoining parents to conceive and have children. The original context of Malachi makes it more likely that the concerns here are intermarriage and illegitimacy.

3 The reference to a "princess pine" is a bit puzzling. My dictionary identifies a "prince's-pine" as identical with the evergreen called in Cree *pipsissewa* (in Latin *Chimaphila umbellata*). Peterson's *Field Guide* does not mention either a "princess pine" or "prince's-pine," but it describes the Common Pipsessewa as a "creeping evergreen, hardly woody, with short *upright* stems. . . . Height to 10" [i.e., inches]" (*A Field Guide to Trees and Shrubs*, ed. George A. Petrides, 2nd ed. [Boston: Houghton Mifflin, 1972], 179).

4 A student of mine, Neill Carson, did an excellent comparative paper on "The Pattern of Conversion" in Augustine, Bunyan, and C. S. Lewis. He noted that "the unconverted self is trapped in a disturbing frenzy which abruptly stops in the moment of conversion and which is transformed into a productive dynamism in the period after conversion" (Religious Studies 381, "The Transformation of the Self" at Queen's University).

CHAPTER 10

MUTUALITY AND THE SACRED: JOY KOGAWA

FROM DIVINE ABANDONMENT
TO HUMAN SOLIDARITY

IN JOY KOGAWA'S FICTIONAL EFFORTS to find the location of the sacred sometimes cultural traditions blend and reinforce each other, while at other times they conflict and clash. From her Japanese-Canadian perspective she affirms and criticizes aspects of her dual heritage in an admixture and interpenetration of different cultural symbols—Christian and Buddhist, North American and Asian. In *Obasan* (1981) Joy Kogawa seeks the abode of sacrality in a quest for cosmic meaning during a period of suffering and hardship for Japanese Canadians. In *Itsuka* (1993) she continues her search into a realm where the sacred requires a political resolution and justice for her community. Kogawa's third novel, *The Rain Ascends* (1995), though it does not deal with Japanese Canadians, continues the examination of the conflict between love and justice in a woman who discovers that her clergyman-father has been a persistent sexual abuser of boys.[1]

As in the case of the crisis among the Belcher Islands Inuit examined in chapter 5 above, Kogawa's fiction displays the complex and sometimes ambiguous relationship between a Canadian minority (this time of Asian origin) and the dominant culture of European ancestry. The Belchers Inuit also struggled to preserve their identity in the face of cultural dominance and claims of Christian exclusivity. The descriptions in *Obasan* of the removal, internment, deportation, and expulsion during World War II, and in *Itsuka* of the movement for redress during the 1980s, partially incorporate mainstream Canadian conventions from a largely

---

Notes to Chapter 10 are on pp. 237-39.

Christian religious milieu while simultaneously representing the Japanese-Canadian attempt to maintain their distinctive traditions.

Joy Kogawa's first two novels, *Obasan* and *Itsuka*, are set amidst the two major events in the history of Japanese Canadians in the twentieth century. While *Obasan* portrays all the negative effects of their relocation, internment, and dispersal in the 1940s, its sequel *Itsuka* describes the success of their movement for redress in the 1980s. In *Obasan* Naomi narrates her experiences between 1941 and 1954: her family's relocation in 1942 from Vancouver to Slocan in the British Columbia interior and the subsequent removal in 1945 to a sugar-beet farm near Granton, Alberta. *Itsuka* displays, again from Naomi's narrative perspective, the persistency of Japanese Canadians in the face of setbacks, internal dissensions, and other obstacles during the 1980s leading up to the Canadian government's acknowledgment of its injustices. After a consideration of its context in Kogawa's life and later writing, this essay will be concerned principally with an interpretation of *Obasan*.

In these first two novels, where the subject is the Japanese-Canadian experience, Kogawa's skilful and sophisticated fictional treatment exemplifies a problem familiar within the study of postcolonial literatures. The minority culture, as part of the strategy for maintaining its distinctiveness, must differentiate itself from the mainstream dominant culture. Such maintenance of difference inevitably entails critique of the dominant majority, its values and practices. But, the minority portrays its difference in terms recognizable within the cultural context of the mainstream. Kogawa's novels follow the conventions of Euroamerican fiction in a Canadian context and setting where Japanese Canadians have gone through several generations of acculturation (she is always conscious of the differences between successive generations, the Issei, the Nisei, the Sansei). Because the minority is both similar to and different from the majority Kogawa goes far beyond a simpleminded bifurcation in which Japanese Canadians are morally superior to Canadians of other than Japanese ancestry.[2] Rather than choosing to "deconstruct an existing subjectivity or posit an essentialist, universal, unitary subject," she investigates multiple identities situated at "the intersection of nation, gender, sexuality, class, and race, as well as history, religion, caste, and language" (Hutcheon 1995, 11).

In *Obasan* Naomi, looking back from her vantage point in 1972, sifts through her childhood memories, losses, and sufferings. Naomi's childhood consciousness filters these hardships as they are wrought through her emotions, experiences, and perceptions. Documents and letters from her Aunt Emily provide an historical context and adult perspective, expanding the domestic surroundings Naomi shares in her life with her aunt and uncle, Aya Obasan and Isamu. *Itsuka* resumes Naomi's story in Toronto in 1984, both recapitulating events since her arrival there in 1976, with further background from her teen years in Alberta, and then following the organized efforts to seek compensation and amends for the injustices of the 1940s, culminating in the government apology of September 1988. Naomi's adult sensibility registers these activities as she moves gradually from her passivity and solitude into a community, sharing its labours to attain justice. At the same time, now in the middle years of her life, Naomi takes the risky first steps of trust and love in a relationship with Cedric, an Anglican chaplain at one of the colleges of the university.

In both novels the political and communal dimensions of life among Japanese Canadians are given personal depth by conveying their effects on the narrator. But Naomi's uniquely personal problems intensify the difficulties she shares in common with her Japanese-Canadian friends and family members. In *Obasan* the interior counterpart of the cataclysmic losses the community undergoes is Naomi's loss of her mother, who left for Japan in 1941 and who, so Naomi at last discovers in 1972, eventually died there from the effects of the atomic bomb dropped on Nagasaki in 1945. But four-year-old Naomi, with a child's logic, believed she had caused her mother's departure because of her "secret," that is, the sexual abuse inflicted on her by a next-door neighbour, Old Man Gower.

Naomi's aunt, Aya Obasan, the novel's title character, becomes the emotional anchor of Naomi's life during the years in Slocan and Granton. Naomi's father too is absent for much of this time, separated from his son and daughter during the relocation, then hospitalized with tuberculosis, until his death in 1951. The novel ends when, after the death of her Uncle Isamu, Naomi learns about her mother's fate, at last understanding that her silence was a way of protecting her children. Indeed, throughout the novel the protective silence of Japanese Canadians is seen as a way of shielding children from the horrors of the 1940s—the refrain *kodomo ne tame* (for the sake of the children) recurs throughout. At the end Naomi experiences the epiphany of knowing and of prayerful communion with her absent, silent mother: "Because I am no longer a child I can know your presence though you are not here" (243).

Kogawa has claimed this as her favourite passage in *Obasan*. In an interview with Val Ross about *Itsuka* she connects this notion of presence in absence with a quotation from theologian Rosemary Ruether that was to become the epigraph of *The Rain Ascends*: "Each of us must discover the secret key to divine abandonment— that God has abandoned divine power into the human condition utterly and completely, so that we may not abandon each other." At the same time she goes on to remark of *Obasan*, "It's about the death of God" (Ross 1992, C15). Here, as elsewhere, and uncharacteristic of many other writers, Kogawa proves to be an insightful and reliable guide to the meaning of her own art. Her fictional domain is the relation between art and politics, that relation being understood and interpreted in theological terms. Joy Kogawa, both existentially and within the context of the Japanese-Canadian community, wants to know what trust means when one's basic trust in life has been undermined by metaphysical abandonment, experienced amidst racism and persecution. She wants to find out what embodied love means when the body of the other is absent and when one's own body has been abused in loveless exploitation. She wants to explore the terrible conflict between the love of a child for her parent and the need for justice in the community.

Among the constancies and continuities between *Obasan* and *Itsuka* is the bond of Naomi with her dead mother, though the sense of her mother as an embodiment of the sacred diminishes in the sequel. *Itsuka* tells of a journey Naomi makes in 1976 to visit her mother's grave near Tokyo: "Within this one hour at Mama's grave, I meet the one I need to meet" (83). Oddly, though, there is almost no mention in *Itsuka* about her father's influence or her recollections of him (but see page 10), though in *Obasan* Naomi loves him deeply. For some months she is unable to acknowledge openly his death to a schoolmate. In *Obasan* Stephen, who continually rejects anything Japanese, fled Granton for a career in music immediately after high school and returns only briefly; in *Itsuka* contact with Stephen remains intermittent and strained—he refuses to have anything to do with the redress movement.

The portraits of Aya Obasan and her husband, Isamu, are likewise consistent in the first two novels, though now her other aunt, Emily, strident and outspoken, comes to the fore in *Itsuka*. Kogawa has commented that whereas *Obasan* is Aya Obasan's story, *Itsuka* is Emily's. The contrast drawn in *Obasan* stands in *Itsuka* also: "How different my two aunts are. One lives in sound, the other in stone. Obasan's language remains deeply underground but Aunt Emily, BA, MA, is a word warrior" (32). In *Itsuka* too we recognize certain traits of the Naomi of the earlier novel—her withdrawal into silence, her social awkwardness, and her emotional distance, especially from men. What differs is a changed voice or tone on the part of Emily and especially Naomi—both are less gentle, less patient, less tolerant, less innocent. *Itsuka* adds to Naomi's past a largely negative experience of Christian fundamentalism during her teens in Granton. The geographical setting has changed from the mountains of British Columbia and the farms of rural Alberta to the streets of downtown Toronto. Japanese Canadians have become active and politically engaged in *Itsuka* as they take up the struggle for the reparations of wrongs done them during and after World War II, the period represented in *Obasan*.

In *Itsuka* there is no mention either of the childhood sexual abuse by Old Man Gower that figures so prominently in *Obasan*. The second novel relates how during Naomi's teens in Granton she was approached by someone whose appearance is similar to Gower's, "a fat bald man who has blown into the area with the chinook" (*Itsuka*, 25-26). Mr. Gower is described in *Obasan* as having a "large and soft" belly and "a shiny skin cap" on the top of his head (61). The look-alike stranger in *Itsuka* is rumoured to have fondled a girl behind the Granton curling rink. He stops his car one Saturday morning beside the sugar-beet field, where Naomi is working some distance from her uncle and brother, and offers her a five-dollar bill. Naomi flees in nausea, a pattern repeated with her cowboy suitor Hank (42, 44) and, to a lesser extent, when Father Cedric first touches her.

In *Obasan* the adult Naomi wonders at one point whether Mr. Gower (referring presumably to some subsequent and metaphoric reincarnation of that abusive persona) still walks "through the hedges between our houses in Vancouver, in Slocan, in Granton and Cecil" (62). Perhaps this figure of the abuser has become a composite in Naomi's mind, still inhabiting her nightmares. In Lethbridge in 1945 a stranger in a restaurant kept beckoning to Naomi while holding out five dollars (*Obasan*, 190). But it is the recollection of the stranger approaching her in the sugar-beet field that Naomi summons up in *Itsuka*, as well as the attendant encounter with Hank, in the immediate aftermath of her flight from Cedric's embrace.

While Kogawa knew in 1987 that the novel would concern Naomi's sexuality and her fundamentalist Christian background, she was not then sure that it would deal with the Japanese-Canadian community ("although it's likely it will"). When an interviewer asked Joy Kogawa how Naomi was going to develop in this forthcoming novel (*Itsuka* was then in progress), Kogawa answered: "I'm going to struggle with Naomi's sexuality, just as I struggle with my own. Whether I'll be able to do that successfully, in my life or in this book, I do not know" (Komori 1987, 63).

If, as Kogawa has suggested, using the words of Rosemary Ruether, *Obasan* is about divine abandonment whereas *Itsuka* is about human solidarity, the character of Naomi provides both the negative and affirmative connections with the sacred in both novels. In Hugh MacLennan's *The Watch that Ends the Night* and Ignazio Silone's *Bread and Wine* the protagonists move through similar stages, from a childhood religion that gives way to political involvement until that in turn is supplanted by a radical experience of human love. MacLennan's George Stewart finally arrives at a further stage of return to transcendence with the death of the beloved; Silone's Pietro Spina experiences the sacralization of companionship among human beings. At the end of *Itsuka* it is in doubt whether Naomi's experience of either political involvement (and its fulfilment) or Father Cedric's love will suffice for her. After the triumphant ecstasy of the success of the redress movement, whose struggles Naomi has made her own, what will ordinary life mean for her? *The Rain Ascends* problematizes this relationship between the political and the personal by putting the bonds of a daughter's love for an aged parent in conflict with the obligations of justice to others.

But Kogawa does not think that political reality holds any importance for Naomi at the end of *Obasan*: "What to her matters is the cosmic quest, the capacity for faith and meaning" (Ackerman 1993, 222). At the same time she acknowledges that Naomi's experience of separation from her mother's love is "my (fairly conscious) analogy of postholocaust experience of *faith*." She explains: "The preholocaust experience is the presence of God, the God of history, the God who saves; the postholocaust experience, or the reaction of the Christian Church, at any rate, is the feeling that God is dead. There is a sense of abandonment. They abandoned their faith or their faith abandoned them" (ibid., 220-21).

With these terms Kogawa locates the fictional experience of her narrator, Naomi—whatever relation that experience may bear to her own—alongside that of Elie Wiesel and other Holocaust survivors. François Mauriac, in his Foreword to Wiesel's classic memoir of the Holocaust, *Night*, declares that among other outrages "the worst of all to those of us who have faith [is] the death of God in the soul of a child who suddenly discovers absolute evil" (Wiesel 1960, 9). "For a child," the adult Naomi reflects, "there is no presence without flesh" (*Obasan*, 243). While Naomi does not experience "absolute evil" in the manner of Eliezer, the child in *Night*, she does experience prejudice, injustice, hardship, and dislocation. For Eliezer what made the comparatively greater sufferings of Auschwitz even bearable was the presence of his father whose welfare and care became the focus of his life's meaning. The death of the elder Wiesel towards the end of the war removed from Eliezer his last reason to go on living. The younger Naomi had a surrogate mother in the form of her aunt, but even so the inexplicable absence and silence of her mother form the cloud under which she lives and which, in effect, eclipses the divine in her life. Naomi's experience of the absence of the divine in *Obasan*, whose immediacy is given in the absence of her mother, and the means by which she copes with those absences, need exploration.

Kogawa and Wiesel, in spite of these similarities, differ decisively in their attitudes towards the perpetrators of the injustices against them. Both authors share an understanding of the meaning of silence (although perhaps Kogawa sees more of its positive aspects than does Wiesel), and both share a sense of obligation—even compulsion—about bearing testimony and telling their story. For Kogawa, however, the continuing life of Japanese Canadians in Canada means coming to terms with those who perpetrated injustice and denied human rights. That, coupled with a strong sense of the Christian meaning of forgiveness and reconciliation, motivated her work within the redress movement. For Elie Wiesel, siding with the victims means opposing the murderers. He sees it as no part of his enterprise to explain why the Holocaust came about or to understand the viewpoint of the oppressors: "If the victims are my problem the killers are not. The killers are someone else's problem" (Wiesel 1990, 17).

Joy Kogawa, on the other hand, feels it necessary to understand the enemy. As she states in a 1992 film, *The Pool: Reflections of Japanese-Canadian Internment*, victims should take on "the imaginative exercise of being part of the victimizer." She wants "both victims and victimizers to be in dialogue, in communication, in communion, and in recognition mutually of each other's positions." In another interview, with Rita Deverall on Vision TV in 1994, Joy Kogawa speaks of the necessity of overcoming blindness by taking on the enemy's viewpoint. She elaborated her position in response to the question, "Can you see through the enemy's eyes now?" Kogawa spoke of being on a journey towards mercy, having discovered that "the Goddess of Mercy is the goddess of abundance." Kogawa believes that if you have "a sufficient sense of the abundant life—if you are able to perceive with genuine gratitude, if you can have that largeness within yourself—you can so see the other that they cease to be the enemy." This kind of transformative vision of the other she takes even further, to the point that it reaches a kind of transference:

> You can so see them that you can become them. . . . That we ought to be able to live a part of Hitler inside of ourselves, that we ought to be able to see that—or the Ku Klux Klan, or whoever we all are. I mean we are all humans and in some way we are all connected and we are all capable of anything given the right circumstances.

Millicent, the loving daughter in *The Rain Ascends*, finds herself in the position of Hitler's cat, who on Judgment Day "can stand in front of that awesome cloud of witnesses and yowl its unacceptable tale of affection" (1995, 12).

Whether or not Kogawa's argument for mutuality is applicable in the case of Japanese Canadians in relation to the rest of Canadians, it is doubtful that a merciful seeing through the eyes of the enemy can be applied to the case of the Jews and Hitler. In the first place the scale and nature of the atrocities differ, occurring in a context where the relation between victims and victimizers cannot be resumed. How are the six million dead to see through the eyes of their murderers? And perhaps too, as Cynthia Ozick points out, quoting from the rabbis, "Whoever is merciful to the cruel will end by being indifferent to the innocent." Victims and victimizers can only be in dialogue and communion, can only experience mercy and reconciliation, in cases other than murder. As Ozick states: "Murder is irrevocable. Murder is irreversible. With murder there is no 'next time'" (1976, 185-86). Early in 1995, on the fiftieth anniversary of its liberation, Elie Wiesel prayed at Auschwitz-Birkenau: "God, merciful God, do not have mercy on murderers of Jewish children. . . . Do not have mercy on those who created this place. Do not forgive the people who murdered here" (*Globe and Mail* 27 January 1995, A14).

The connections—and disjunctions—between Joy Kogawa's first two novels create opportunities for comparison and commentary as well as interpretive difficulties. *Itsuka* as a sequel of *Obasan* provides an effective opportunity for the resolution of the injustices of the evacuation and dispersal policies of the Canadian government in the 1940s with the redress and apology of the 1980s. But as a continuation of Naomi's story *Itsuka* is less effective, failing as it does to take up, continue, and perhaps resolve the problems that were Naomi's own within the context of the first novel. Childhood sexual abuse and abandonment by her mother give way to the legacy of fundamentalism and a teenaged encounter with a seducer. Political issues are engaged in *Obasan* principally at the artistic, imaginative, and personal level through the consciousness and experience of Naomi and are resolved in those terms. Naomi's childhood perspective makes *Obasan* work effectively. But Kogawa has confessed that she continues, even after the publication of *Itsuka*, to find difficulties with its narrative point of view.

The problem, it seems to me, is that in *Itsuka* Joy Kogawa has it as her principal aim to recount the events with which she was directly and personally involved attending the redress movement. Perhaps what is lacking here is an appropriate persona (like the childhood Naomi) from which she is properly distanced, at least temporally (and temporarily), and whose story matters to the reader in and for itself, not only as an entrée into political events in which she participated. In *Itsuka* Aunt Emily states—and the author has quoted her character in several contexts afterwards—"When we follow the light, we extinguish the night, and we do this through politics as much as through art" (248). Notwithstanding Kogawa's appreciation for this statement as a legitimation for other means than art to banish darkness, ironically it can also be an artist's rationale for abandoning art. But the appearance of a third novel at this point in her career differentiates Kogawa from Margaret Laurence who, after *The Diviners*, turned away from fiction writing to such causes as the antinuclear movement and Pollution Probe. The literary artist's task, even when her subject is politics, is to render artistically the effects and efficacy of political involvement in the lives and on the pulses of her characters.

In her 1983 address "My Final Hour" Margaret Laurence expresses some of her own views about the relation of artistic endeavour to human survival: ". . . the artist affirms the value of life itself and of our only home, the planet Earth. Art mirrors and ponders the pain and joy of our experience as human beings" (1988, 260). Laurence continues by reflecting that we face the possibility of a world in which all the works of the human imagination might be destroyed, and then goes on to state that her responsibility as a writer is "not to write pamphlets; not to write didactic fiction" (ibid., 261). Laurence feels that would "a betrayal of how I feel about my work" and that her responsibility is "to write as truthfully as I can, about human beings and their dilemmas, to honour them as living, suffering and sometimes joyful people" (ibid.).

In *Itsuka*, contrary to the methods and expression of *Obasan*, Joy Kogawa confuses the realms of politics and art. To paraphrase a comment of R. W. B. Lewis about the relative importance of religion and literature, on an absolute scale it may be that politics is more important than art, but in the literary realm, politics ought to follow art, and to do so naturally. The metaphysics of divine abandonment, where the sacred is found in the void of absence, functions as the theological correlate of the communal experience of exile and of the individual experience of sexual abuse and the loss of the mother. This relocation of sacrality succeeds admirably in *Obasan*. But in *Itsuka*, though the experience of human solidarity may function as consolation for the earlier abandonment, and the redress movement may be a historical example of that solidarity, the novel lacks a correspondingly convincing resolution on the individual level for Naomi who, though she falls in love with Cedric, remains something of a bystander and observer in relation to the search for justice. In *The Rain Ascends* Millicent is fully engaged on both the individual and political levels.

BREAD AND STONES AND NAMES IN *Obasan*

JOY KOGAWA HAS SAID THAT SHE does not know what part of
her is Japanese; but at the same time she thinks that the "deepest
aspect" of her is Christian (see Redekop 1990, 96-97). In *Obasan*
that "deepest aspect" may be conveyed most immediately in the
novel's biblical epigraph: "To him that overcometh will I give to eat
of the hidden manna and will give him a white stone and in the
stone a new name written" (Rev. 2:17; cf. *Obasan*, v). The biblical
context assures faithful Christians of rewards if they endure suffering, hardship, and persecution. "Manna" refers originally to the
food provided to the Israelites during their wanderings in the
wilderness (see Exodus 16:35), a supernatural sustenance that
becomes, metaphorically, in the New Testament gospels Christ as
the bread of life come down from heaven (John 6:31). In the epigraph from Revelation this "hidden manna" is a form of eschatological spiritual food, a christianized version of rabbinic legend in
which the manna was concealed during the destruction of the Temple until the dawn of the messianic age.

The "white stone" (Greek *psephos*, pebble) may be an amulet
engraved with a name—perhaps a Christian adaptation of the protective charm used in mystery cults—or a commonly used ancient
admission token (here, for example, for entrance to a heavenly ban-
quet). The "new name" may be Christ's name, shared by those
who participate in his sufferings, or a new identity following a new
birth.[3] Kogawa uses the terms of this epigraph—hidden manna,
white stone, new name—as thematic links throughout the story,
indexes of her own preoccupations and insights about the religious
significance of this persecuted and exiled Canadian minority. Her
use of these symbols in *Obasan* is partially controlled and shaped
by their biblical use; Kogawa also transports biblical metaphors
across cultural boundaries and infuses new meaning into them.

In the Hebrew scriptures "bread" signifies food in general.
Manna and the unleavened bread of the Exodus are the prototypes
of bread used in religious feasts and celebrations (e.g., Passover).[4]
The connection is explicit in Exodus 16:15: "They said to one
another, It is manna; for they wist not what it was. And Moses said
unto them, This is the bread which the Lord hath given you to
eat." A stone, though usually suggesting hardness, immobility, and
endurance (and perhaps eternity, as when memorial stones are
heaped up to commemorate an event) is often the antithesis of

living or biological entities. (An interesting exception is 1 Peter 2:5 where the rejected "living stones" become a spiritual priesthood and the materials for building a new edifice.) In Kogawa's epigraph stone is antithetical to bread and the nourishment it provides. In Luke's Gospel Satan tempts Jesus in the wilderness to prove that he is the Son of God by turning a stone into bread (4:3). And Jesus asks, "If a son shall ask bread of any of you that is a father, will he give him a stone?" (Luke 11:11; cf. Mt. 7:9).

Aunt Emily quotes the words of Habakkuk to Naomi— "Write the vision and make it plain." But she does not quote the succeeding words—"upon tables," that is, tablets, probably of stone, like those on which Moses received the Ten Commandments (cf. Deut. 9:9). The writer's task parallels the prophet's (or even the divine lawgiver's) who engraves something new in stone. The novelist as seer listens to silence, turns stones into bread, confers names upon the unnameable, writing it all down upon an unreceptive and flinty surface, generally struggling to redeem materials often unpromising and resistant. King-Kok Cheung interprets Kogawa as reevaluating both language and silence and thereby undermining logocentrism: "She reveals the strengths and limits of discursive power and quiet forbearance alike; in doing so, she maintains the complementary functions of verbal and nonverbal expression" (1993, 128).

Kogawa shows mainstream majority Canadians (those of European descent) their failure to live up to their own ideals in their treatment of Canadians of Japanese ancestry. Her view is that minorities can be the healing "leaven" within society, perhaps paralleling and legitimating her own prophetic artistry, providing the majority with the means of their own restoration and salvation. Evoking John 9:1-12, the narrator poetically describes the evacuees as being "sent to the sending, that we may bring sight" (111). The practice of Christianity by Japanese Canadians proves to be more active and forgiving than that of other Canadians. Because, as she writes in the Preface to her father's book, the Issei refused to see Canada as the enemy, they created (and preserved) the possibility of friendship, "by persisting in seeing the face of the friend even when it was not there." She affirms, in terms paralleling what she says elsewhere about the relationship between the victim and the victimizer, that "that capacity to transform a broken reality and to make it whole can only come from strength—the most deeply powerful spiritual strength available to us, superseding all political power" (Nakayama 1984, 8). At a conference in Japan in 1992 Joy Kogawa spoke of the various ways in which minorities continue to fulfil this role.[5]

Of the three central terms of the epigraph (bread, stone, name) the prefatory narrative comment (on the page opposite the opening page of the first chapter) invokes only one, stone. That stone is for Naomi a negative silence that, here at the outset, is the opposite of the word: "I hate the stillness. I hate the stone. I hate the sealed vault with its cold icon. I hate the staring into the night" (vi). Naomi can neither embrace the absent voice in its silence nor follow the underground stream down to the hidden voice and the freeing word. At the opening of chapter 1 Naomi at age thirty-six visits the coulee on the virgin prairie with her uncle, as she has done for many years without knowing the purpose of this annual visit. The magnitude of his remembered loss on the anniversary of the bombing of Nagasaki and of his silence about the death of Naomi's mother are only hinted at. The rippling prairie grasses are reminiscent of other personal losses—the sea he has left behind and his confiscated boat. When Naomi leaves him briefly to descend into the gulch, she listens to the water of the intermittent underground stream for its "hidden voice" and "freeing word." Yet the natural context here remains a cosmic silence as steadfast and secretive as her uncle's.

As Erika Gottlieb has put it so well, "the natural setting in the first chapter is more than background: it represents the stillness and tension in the cosmos and the soul" (1986, 35). Gottlieb explains that the three landscapes of the novel's opening proceed from the universality evoked by the "cosmic-mythical symbols" quoted in the epigraph from Revelation, through the "narrator's soul as wasteland" depicted in the prefatory narrative comment, to the actual Canadian prairie landscape of chapter 1 as described on the evening of 9 August 1972 (ibid., 34-35). These interrelated landscapes introduce us to the novel's concentric system of puzzles.

If initially silence is negative in its connotations, the "stony silence" of a universe largely indifferent, so too are Naomi's uncle's attempts at breadmaking at first depicted as pathetically failed efforts to assimilate. He received his bread recipe just after the war at the local grocery store with the purchase of a bag of flour.

Naomi's response, at age ten, to her uncle's first attempt at baking is to ask, "How can you eat that stone?" (12). She continues to refuse his "stone burreddo," even when offered with butter by her brother Stephen. No matter what her uncle added to it, whether oatmeal, barley, potatoes, or carrots, "it always ended up like a lump of granite" (13). She declares: "If you can't even break it, it's not bread." When Obasan ate her husband's bread, she soaked it in homemade "weedy tea," though both children prefer Japanese tea on their cold rice with salted pickles late at night. At the gathering after his death Naomi wonders if the baking that loaf of black bread was her Uncle Sam's last act.

Early on in the novel also introduces bread as a symbol whose initial meaning, like word and silence, is negative, interpreted as being like rock or stone, and an illustration of a miserable and failed attempt to integrate themselves into a Canadian lifestyle. Here Naomi interprets Stephen's offering bread to her in terms of his "always ordering me around." But she later makes a kind and sympathetic response to his preference for bread over rice during the evacuation. On the train to Slocan Naomi has her doll offer Stephen a sandwich. Part of his efforts to distance himself from anything Japanese, Stephen had rejected his aunt's earlier offer of a rice ball with the angry retort, "Not that kind of food."

During the evacuation Stephen's obdurate silence shields and betrays his fractured identity. Naomi—herself likewise silent, but also perceptive and observant—sees Stephen as broken, like Humpty Dumpty, his leg in a cast and using a single crutch. He is also "half in and half out of his shell," not knowing who he is, and ashamed of his Japanese background because of racial slurs and taunts suffered at school. When Naomi (or her doll speaking for her) recites aloud the first two lines of the nursery rhyme, the final two lines are implicitly present also: "All the King's horses and all the King's men / Couldn't put Humpty together again."[6] This irony alludes to Aunt Emily's comment about her loss of faith in the Royal Canadian Mounted Police after Japanese Canadians were beaten at Hastings Park—"At one time, remember how I almost worshipped the Mounties?" (100). Her letters reflect the hurt and sense of betrayal experienced by Canadians of Japanese ancestry that the Canadian government and the agents of the British crown—the institutions in which they believed ("all the King's horses and all the King's men")—are now arrayed against them.

Itsuka mentions Obasan's scrapbook of royal-family clippings and her response to the King's death: "The day King George VI died, no one in Granton mourned more than Obasan. She sat by the radio, head bowed, hands folded in prayer, listening to CJOC Lethbridge" (10). On the train en route to Slocan Naomi imagines that rice paste (Obasan uses a single grain to seal an envelope) might be enough to put Stephen back together again. Their ancestral culture has the potential of healing for Stephen, by life-sustaining means not available in Canada. Western-style bread has not been the staff of life for Japanese Canadians, and no replacement for the rice of Asia.

The symbolic significance of a name—and the negative power of misnaming, as in the epithets endured by Stephen—also arises early in the novel. Teaching her class, just before she receives the summons to return home after her uncle's death, Naomi corrects a student's pronunciation: the class troublemaker insists on saying her surname, Nakane, as "Nah Canny." When the next question is whether she has ever been in love, Naomi deflects it with a question of her own about what it means to be "in" something.[7] Naomi ponders the negative meaning of "spinster" (or "old maid" or "bachelor lady") as a designation for herself, contrasting her reaction with Aunt Emily's assertion that "if we laundered the term properly she'd put it on" (8). The questions from the class persist, evoking memories for Naomi of being interrogated on a date about her birthplace and length of residence in Canada and the meaning of "Nisei."

The schoolgirl who tells Naomi's brother Stephen that "all the Jap kids at school are going to be sent away and they're bad and you're a Jap" (70) prefigures the name-calling of the Canadian newspapers and of politicians and citizens in general. Typical of many victims, Stephen passes on the abuse he has received, telling Naomi that she also is "bad" and a "Jap." (Her father informs her that this is wrong, they are Canadians.) The most injurious instances of name-calling occur in the context of the deportation of the Japanese-Canadians away from the British Columbia coast. Aunt Emily recognizes this for what it is: "None of us, she said, escaped the naming. We were defined and identified by the way we were seen" (118). Identified as "a stench in the nostrils of the people of Canada," the Japanese Canadians "are therefore relegated to the cesspools" (ibid.). Aunt Emily comments on the appropriateness of the term "evacuation:" it was an "evacuation" (in the sense of emptying the bowels) because the Japanese Canadians were "flushed out of Vancouver" like "dung drops." As so often in the horrible history of racism, a negative label that differentiates "them" from "us," that shows that "they" are not people like "us," then legitimates "them" being treated as if they were not fully human.

Stephen reacts to his schoolmates' treatment by attempting to distance himself from his Japanese identity (when he refuses to eat rice, for instance) or by passing on his own victimization to Naomi. On arrival at the little house in Slocan Stephen retreats to the backyard where, using his crutch, he slaughters the butterflies in revenge for his own hurt. They are "gold and brown winged things,"[8] but by (mis-)naming them "moths," he repeats the insults his schoolmates inflicted on him: "They're bad. . . . They eat holes in your clothes" (123). "Bad" things like "Japs" and "moths" deserve to be sent away or destroyed.

FROM SILENCE TO COMMUNION

NAOMI GIVES INDICATIONS OF BEING less deeply wounded than her brother, even though she is the silent one who almost never speaks. On the train she is unable to comply when her aunt urges her to take an orange as a gift to the young woman with the baby. But she watches as first Obasan and then the old woman preserve the Japanese custom of gift-giving even in their present extremity of scarcity and deportation. Returning to the ancient rhythms of traditional Japanese life provides reassurance and healing amidst the wounds and insults of their present crisis. A little later Naomi follows the example of Obasan by responding to Stephen's hurt and isolation. She puts her treasured rubber ball in his jacket pocket. At their new home Naomi observes her brother's slaughter of the butterflies; she observes as well something outside the field of his vision: "One butterfly he cannot see is hovering over his head" (123). Perhaps too she recognizes the butterfly in its traditional symbolic role as an image of hope, eternity, and the human spirit. While Stephen cannot stand the silence of Obasan's house, and has to get away from it, finding partially at least his voice and his refuge in music, Naomi appreciates the positive aspects of her aunt's quiet ways, reminiscent of her mother's protective and accepting silence that did not scold, blame, criticize, or invade. King-Kok Cheung notes that most reviewers have seen silence in *Obasan* in exclusively negative terms, a Eurocentric bias that favours speech and condemns silence (Cheung 1993, 126-27). She maintains that Kogawa distinguishes among various forms of silence and stresses "the positive use of nonverbal behavior as a corrective to the prevailing critical trend that privileges speech" (ibid., 128).

The eloquent complement to Naomi's mother's silence is her visual language: "Her eyes are steady and matter of fact—the eyes of Japanese motherhood. They do not invade and betray. They are eyes that protect, shielding what is hidden most deeply in the heart of the child" (59). In contrast, Mrs. Sugimoto's eyes, on the day that Naomi put the (yellow) baby chicks in the cage with the (white) mother hen, "search my face:" "Her glance is too long. She notes my fear, invades my knowing" (60). With her invasive stare and her fussing over her sons Mrs. Sugimoto reminds Naomi of the white hen who kills her own chicks. While the politics of colour here contrast white and yellow, Caucasian and Japanese, modes of behaviour, Kogawa does not make these absolute moral categories that are rigidly distinct.

Mrs. Sugimoto falls short of the ideal and practice of Japanese motherhood and, at least implicitly, behaves in a manner typical of a non-Japanese mother. Similarly, neither prejudice nor kindness is the exclusive property of either racial group. Although the next door neighbour, Old Man Gower, sexually abuses Naomi in Vancouver, and although in Slocan she has a similar experience, again involving a white male (her schoolmate Percy), her experience with white males is not restrictively negative. In Slocan, Rough Lock Bill provides a positive counterpart to Old Man Gower's harmful treatment of Naomi. Bill gently exchanges names (written in the sand) with the silent Naomi, tells her a story that is accepting of her silence ("smart people don't talk too much"), and ends up by saving her from drowning. When Naomi recovers she finds "he is peering at me, his face close to mine," but even this looking is only in the matter-of-fact way she prefers, in accordance with her mother's example.[9]

Furthermore, the ignorance and prejudice evident in the name-calling Stephen experiences from white schoolmates in Vancouver also has its Japanese parallel in Slocan. Naomi is shunned in the bath by Reiko and Yuki whose mother believes that Naomi's family has tuberculosis because of her father's hospitalization and Stephen's limp. When Naomi asks her uncle for an explanation he replies that illness "is a matter of misfortune, not shame" (166). And the incident of the white mother hen killing her own yellow chicks, an allegory of what the "mother" country has done to her Japanese-Canadian "children," also has its dark vengeful reversal in Slocan when Stephen and Naomi watch six schoolboys, all of them apparently of Japanese ancestry, participate in the prolonged killing of a white hen ("Got to make it suffer" [155]). One of Kogawa's poems has a similar incident set in Japan, its imagery reminiscent of a scene of torture. A chicken is slaughtered by five men, "One with knife, one grinning toothless." The poet imagines herself "dangling feet first from the sky" and wonders if she should struggle ("The Chicken Killing" in Kogawa 1974, 21). In the same collection another section, headed "Forest Creatures," has several poems evoking Joy Kogawa's experience of the evacuation.

For Naomi this business of yellow chicks and white hens becomes a confused mélange of associations and images attending issues of motherhood and racism and victimization and death. When Naomi is in the hospital after her near-drowning her aunt gives her the story of Chicken Little, "an oversized baby chick." Naomi connects this story of the alarmist chicken with Stephen's "Yellow Peril" board game where "a few brave defenders" are pitted against a large number of Japanese enemies: "There are fifty small yellow pawns inside and three big blue checker kings" (152). Naomi's understanding is that to be yellow is to be small and weak—in a word, "chicken"—but yellow chicks turn white when they grow up (and the former victims become victimizers?).

On a personal level these negative experiences of Naomi's early years leave her with a legacy of abuse, internalized guilt, and a sense of abandonment. She has experienced the hardship and dis-locating upheaval of the evacuation, the racism of schoolmates and society at large, the inexplicable departure of her mother (and her subsequent silence as well as uncertainty as to her fate), the death of her father, and, after the end of the war the tragedy of another removal from the British Columbia interior to Alberta with the renewal of hardships that are if anything more inexplicable and intense. The accuracy of Kogawa's description of *Obasan* as being about the death of God means that for Naomi all that is ultimate in her world is shattered or gone. The reaction of Naomi and of Aya Obasan and her uncle Isamu is chiefly one of passive endurance of their suffering. Its redemptive aspects come through a fusion of cultural symbols and through the unlocking of the secrets of Naomi's mother, whose silence has both a negative and a positive impact on her daughter.

Naomi believes that the secret of her abuse by Gower is the explanation for her mother's absence. Even as an adult Naomi seems hesitant to probe this mystery and to discover the truth. Her links with her absent mother are through her father (until his death), her favourite doll (until its loss just after arrival in Slocan), and through her aunt (Obasan). Other objects—"transitional objects" a psychologist would term them—bridge the gulf of her mother's absence and ease the passage to her new home. She takes with her a rubber ball found beneath a cot the night she overheard an adult discussion of the measures against the Japanese Canadians. But she gives the ball as a gift to her brother when she sees his hurt. She retains the two yellow toy Easter chicks previously stowed in the drawer of her mother's sewing machine, intended as a surprise for her upon her return. Perhaps Naomi intended at some level these toy chicks to be an apology and redemption for the ones whose deaths her carelessness had caused.

Just before the departure from Slocan friends and relatives are gathered in the Nakane house for a communion service conducted by Nakayama-sensei (an Anglican priest who shares both the name and profession of Joy Kogawa's own father). As the service proceeds in a mixture of Japanese and English he finishes praying for "all Christian Kings, Princes and Governors" when Stephen's weight on an open box of belongings results in a loud crack. He has broken his mother's favourite record, "Silver Threads Among the Gold," from which "one small piece is broken off like a bite off a giant cookie" (176). While the service proceeds Stephen passes the broken piece to his father just before the communion wafer is broken and distributed: "Sensei carries a small silver box in one hand and lifts out a tiny paper-thin white square which he snaps in half" (177). Kogawa thereby suggests a connection between these broken discs taken from their respective boxes and passed around as tokens of love in absence. (Later the link is made between the communion wafer and Aunt Emily's letters as means of communion; cf. 182—"white paper bread for the mind's meal").

Here Kogawa portrays the ironies and ambiguities of the situation in a rich and complex tapestry. In a Christian communion service, under conditions of internment and just prior to removal to begin worse sufferings, these Japanese Canadians pray that their King may govern them in a "quiet and godly" manner. Simultaneously Stephen fractures the means of his own communion with his absent mother. Significantly, his connection with her, and with his father with whom he plays the flute during a brief reunion visit in Slocan (171), is through the medium of music. In an early part of the story Naomi describes Stephen's listening with rapt attention to his mother's records, though of her favourite she remarks: "It does not occur to me to wonder why Mother would have liked this song. We do not have silver threads among the gold" (126).

Whenever Nakayama-sensei prays he stresses their mutual support of one another. On arrival at Slocan he says, "together . . . by helping each other," and gives thanks "that we are together again" (122); at the close of the communion service upon departure he says, "We will not abandon one other" (178). After Naomi's discovery of her mother's fate the Rev. Nakayama says, "That there is brokenness. . . . That this world is brokenness. But within brokenness is the unbreakable name" (240). A little later he prays again: "Father, if your suffering is greater than ours, how great that suffering must be. . . . How great the helplessness. How we dare not abandon the ones who suffer, lest we abandon You. . . . Teach us to see Love's presence in our abandonment" (243). Having emphasized to an interviewer that "Nakayama-sensei is a real character, a real Anglican minister—he's my real father," Kogawa continues: "Those services really happened, those words really happened, those prayers really happened" (Ackerman 1993, 219). Given her insistence on the authenticity of this theological formulation as her father's own, we must take it that Rosemary Ruether's view that God has abandoned divine power so that we might not abandon one another is a post facto verification of a position that Kogawa already held, one she got from her father. Ruether's liberation theology has women, in company with other oppressed peoples, leading the way in a revolution against transcendence and dominance and technological power towards "communal personhood" (Reuther 1979, 51).

King-Kok Cheung uses the word "double-voicing" (in the sense of "more than one" voice) to describe Joy Kogawa's "discourse(s) of silence" which brings together both Western and Asian sensibilities: "Kogawa fuses the Japanese legacy of attentiveness and intuitive knowing with Buddhist and Christian meditations" (1993, 20). Elsewhere though Cheung sees more opposition between Christianity and Buddhism than actually exists. She overemphasizes their differences when she claims they hold "contradictory attitudes towards word (logos) and silence. Whereas the Christian prophetic tradition stresses the importance of voice, Buddhist meditation evinces reverence for silence" (ibid., 129 n). Cheung might have found a similar reverence for silence in Christian meditative traditions. In October 1992 the abbot of Tenryuji, a temple in western Kyoto, gave a lecture in which he described a European visit by some Japanese Zen Buddhists to share their experiences of meditation in dialogue with Roman Catholic priests.

Sau-ling Cynthia Wong, referring to the "stone bread" as a "religious symbol devoid of specifically ethnic connotations," is precisely right when she states that "Christianity in *Obasan* is never portrayed as 'Western,' as opposed to 'Oriental'" (Wong 1993, 23). Wong, however, restricts the meaning of the Eucharistic bread to a reenactment of Christ's sacrifice whose parallel in the novel is to be found in the Christlike sacrificial figure of Naomi's mother "who literally loses her flesh and blood" (ibid., 23). In fact it would seem that the communion through love in absence is Nakayama's (and Kogawa's) Eucharistic theology in *Obasan*, not sacrificial reenactment. The concern is more pastoral than priestly or ritualistic.

Nakayama-sensei's celebration of the Anglican form of the Eucharist in *Obasan* tends towards a "horizontal" Protestant interpretation in its emphasis on Christians gathering together in "communion," not even so much with God as with each other. There is little evidence of the more "vertical" Roman Catholic stress on Christ's sacrifice as means of atonement between God and humanity. There is little discourse about sin and redemption in these prayers and services. Aunt Emily, speaking to Naomi about Nakayama-sensei's "desperation to keep the community together," describes him as "a deeply wounded shepherd trying to tend the flock in every way he could." She maintains that the postwar repatriation and dispersal policies were worse in their effects than the evacuation: "To a people for whom community was the essence of life, destruction of community was the destruction of life" (186).

This interpretation of the communion service emphasizing its dimensions as communal meal illustrates the liturgical adaptation of a Western religious form accommodating Japanese meanings. In monotheistic traditions such adaptation to incorporate different cultural values verges on syncretism. For Japanese people, used to moving back and forth between Shinto and Buddhist—and now Christian—practices, religious exclusivity seems strangely restrictive. There is a Japanese saying to the effect that one is born as a Shinto, marries as a Christian, and dies as a Buddhist, an expression conveying how each of these three religions comes to prominence with a particular rite of passage. In fact, "it is well known among Japanologists that at present the major role of Buddhism in Japanese society is its near monopoly of funeral services for the dead" (Lai 1993, 73).

As one scholar of Japanese religions, Ian Reader, explains, "The Japanese do not live in a system that demands full-blooded, belief-orientated and exclusive commitment that precludes any other. Rather, their orientations are situational and complementary: the necessity of dealing with the problem of death demands one set of responses and orientations while the time of year or birth of a child requires another" (Reader 1991, 16). In *Obasan* Japanese Canadians seem readily able to incorporate both Christian and Buddhist practices at the funeral of Naomi's Grandmother Nakane. Japanese people who have converted to Christianity frequently report missing in their new religion the death practices, and especially the connection with their ancestors, provided in Buddhism. After Nakayama-sensei conducts the Christian funeral service the grandmother's body is cremated in the Buddhist manner on a pyre of logs, a practice Aya Obasan relates both to the appearance of the angel in the fiery furnace of the Book of Daniel and to the tempering of samurai swords. The Buddhist practice of cremation drives out the impurity attending death, transforming, with the accompaniment of other rituals, the corpse into the purified spirit of the ancestor. As part of this process the priest grants a posthumous name ("a Buddhist name") to the dead person. The ancestor thus becomes a source of blessings for the descendants, available to be prayed to for protection (see Earhart 1984, 60-61; cf. Reader 1991, chap. 4).

In *Obasan* Naomi incorporates Buddhist beliefs and practices into her own observances for the deaths of both her parents. In

Granton Naomi returns home one evening with a captured frog to hear of her father's death, news that comes during a now-rare visit from Nakayama-sensei. Naomi has decided to call her frog "Tad," "short for Tadpole or Tadashi, my father's name" (206). She thinks of the frog as a messenger from her father until one day it disappears. The next sentence is: "My last letter to father has received no answer" (208). Her pet frog functions as another transitional object for her, unable as she is to acknowledge fully at this point her father's death—"for years I simply do not believe it." But there is a deeper symbolic significance here too. In general the frog, amphibious and lunar in nature, appearing and disappearing, is connected with creation and resurrection, and placed on Egyptian mummies (see Cirlot 1971, 114-15). More specifically, many Japanese temples and shrines sell lucky frog figurines. According to one scholar, "the symbolic efficacy of this frog derives from a linguistic pun, for the word for frog, *kaeru*, is pronounced the same as the verb *kaeru*, to return" (Reader 1991, 178).[10] The frog symbolizes the hope for a safe return from a journey as well as the safe return to health from illness. Perhaps here Naomi's wish is for her father to return from death as ancestral spirit to guide and protect her.

For Joy Kogawa, as for her narrator Naomi Nakane, dreams figure in a prominent way as warnings, means of communication, signposts of directions to be taken. Kogawa relates that in a dream she was directed to go to Ottawa and to the Archives. There she received the Muriel Kitagawa papers that became the basis for Emily's letters in *Obasan*, chapter 14 (see Ackerman 1993, 217-18). As a schoolteacher in Cecil Naomi has recurring dreams of "flight, terror, and pursuit," and one in which three Asian women attempt to forestall their deaths at the hands of soldiers by seductive behaviour: "It was too late. There was no hope. The soldiers could not be won" (62). In the context of these nightmares of "abject longing, wretchedness, fear, and utter helplessness" Naomi describes, for the first time in her story, her abuse by Gower at age four, wondering, "Is this where the terror begins?" At the time of her uncle's death Naomi has a dream about stairs to "a courtyard and the place of the dead" in which the Grand Inquisitor, looming over her and her mother, is depicted in the same terms as Old Man Gower—"the top of his head a shiny skin cap" (228; cf. 61). He is trying to pry open Naomi's eyes and her mother's lips: "What the

Grand Inquisitor has never learned is that the avenues of speech are the avenues of silence. To hear my mother, to attend her speech, to attend the sound of stone, he must first become silent. Only when he enters her abandonment will he be released from his own" (228).

This dream is a prelude to Naomi's discovery of her mother's fate—the nightmare of her dying and the reason for her "vigil of silence"—when she hears her mother's voice in Nakayama's reading of the letters from Grandma Kato. This gathering with Nakayama-sensei, Stephen, Aunt Emily, and Obasan parallels previous ones, becoming as much a memorial for Naomi's mother as a wake for her Uncle Isamu. It echoes the liturgical setting of the communion at Slocan, for instance, as Naomi slices her uncle's stone bread to serve with the green Japanese tea, a cultural transposition of the elements of the Eucharist. (There is even the parallel incident of Stephen breaking off, "then changing his mind," a piece of his uncle's bread during Nakayama's praying.)

Grandma Kato's words become sacred scripture: "Sensei pauses as he reads. 'Naomi,' he says softly, 'Stephen, your mother is speaking. Listen carefully to her voice'" (233). Naomi learns too from Aunt Emily of her mother's grave, the memorial stone with no date, the plaque with her name, and the Canadian maple tree planted by missionaries. The entire three pages comprising chapter 38 are a prayer addressed to her mother in various terms—"Silent Mother," "Martyr Mother," "Young Mother at Nagasaki," "Maypole Mother," "Gentle Mother." Following the pattern of a Buddhist observance of death, Naomi's mother undergoes transformation from scarred and suffering body, tortured with a radiation sickness—from one, that is, who cannot be properly remembered and honoured while her story remains untold—to a purified spirit present to guide and bless Naomi in the role of ancestor. On the novel's penultimate page as Naomi grieves she addresses her song of mourning to "Father, Mother, my relatives, my ancestors" (246).

With the discovery of love's presence in her abandonment Naomi discovers positive meaning in the symbols understood negatively at the novel's outset. Her uncle's stone bread, first understood as a sign of Issei defeat and assimilation, becomes a means of communion for Naomi—with other friends and other family members, with him, and as mediating element for Japanese Canadians with the mainstream Canadian culture. Even "the world of stone" in which the Issei lived now becomes their place of rest (246), a memorial to their endurance and their memory. And in fulfilment of the biblical promise, perhaps here best understood in terms of the Buddhist posthumous name, those who endure receive a "new name," either concealed in a stone for Christians or written in a memorial tablet for Buddhists: "This honorary name indicates, in Buddhist terms, that the material aspect of the dead person has been extinguished, and the person has gone on to enlightenment, or paradise" (Earhart 1984, 61). On the concluding page Naomi returns to the coulee where she had been with her uncle a month earlier, now able to hear the hidden voice and the freeing word in the underground stream.

Obasan ends with Naomi finally being released from a stony and imprisoning silence of prolonged grief for her mother into true mourning. The hope that tears will one day become laughter is carried forward and realized in the next novel, *Itsuka*, where the success of the redress movement becomes vindication of the Issei sufferings. Joy Kogawa in her quest for the sacred amidst the personal and communal sufferings of the past fifty years finds ways of combining her ancestral traditions with those extant in Canada derived from European and Christian roots. Her particular kind of synthesis or syncretism favours a blend whose promise is for a future of mutuality in fulfilment of the highest hopes Canadians have for themselves.

NOTES

1 Kogawa, *Obasan* (1983), and Kogawa, *Itsuka* (1993). The Penguin paperback edition of *Obasan* is a reprint of the Lester & Orpen Dennys edition, having identical pagination. The Penguin paperback edition of *Itsuka* is a revised version of the hardcover edition published by Viking. Page references to the respective Penguin paperback editions are cited parenthetically here.

2 Stuart Hall, writing about ethnicity in the representation by and of blacks in English cinema, says "you can no longer conduct black politics through the strategy of a simple set of reversals, putting in the place of the bad old essential white subject, the essentially good black subject" ("New Ethnicities," in Institute of Contemporary Arts 1988). Such a strategy, according to Hall, makes all black people either good or at least "the same," and that is "one of the predicates of racism."

3 See *Dictionary of the Bible, s.v.* "stone," "manna" (Hastings 1963). See too Caird 1966, 42. T. Schrire comments that amulets, not mentioned in the Old Testament, were common by the time of the Maccabees. He continues: "The Jewish approach to protection from the Evil Eye is based on ... the firm belief in the tremendous power of the written Names of God, of angels, and of biblical quotations generally" (1966, 9). While Jewish amulets were usually parchment, Arabs used silver, which "because of its white colour and brightness was considered to be a lucky metal" (ibid., 24).

4 In the eleventh century the "Azyme Controversy" focussed on whether the bread of the Eucharist should be leavened or unleavened. Does leavened bread better represent the risen body of Christ than the "dead bread" of Israel? (Smith 1978).

5 Joy Kogawa was keynote speaker at the Canadian Studies Seminar at Kwansei Gakuin University, Nishinomiya, Japan, held 21-22 November 1992. She suggested five roles for minorities: to be a bridge; to critique the dominant position; to bring healing through mutuality; to stand with other minorities on the side of justice; and, to give voice to alternate perceptions. With respect to the third role—mutuality—she indicated that the redress movement was a struggle for mutuality, whose alternative is silence. She quoted from *Itsuka*: "What heals people is the power of mutuality."

6 While teaching *Obasan* I came across a cartoon based on the Humpty Dumpty nursery rhyme. The queen, with a pot of glue, surveys a smiling and restored Humpty. The caption reads: "I know all the king's horses and all the king's men couldn't do it—but that didn't mean it couldn't be done." If Marshall McLuhan is right that every joke conceals a grudge, here the grudge turns on gender whereas in Kogawa it is about government.

7 Ann-Janine Morey links food and sex and salvation as problematic areas for women (see Detweiler and Doty 1990, 169-79). If the body is seen as a bounded container, what passes in and out of it is important. Thus food is significant for Naomi because of her childhood sexual abuse by a neighbour. Eating disorders among women, especially anorexia nervosa, have recently been related to rape or sexual abuse. The issue, presumably, is control over one's body, at least through the regulation of food intake because of unwanted sex. Naomi's sexual abuse is one of the main reasons for her silence—her refusal to let words pass from her.

8 Though it seems unlikely from their description, it would be symbolically significant if these were Monarch butterflies, thereby suggestive once more of the negative authority of the British Crown.

9 Marilyn J. Legge refers to Rough Lock Bill as "an Indian living on Slocan Lake" (1992, 190). There is no clear evidence of his native ancestry, though his brown skin is darker than Naomi's and Kenji's and

though he tells a story of the first Indians who came to the area. Significantly, he distinguishes his own family's history from that of the natives who preceded them: "When my Grandad came, there was a whole tribe here. . . . But last I saw—one old guy up past the mine—be dead now probably" (146).

10 The frog's progression through various stages of metamorphosis makes it a widespread symbol of transformation (see Margaret Atwood, *Surfacing*, for example). Ian Reader mentions that frog figurines are sold at the Buddhist temple at Kiyoshi Kojin near Takarazuka, where I bought one without knowing its significance.

Conclusion

EVEN IF, AFTER SEARCHING OUT Canadian religion and culture, the locations of the sacred are found to be everywhere and nowhere, multiple rather than single, fluid rather than fixed, ephemeral rather than permanent, or at the margins rather than the centre, there still remains a persistent kind of disjunction between this discovery and some of our usual habits of mind on these matters. I am thinking of the problems raised by the kind of exclusive demands that Western monotheistic traditions have made on the religious allegiance of individuals. One is not supposed to be a Christian or a Jew or a Muslim and at the same time be something else. Monotheism warns sternly against idolatry, against putting other gods before the one supreme God, against raising penultimate concerns to the level of ultimacy.

So it is that any kind of synthesis or syncretism that might involve monotheism coming into combination with something else is frowned on. To revert to two of the examples taken up in the preceding essays, namely, the situation of the Belchers Inuit or of Japanese Canadians, both these groups were faced with the obstacles of a triple impossibility: they could not simply maintain their ancestral traditions (whether shamanism or Buddhism); they were unable totally to assimilate themselves to the new style of life characteristic of the majority culture (that is, some form of Christianity); yet neither were they encouraged to combine the old and the new. Here "the old" is their ancestral religious and cultural traditions and "the new" represents the prevailing culture of Canada dominated largely by Christian assumptions and a Western religious ethos. A. M. Klein, with his "seconding of a testament already seconded," could also be seen to some extent to be attempting a post-Holocaust synthesis of Judaism with Christianity.

From another point of view, Canadians of European descent take it for granted that their religion, usually Christianity, exists (whether actually or potentially) in some pure form untrammelled with any kind of contamination from "culture." Perhaps they

241

assume this most readily if they are born and grow up within
Canada. Yet even they struggle (or perhaps they do not struggle,
being unconscious of the issues) to reconcile the old (their inherited Christianity) with some form of the new (whether feminism,
political beliefs, or New Age spirituality, to cite a few examples).
Within Western religions syncretism tends to be a bad word; religious pluralism tends in practice sometimes to mean, not the coexistence of different religions, but subsuming the other under
Christian "inclusiveness." For instance, to incorporate the native
practice of burning sweetgrass into a Christian communion service
is more takeover or cultural appropriation (if practised by non-
natives) than it is interreligious dialogue and reciprocity.

Cornelius Jaenen and John Webster Grant have both pointed
out the great gulf between what missionaries thought they were
offering to natives and what the native peoples thought they were
doing when they accepted Christianity. In a suggestive typology
Jaenen delineates eight possible native responses to missionaries
ranging from aggressive rejection to complete acceptance of Christianity (Jaenen 1985). One of these responses is what he terms
"religious dimorphism," that is, "simultaneous assent to both the
old ways and the 'new religion,' each compartmentalized and called
upon as circumstances and needs dictated" (ibid., 192). This "internalized dualism" was, according to Jaenen, the response of most
"so-called converts." Religious dimorphism enabled natives to
draw upon both Christianity and their own inherited traditions
selectively and situationally, going back and forth between the two
as the occasion demanded, but without bringing them together to
forge some kind of synthesis or syncretistic unity.

Because of the exclusive nature of Western religions, they do
not combine well with other, potentially competing, ways of being
religious. Yet in practice perhaps religious dimorphism (or even
polymorphism) is the characteristic method by which most Canadians encounter and live out their experience of the sacred as it
manifests itself in a myriad of forms and places. As Jaenen comments, "Probably all individuals hold beliefs which are mutually
contradictory but these produce no behavioural crises so long as
they remain compartmentalized" (ibid., 193). Tom Sinclair-
Faulkner, writing about the possibility of hockey having religious
meaning for Canadians, says that people have to find ways of moving among the worlds of business, sports, church, and academy,

"donning and abandoning new roles as required." He maintains that "the person does not have available to her one sacred cosmos which convincingly superordinates all reality." Instead, he argues, "she must cobble together her own religion, constructing it from material borrowed from her encounter as a sort of consumer with the different sacred cosmoses made available to her by the different competing *ecclesiae* of her society" (1977, 388).

It seems to me that the constructive or synthetic effort of "cobbling together" one's own religion, if that means reconciling and harmonizing all of the disparate elements, seldom actually takes place, or if it does, then it is a largely intellectual endeavour. For instance, a theologian might struggle to work out the contradictions between her feminism and her Christianity, or another very thoughtful Christian might try to think through an existential encounter with the sacred in the natural world in terms of what the biblical record says about divine revelation in history. In general, though, people tend more often to don and abandon various roles as required and thereby to keep them compartmentalized and out of conflict with one another.

For sociologist Reginald Bibby the consumer's tendency to pick and choose what is placed in the shopping basket signals the decline or fragmentation of organized religion in contemporary culture. To select first a bit of this and then a bit of that may be lamentable from the standpoint of an older religious hegemony with its vision of a single superordinating sacred cosmos identifiable and available within a unified culture. Recognizing manifold locations of the sacred means taking religious pluralism in its modern context seriously. It also means that demands for integrity and consistency may inhibit or contradict the freedom to seek out and discover the sacred in all its modalities.

Religion in Canada late in the twentieth century is highly personal and individual, characterized more by an eclectic spirituality cobbled together from various sources rather than a monolithic and unitary superordinating system of belief. Accordingly, to find the sacred located in the nooks and crannies of contemporary life, especially at the horizons of the ordinary, taken-for-granted world of everyday, is what we should expect to be the future of religion in Canada into the next millennium.

References

Abell, Sam. 1977. "Foreword." *Still Waters, White Waters: Exploring America's Rivers and Lakes*. By Ron Fisher. Washington: National Geographic Society.

Abrams, M. H. 1958. "Belief and the Suspension of Disbelief." In *Literature and Belief: English Institute Essays, 1957*, 1-30. New York: Columbia University Press.

Ackerman, Harold. 1993. "Sources of Love and Hate: An Interview with Joy Kogawa." *American Review of Canadian Studies* (Summer): 217-29.

Albanese, Catherine L. 1990. *Nature Religion in America: From the Algonkian Indians to the New Age*. Chicago: University of Chicago Press.

Atwood, Margaret. 1971. *Power Politics*. Toronto: Anansi.

_____. 1972. *Survival: A Thematic Guide to Canadian Literature*. Toronto: Anansi.

_____. 1987a. *Surfacing*. 14th printing. Toronto: General Publishing, PaperJacks. Originally published in 1972.

_____. 1987b. "True North." *Saturday Night* (January): 141, 143-44, 146, and 148.

_____. 1991. *Wilderness Tips*. Toronto: McClelland & Stewart.

Auden, W. H. 1967. *The Enchafèd Flood or the Romantic Iconography of the Sea*. New York: Random House, Vintage Books.

_____. 1968a. *The Dyer's Hand and Other Essays*. New York: Random House, Vintage Books.

_____. 1968b. "The Quest Hero." In Neil D. Isaacs and Rose A. Zimbardo, eds., *Tolkien and the Critics: Essays on J. R. R. Tolkien's The Lord of the Rings*, 40-61. Notre Dame: University of Notre Dame Press.

Augustine, Saint, Bishop of Hippo. 1991. *Confessions*. Translated by Henry Chadwick. Oxford: Oxford University Press, World's Classic, 1992.

Avison, Margaret. 1992. "Reading Morley Callaghan's *Such Is My Beloved*." *Canadian Literature* no. 133: 204-208.

Berger, Peter L. 1969. *A Rumour of Angels: Modern Society and the Rediscovery of the Supernatural*. Markham, ON: Penguin.

Bibby, Reginald W. 1987. *Fragmented Gods: The Poverty and Potential of Religion in Canada*. Toronto: Irwin.

Blaise, Clark. 1986. *Resident Alien*. Markham, ON: Penguin.

Boire, Gary. 1995. *Morley Callaghan: Literary Anarchist*. Toronto: ECW Press.

Bonisteel, Roy. 1980. *In Search of* Man Alive. Toronto: Collins, Totem.

Boyd, Stephen B. 1990. "Domination as Punishment: Men's Studies and Religion." *Men's Studies Review* 7(2): 3-9.

Brenner, Rachel Feldhay. 1989. "A. M. Klein and Mordecai Richler: Canadian Responses to the Holocaust." *Journal of Canadian Studies* 24(2): 65-77.

———. 1990. "A. M. Klein and Mordecai Richler: The Poetics of the Search for Providence in the post-Holocaust World." *Studies in Religion/Sciences Religieuses* 19(2): 207-20.

Brody, Hugh. 1975. *The People's Land: Eskimos and Whites in the Eastern Arctic*. Markham, ON: Penguin.

———. 1983. *Maps and Dreams: Indians and the British Columbia Frontier*. Markham, ON: Penguin.

———. 1987. *Living Arctic: Hunters of the Canadian North*. Vancouver: Douglas & McIntyre.

Brown, Michael. 1978. "On Crucifying the Jews." *Judaism* 27(4): 476-88.

Buckley, Vincent. 1968. *Specifying the Sacred*. London: Chatto & Windus.

Burridge, John W. 1992. "Religion in Morley Callaghan's *Such Is My Beloved*." *Journal of Canadian Studies* 27(3): 105-14.

Butala, Sharon. 1994. *The Perfection of the Morning: An Apprenticeship in Nature*. Toronto: HarperCollins.

———. 1995. *Coyote's Morning Cry: Meditations and Dreams from a Life in Nature*. Toronto: HarperCollins.

Caird, G. B. 1966. *The Revelation of St. John the Divine*. New York: Harper & Row.

Callaghan, Morley. 1934. *Such Is My Beloved*. Toronto: McClelland & Stewart, New Canadian Library, 1957.

———. 1937. *More Joy in Heaven*. Toronto: McClelland & Stewart, New Canadian Library, 1970.

———. 1951. "It Was News in Paris—Not in Toronto." *Saturday Night*, 5 June, 8, 17, 18.

———. 1963. *That Summer in Paris*. Toronto: Macmillan.

———. 1978. *No Man's Meat & The Enchanted Pimp*. Toronto: Macmillan.

———. 1985. *Our Lady of the Snows*. Toronto: Macmillan.

Callhoun, Fill. 1941. "Eskimo Murders at Hudson Bay." Life's Reports. *Life*, 9 June, 14, 16, 18, 22, 24.

Cameron, Elspeth, ed. 1978. *The Other Side of Hugh MacLennan: Selected Essays Old and New.* Toronto: Macmillan.

———. 1981. *Hugh MacLennan: A Writer's Life.* Toronto: University of Toronto Press.

Campbell, Joseph. 1956. *The Hero with a Thousand Faces.* New York: Meridian.

———, with Bill Moyers. 1988. *The Power of Myth.* New York: Doubleday.

Camus, Albert. 1955. *The Myth of Sisyphus and Other Essays.* New York: Vintage.

Canadian Encyclopedia Plus. 1995. CD-ROM. S.v. "Religion." Toronto: McClelland & Stewart.

Carpenter, Edmund. 1968. "Witch-Fear Among the Aivilik Eskimos." In Victor F. Valentine and Frank G. Vallee, eds., *Eskimo of the Canadian Arctic*, 39-42. Toronto: McClelland & Stewart.

Chambers, Robert D. 1967. "The Novels of Hugh MacLennan." *Journal of Canadian Studies* 2(3): 3-4.

Cheung, King-Kok. 1993. *Articulate Silences: Hisaye Yamamoto, Maxine Hong Kingston, Joy Kogawa.* Ithaca: Cornell University Press.

Christ, Carol. 1979. "Spiritual Quest and Women's Experience." In Christ and Plaskow 1979, 228-45.

———, and Judith Plaskow, eds. 1979. *Womanspirit Rising: A Feminist Reader in Religion.* New York: Harper & Row.

Cirlot, J. E. 1971. *A Dictionary of Symbols.* 2nd ed. London: Routledge & Kegan Paul.

Clift, Dominique. 1989. *The Secret Kingdom: Interpretations of the Canadian Character.* Toronto: McClelland & Stewart.

Cohen, Matt. 1975. "Morley's Coy Mythtress." *Books in Canada* (July): 3-5.

———. 1984. "Notes on Realism in Modern English-Canadian Fiction." *Canadian Literature* no. 100: 65-71.

Coles, Robert. 1989. *The Call of Stories: Teaching and the Moral Imagination.* Boston: Houghton Mifflin.

Conron, Brandon. 1966. *Morley Callaghan.* Twayne's World Authors Series. New York: Twayne.

———, ed. 1975. *Morley Callaghan: Critical Views on Canadian Writers.* Toronto: McGraw-Hill Ryerson.

Crane, R. S., ed. 1957. *Critics and Criticism: Essays in Method.* Abridged ed. Chicago: University of Chicago Press.

Cruikshank, Julie. 1979. *Athapaskan Women: Lives and Legends.* Ottawa: National Museums of Canada.

Davey, Frank. 1983. *Surviving the Paraphrase: Eleven Essays in Canadian Literature*. Winnipeg: Turnstone Press.

Davidson, Arnold E., and Cathy N. Davidson. 1981. *The Art of Margaret Atwood: Essays in Criticism*. Toronto: Anansi.

Davidson, James West, and John Rugge. 1976. *The Complete Wilderness Paddler*. New York: Knopf.

Davies, Robertson. 1976. *The Manticore*. Markham, ON: Penguin. Originally published in 1972.

————. 1977. *Fifth Business*. Markham, ON: Penguin. Originally published in 1970.

————. 1981. *The Well-Tempered Critic: One Man's Views of the Theatre and Letters in Canada*. Edited by Judith Skelton Grant. Toronto: McClelland & Stewart.

————. 1985. *What's Bred in the Bone*. Toronto: Macmillan.

————. 1987. "Keeping Faith." *Saturday Night* (January): 187-90, 192.

————. 1994. *The Cunning Man*. Toronto: McClelland & Stewart.

Davis, Winston. 1992. *Japanese Religion and Society: Paradigms of Structure and Change*. Albany: State University of New York Press.

Des Pres, Terrence. 1976. *The Survivor: An Anatomy of Life in the Death Camps*. New York: Oxford University Press.

Detweiler, Robert, and William G. Doty, eds. 1990. *The Daemonic Imagination: Biblical Text and Secular Story*. Atlanta: Scholars Press.

Dewdney, Selwyn, and Kenneth Kidd. 1967. *Indian Rock Paintings of the Great Lakes*. 2nd ed. Toronto: University of Toronto Press.

Dillard, Annie. 1974. *Pilgrim at Tinker Creek*. New York: Harper & Row, Perennial Library, 1985.

Dillenberger, John, and Claude Welch. 1958. *Protestant Christianity: Interpreted through its Development*. New York: Scribner's.

Donaldson, Mara E., and Max Harris. 1994. "Retrospective on the Work of Nathan A. Scott, Jr." *Religious Studies Review* 20(4): 117-25.

Dooley, D. J. 1979. *Moral Vision in the Canadian Novel*. Toronto: Clarke, Irwin.

Eagleton, Terry. 1983. *Literary Theory: An Introduction*. Minneapolis: University of Minnesota Press.

Earhart, H. Byron. 1984. *Religions of Japan: Many Traditions Within One Sacred Way*. Harper: San Francisco, 1984.

Eliade, Mircea. 1959. *The Sacred and the Profane: The Nature of Religion*. New York: Harcourt Brace & World.

————. 1963. *Patterns in Comparative Religion*. Cleveland and New York: Meridian Books.

_____. 1967. *Myths, Dreams, and Mysteries: The Encounter between Contemporary Faiths and Archaic Realities*. New York: Harper & Row, Harper Torchbooks.

Eliot, T. S. 1964. *Selected Essays*. New ed. New York: Harcourt Brace & World.

Engel, Marian. 1977. *Bear*. Toronto: Seal Books. Original edition, Toronto: McClelland & Stewart, 1976.

_____. 1983. "Steps to the Mythic: *The Diviners* and *A Bird in the House*." In Woodcock 1983, 236-40.

_____. 1984. "Why and How and Why Not and What Is This, About Starting Another Novel. . . ." *Canadian Literature* no. 100: 98-104.

Fabre, Michel. 1983. "Words and the World: *The Diviners* as an Exploration of the Book of Life." In Woodcock 1983, 247-69.

Fager, Charles. 1977. "Small Is Beautiful, and So Is Rome: The Surprising Faith of E. F. Schumacher." *Christian Century*, 6 April, 325-28.

Fairbanks, Carol. 1990. "Joy Kogawa's *Obasan*: A Study in Political Efficacy. *Journal of American and Canadian Studies* 5 (Spring): 73-92.

Falcon Films. 1992. *The Pool: Reflections of Japanese-Canadian Internment*. With Joy Kogawa. Directed by Mark de Valk. Produced by Mark de Valk and Joan Griffin.

Farmiloe, Dorothy. 1973. "Hugh MacLennan and the Canadian Myth." In Goetsch 1973, 145-54.

Fee, Margery. 1987. "Romantic Nationalism and the Image of Native People in Contemporary English-Canadian Literature." In King et al. 1987, 15-33.

Fenge, Terry. 1992. "Damning a People? The Great Whale Project and Inuit of the Belcher Islands." *Alternatives* 19(1): 48-49.

Fleming, Archibald Lang. 1965. *Archibald the Arctic*. Toronto: Saunders.

Foster, John, and Janet Foster. 1975. *To the Wild Country*. Toronto: Van Nostrand.

Frankl, Viktor E. 1984. *Man's Search for Meaning*. Revised and updated. New York: Washington Square.

Franks, C. E. S. 1977. *The Canoe and White Water: From Essential to Sport*. Toronto: University of Toronto Press.

Fraser, Blair. 1955. "The Fairy Tale Romance of the Canadian Shield." *Maclean's*, 24 December, 7, 42-45.

Frye, Northrop. 1957. *Anatomy of Criticism*. Princeton: Princeton University Press.

_____. 1964. *The Educated Imagination*. Bloomington: Indiana University Press.

_____. 1971. *The Bush Garden: Essays on the Canadian Imagination*. Toronto: Anansi.

————. 1977. "Haunted by Lack of Ghosts: Some Patterns in the Imagery of Canadian Poetry." In Staines 1977, 22-45.

————. 1982. *Divisions on a Ground: Essays on Canadian Culture.* Toronto: Anansi.

————. 1991. *The Double Vision: Language and Meaning in Religion.* Toronto: University of Toronto Press.

————, Sheridan Baker, and George Perkins. 1985. *The Harper Handbook to Literature.* New York: Harper & Row.

Fulford, Robert. 1990. "Hugh MacLennan Sacrificed His Talent to a Calvinist God." *Financial Times of Canada*, 19 November, 37.

Gerhart, Mary. 1990. "Whatever Happened to the Catholic Novel? A Study in Genre." In Gerhart and Yu 1990, 183-201.

————, and Anthony C. Yu, eds. 1990. *Morphologies of Faith: Essays in Religion and Culture in Honor of Nathan A. Scott, Jr.* Atlanta: Scholars Press.

Gibson, Douglas, ed. 1991. *Hugh MacLennan's Best.* Toronto: McClelland & Stewart.

Gill, Sam D. 1982. *Beyond "The Primitive": The Religions of Nonliterate Peoples.* Englewood Cliffs, NJ: Prentice-Hall.

Gilkey, Langdon B. 1969. *Naming the Whirlwind: The Renewal of God-Language.* Indianapolis: Bobbs-Merrill.

Girard, René. 1977. *Violence and the Sacred.* Translated by Patrick Gregory. Baltimore: Johns Hopkins University Press.

"God Is Alive: Special Report, The Religion Poll." 1993. *Maclean's*, 12 April, 32-37, 40-42, 44-50.

"God of the North." 1985. In CBC radio series *The Scales of Justice.* Written by Frank Jones. Produced by George Jonas. Commentary by Edward L. Greenspan. Broadcast 7 July.

Goetsch, Paul, ed. 1973. *Hugh MacLennan.* Toronto: McGraw-Hill Ryerson.

Gold, Joseph. 1990. *Read for Your Life: Using Literature as Life Support System.* Markham, ON: Fitzhenry & Whiteside.

Goldman, Marlene. 1993. "Earth-quaking the Kingdom of the Male Virgin: A Deleuzian Analysis of Aritha van Herk's *No Fixed Address* and *Places Far from Ellesmere.*" *Canadian Literature* no. 137: 21-38.

Gottlieb, Erika. 1986. "The Riddle of Concentric Worlds in *Obasan.*" *Canadian Literature* no. 109: 34-53.

Grace, Sherrill E., and Lorraine Weir. 1983. *Margaret Atwood: Language, Text, and System.* Vancouver: University of British Columbia Press.

Grant, John Webster. 1980. "Missionaries and Messiahs in the Northwest." *Studies in Religion/Sciences Religieuses* 9(2): 125-36.

————. 1984. *Moon of Wintertime: Missionaries and the Indians of Canada in Encounter since 1534*. Toronto: University of Toronto Press.

Grant, Judith Skelton. 1994. *Robertson Davies: Man of Myth*. Toronto: Penguin.

Greenstein, Michael. 1989. *Third Solitudes: Tradition and Discontinuity in Jewish-Canadian Literature*. Kingston and Montreal: McGill-Queen's University Press.

Grene, David. 1968. "The *Odyssey*: An Approach." *Midway* 9(4): 47-68.

Grey Owl. 1976. *The Men of the Last Frontier*. Toronto: Macmillan, Laurentian Library.

Gualtieri, Antonio R. 1977. "Towards a Theological Perspective on Nationalism." In Slater 1977, 507-24.

————. 1984. *Christianity and Native Traditions: Indigenization and Syncretism Among the Inuit and Dene of the Western Arctic*. Notre Dame: Cross Roads.

Guédon, Marie-Françoise. 1983. "*Surfacing*: Amerindian Themes and Shamanism." In Grace and Weir 1983, 91-111.

Gunn, Giles B., ed. 1971. *Literature and Religion*. London: SCM.

Hall, John Douglas. 1980. *The Canada Crisis: A Christian Perspective*. Toronto: Anglican Book Centre.

Harcourt, William, and Garth Price, producers. 1971. "Morley Callaghan." CBC-TV *Tuesday Night*. Broadcast 26 October. Cited in Lecker and David 1984, 95.

Harding, M. Esther. 1956. *Journey into Self*. New York: Longmans, Green.

Harrington, Richard. 1981. "Sanikiluaq." *The Beaver* 312(3): 12-17.

Harris, Mason. 1990. "Broken Generations in *Obasan*: Inner Conflict and the Destruction of Community." *Canadian Literature* no. 127: 41-57.

Harvey, Van A., and Marie Augusta Neal. 1979. "Peter Berger: Retrospect." *Religious Studies Review* 5: 9.

Hastings, James, ed. 1963. *Dictionary of the Bible*. New York: Scribner's.

Hewitt, W. E., ed. 1993. *The Sociology of Religion: A Canadian Focus*. Toronto: Butterworths.

Hick, John. 1963. *Philosophy of Religion*. Englewood Cliffs, NJ: Prentice-Hall.

Hoar, Victor. 1969. *Morley Callaghan*. Studies in Canadian Literature. Toronto: Copp Clark.

Hodgson, Maurice. 1967. "The Exploration Journal as Literature." *The Beaver* 298 (Winter): 12.

Hopper, Stanley Romaine. 1971. "The Poetry of Meaning." In Gunn 1971, 221-35.

Horwood, Harold. 1987. *Dancing on the Shore: A Celebration of Life at Annapolis Basin*. Toronto: McClelland & Stewart.

Houston, James. 1995. *Confessions of an Igloo Dweller*. Toronto: McClelland & Stewart.

"How Very Different We Are: A Poll Shows How Canadian and U.S. Attitudes Vary on Family, Politics, and Religion." 1996. *Maclean's*, 4 November, 36-40.

Hultkrantz, Åke. 1979. *The Religions of the American Indians*. Berkeley: University of California Press.

————. 1981. *Belief and Worship in Native North America*. Edited by Christopher Vecsey. Syracuse: Syracuse University Press.

Hutcheon, Linda. 1988. *The Canadian Postmodern: A Study of Contemporary English-Canadian Fiction*. Toronto: Oxford University Press.

————. 1993. Review of *Itsuka*. *Canadian Literature* no. 136: 179-81.

————. 1995. "Introduction: Complexities Abounding." Special Topic: Colonialism and the Postcolonial Condition. *PMLA* 110(1): 7-16.

Ingersoll, Earl G., ed. 1990. *Margaret Atwood: Conversations*. Willowdale, ON: Firefly Books.

Institute of Contemporary Arts. 1988. *Black Film, British Cinema*. ICA Documents 7. London: Institute of Contemporary Arts.

Irwin, Lee. 1990. "Myth, Language and Ontology Among the Huron." *Studies in Religion/Sciences Religieuses* 19(4): 413-26.

Iwama, Marilyn. 1994. "If You Say So: Articulating Cultural Symbols of Tradition in the Japanese Canadian Community." *Canadian Literature* no. 140: 13-29.

Jackson, A. Y. 1964. *A Painter's Country: The Autobiography of A. Y. Jackson*. Toronto: Clarke, Irwin.

Jaenen, Cornelius J. 1985. "Amerindian Responses to French Missionary Intrusion, 1611-1760: A Categorization." In Westfall et al. 1985, 182-97.

James, William Closson. 1977. "A Voyage into Selfhood: Hugh MacLennan's *The Watch that Ends the Night*." In Slater 1977, 315-22.

————. 1981a. "Atwood's *Surfacing*." *Canadian Literature* no. 91: 174-81.

————. 1981b. "'Inuit in Church': Clearing Photographic Misattribution." *Archivaria* 12 (Summer): 59-62.

————. 1981c. "The Canoe Trip as Religious Quest." *Studies in Religion/Sciences Religieuses* 10(2): 151-66.

————. 1981-82. "Inuit in Church—Once More," *Archivaria* 13 (Winter): 129-30.

_____. 1985a. *A Fur Trader's Photographs: A. A. Chesterfield in the District of Ungava, 1901-4.* Kingston and Montreal: McGill-Queen's University Press.

_____. 1985b. "Religious Symbolism in Recent English Canadian Fiction." In Westfall et al. 1985, 246-59.

_____. 1988. "Canoeing and Gender Roles." In James Raffan and Bert Horwood, eds., *Canexus: The Canoe in Canadian Culture*, 27-43. Toronto: Betelgeuse Books.

_____. 1992. "Nature and the Sacred in Canada." *Studies in Religion/ Sciences Religieuses* 21(4): 403-17.

_____. 1993a. "Two Montreal Theodicies: Hugh MacLennan's *The Watch that Ends the Night* and A. M. Klein's *The Second Scroll.*" *Literature and Theology* 7(2): 198-206.

_____. 1993b. "The Ambiguities of Love in Morley Callaghan's *Such Is My Beloved.*" *Canadian Literature* nos. 138/139: 35-51.

_____. 1996. "'You have to discover it in some other way': Native Symbols as Appropriated by Margaret Atwood and Marian Engel." In Jamie S. Scott, ed., *"And the Birds Began to Sing": Religion and Literature in Post-Colonial Cultures*, 34-46. Amsterdam: Rodopi.

Jameson, Anna Brownell. 1965. *Winter Studies and Summer Rambles in Canada (Selections)*. Toronto: McClelland & Stewart.

Jasper, David. 1989. *The Study of Literature and Religion: An Introduction.* Minneapolis: Fortress.

Johnston, Basil. 1976. *Ojibway Heritage*. Toronto: McClelland & Stewart.

Keen, Sam. 1969. *Apology for Wonder.* San Francisco: Harper & Row, Harper Torchbooks, 1973.

Keith, W. J. 1989. *A Sense of Style: Studies in the Art of Fiction in English-Speaking Canada.* Toronto: ECW Press.

_____. 1993. *Life Struggle: Hugh MacLennan's* The Watch that Ends the Night. Canadian Fiction Studies. Toronto: ECW Press.

Kermode, Frank. 1967. *The Sense of an Ending: Studies in the Theory of Fiction.* New York: Oxford University Press.

Kernan, Julie. 1975. *Our Friend, Jacques Maritain: A Personal Memoir.* Garden City, NY: Doubleday.

Kidd, Bruce. 1987. "Sports and Masculinity." In Michael Kaufman, ed., *Beyond Patriarchy: Essays by Men on Pleasure, Power, and Change*, 250-65. Toronto: Oxford University Press.

King, Thomas, ed. 1990. *All My Relations: An Anthology of Contemporary Canadian Native Fiction.* Toronto: McClelland & Stewart.

King, Thomas, Cheryl Calver, and Helen Hoy, eds. 1987. *The Native in Literature.* N.p.: ECW Press.

Kinsley, David. 1995. *Ecology and Religion: Ecological Spirituality in Cross-cultural Perspective.* Englewood Cliffs, NJ: Prentice-Hall.

Klein, A. M. 1951. *The Second Scroll.* Toronto: McClelland & Stewart, New Canadian Library, 1969.

Klein, Carroll. 1985. "A Conversation with Marian Engel." *Room of One's Own* 9(2): 4-15, 20-31.

Klempa, William, ed. 1994. *The Burning Bush and A Few Acres of Snow: The Presbyterian Contribution to Canadian Life and Culture.* Ottawa: Carleton University Press.

Kogawa, Joy. 1974. *A Choice of Dreams.* Toronto: McClelland & Stewart.

————. *Jericho Road.* 1977. Toronto: McClelland & Stewart.

————. *Obasan.* 1983. Reprint, Markham, ON: Penguin. Originally published in 1981 by Lester & Orpen Dennys.

————. 1985. *Woman in the Woods.* Oakville, ON: Mosaic Press.

————. 1993. *Itsuka.* Rev. ed. Toronto: Penguin. Originally published in 1992 by Viking.

————. 1995. *The Rain Ascends.* Toronto: Knopf.

Komori, Leslie. 1987. "Interview with Joy Kogawa." *Fireweed: A Feminist Quarterly* 24 (Winter): 63-66.

Kreiner, Philip. "Messiah." 1983. In *People Like Us In a Place Like This,* 80-133. Ottawa: Oberon.

Lai, Whalen. 1993. "Buddhism and the Manners of Death in Japan: Extending Aries' *histoire de mentalité de la mort.*" *Pacific World* 9: 69-89.

Landy, Francis. 1983. *Paradoxes of Paradise: Identity and Difference in the Song of Songs.* Sheffield: Almond.

————. 1987. "The Song of Songs." In Robert Alter and Frank Kermode, eds., *The Literary Guide to the Bible,* 305-19. Cambridge: Harvard University Press.

Laurence, Margaret. 1974. *The Diviners.* Toronto: McClelland & Stewart, New Canadian Library, 1978.

————. 1988. "My Final Hour." In Christl Verduyn, ed., *Margaret Laurence: An Appreciation,* 250-62. Peterborough, ON: Broadview Press.

————. 1989. *Dance on the Earth: A Memoir.* Toronto: McClelland & Stewart.

Lecker, Robert, and Jack David. 1984. "Morley Callaghan: An Annotated Bibliography." *The Annotated Bibliography of Canada's Major Authors,* 13-177. Essays in Canadian Writing. Downsview, ON: ECW Press, 1984.

Lecker, Robert, ed. 1991. *Canadian Canons: Essays in Literary Value.* Toronto: University of Toronto Press.

Legge, Marilyn J. 1992. *The Grace of Difference: A Canadian Feminist Theological Ethic.* Atlanta: Scholars Press.

LePan, Douglas. 1987. *Weathering It: Complete Poems, 1948-1987.* Toronto: McClelland & Stewart.

Lewis, C. S. 1959. *Surprised by Joy: The Shape of My Early Life.* London: Collins, Fontana Books.

Lewis, R. W. B. 1971. "Hold on Hard to the Huckleberry Bushes." In Gunn 1971, 87-101.

Long, Charles H. 1990. "The Humanities and 'Other' Humans." In Gerhart and Yu 1990, 203-14.

Lopez, Barry. 1986. *Arctic Dreams: Imagination and Desire in a Northern Landscape.* New York: Charles Scribner's Sons.

Lower, Arthur R. M. 1958. *Canadians in the Making: A Social History of Canada.* Don Mills, ON: Longmans.

———. 1967. "Canadian Values and Canadian Writing." *Mosaic* 1(1): 79-93.

Lucas, Alec. 1983. "Nature Writing in English." In William Toye, ed., *The Oxford Companion to Canadian Literature*, 543-47. Toronto: Oxford University Press.

MacKendrick, Louis. 1983. *Probable Fictions: Alice Munro's Narrative Acts.* Downsview, ON: ECW Press.

MacLennan, Hugh. 1951. *Each Man's Son.* Boston: Little, Brown.

———. 1958. *The Watch that Ends the Night.* Macmillan, Laurentian Library, 1975.

———. 1960a. *Scotchman's Return and Other Essays.* Toronto: Macmillan.

———. 1960b. "The Story of a Novel," *Canadian Literature* no. 3: 35-39. Reprinted in Smith 1961, 33-38.

———. 1969. "Reflections on Two Decades." *Canadian Literature* no. 41: 28-39.

Maritain, Jacques. 1930a. *An Introduction to Philosophy.* London: Sheed & Ward.

———. 1930b. *Le Docteur Angelique.* Paris: Desclée.

———. 1931. *St. Thomas Aquinas, Angel of the Schools.* Translated by J. F. Scanlan. London: Sheed & Ward.

———. 1938. *True Humanism.* New York: Charles Scribner's Sons.

———. 1944. *The Rights of Man and Natural Law.* London: Geoffrey Bles.

———. 1966. *Existence and the Existent.* New York: Random House, Vintage Books.

Marsh, Donald Ben. N.d. [1967?]. *A History of the Work of the Anglican Church in the Area Now Known as The Diocese of the Arctic.* N.p.

Marshall, Tom. 1992. *Multiple Exposures, Promised Lands: Essays on Canadian Poetry and Fiction*. Kingston, ON: Quarry Press.

Mayne, Seymour, ed. 1975. *The A. M. Klein Symposium*. Re-Appraisals: Canadian Writers. Ottawa: University of Ottawa Press.

McClellan, Catharine. 1970. *The Girl Who Married the Bear*. Ottawa: National Museums of Canada.

McDonald, Larry. 1981. "The Civilized Ego and Its Discontents: A New Approach to Callaghan." In Staines 1981, 77-94.

McFarlane, J. A. (Sandy), and Warren Clements. 1994. *The Globe and Mail Style Book: A Guide to Language and Usage*. Toronto: Penguin.

McGregor, Gaile. 1985. *The Wacousta Syndrome: Explorations in the Canadian Langscape*. Toronto: University of Toronto Press.

McLelland, Joseph C. 1994. "Ralph and Stephen and Hugh and Margaret: CanLit's View of Presbyterians." In Klempa 1994, 109-22.

McPhee, John. 1975. *The Survival of the Bark Canoe*. New York: Warner Books.

McPherson, Hugo. 1957. "The Two Worlds of Morley Callaghan: Man's Earthly Quest." *Queen's Quarterly* 64: 350-65. Reprinted in Conron 1975.

Merkur, Daniel. 1985. *Becoming Half Hidden: Shamanism and Initiation Among the Inuit*. Stockholm: Almqvist & Wiksell.

_____. 1989. "Arctic: Inuit." In Deward E. Walker, Jr., ed., *Witchcraft and Sorcery of the American Native Peoples*, 11-21. Moscow, ID: University of Idaho Press.

Miller, J. Hillis. 1965. *Poets of Reality: Six Twentieth-Century Writers*. Cambridge: Harvard University Press.

Miner, Valerie. 1975. "Atwood in Metamorphosis: An Authentic Canadian Fairy Tale." In Myrna Kostash et al., *Her Own Woman: Profiles of Ten Canadian Women*, 181. Toronto: Macmillan.

Mitchell, W. O. 1947. *Who Has Seen the Wind*. Toronto: Macmillan, Laurentian Library, 1972.

Mol, Hans. 1976. *Identity and the Sacred: A Sketch for a New Social-Scientific Theory of Religion*. Agincourt, ON: Book Society of Canada.

_____. 1985. *Faith and Fragility: Religion and Identity in Canada*. Burlington, ON: Trinity Press.

Momaday, N. Scott. 1990. *The Ancient Child*. New York: HarperCollins.

Moodie, Susanna. 1962. *Roughing It in the Bush: Or Forest Life in Canada*. Toronto: McClelland & Stewart.

Moore, Brian. 1985. *Black Robe*. Toronto: McClelland & Stewart.

Morley, Patricia. 1972. *The Immoral Moralists: Hugh MacLennan and Leonard Cohen*. Toronto: Clarke, Irwin.

Morton, W. L. 1961. *The Canadian Identity*. Toronto: University of Toronto Press.

Moss, John. 1983. *Bellrock*. Toronto: NC Press.

―――. 1994. *Enduring Dreams: An Exploration of Arctic Landscape*. Concord, ON: Anansi.

Muir, Edwin. 1975. "The Decline of the Novel." In Tennyson and Ericson 1975, 173-77.

Munro, Alice. 1971. *Lives of Girls and Women*. Scarborough, ON: Signet, New American Library, 1974.

Nakano, Hideichiro. 1995. "Why Did Christianity Fail to Penetrate into Japanese Mind?" In *The Japanese Society: Sociological Essays in Japanese Studies*, 119-46. Tokyo: Kamawanu.

Nakayama, Gordon G. 1984. *Issei: Stories of Japanese Canadian Pioneers*. Toronto: NC Press.

National Archives of Canada (NAC). Historical Branch. File 142299. Volume 2025.

―――. File RG 85. Volume 174.

―――. Department of Northern Affairs and Natural Resources. Northern Administration and Lands Branch. File No. 541-2-1. Volumes 1 and 1A.

National Film Board. 1974. *The New Boys*. Series: *West*. Directed and produced by John N. Smith.

―――. 1977. *Doubles Whitewater*. Series: *Path of the Paddle*. Directed by Bill Mason. Produced by William Brind and Colin Low.

―――. 1982. *Hugh MacLennan: Portrait of a Writer*. Directed by Robert Duncan.

―――. 1984. *Margaret Atwood: Once in August*. Directed by Michael Rubbo. Produced by Michael Rubbo and Barry Howells. A half-hour version is available under the title *Atwood and Family*.

―――. 1991. *The Magic Season of Robertson Davies*. Produced and directed by Harry Rasky.

Nelson, James B. 1988. *The Intimate Connection: Male Sexuality, Male Spirituality*. Philadelphia: Westminster Press.

Nelson, Richard. 1989. *The Island Within*. Vancouver: Douglas & McIntyre.

New, William H. 1966. "The Apprenticeship of Discovery." *Canadian Literature* no. 29: 18-33.

Niebuhr, H. Richard. 1956. *Christ and Culture*. New York: Harper & Row, Harper Torchbooks.

O'Connor, Flannery. 1979. *The Habit of Being*. Edited by Sally Fitzgerald. New York: Farrar, Straus, Giroux.

O'Connor, John J. 1981. "Fraternal Twins: The Impact of Jacques Maritain on Callaghan and Charbonneau." *Mosaic* 14(2): 145-63.

Olney, James. 1972. *Metaphors of Self: The Meaning of Autobiography.* Princeton: Princeton University Press.

Olson, Sigurd. 1974. *The Lonely Land.* Toronto: McClelland & Stewart.

Ong, Walter J. "Voice as Summons for Belief: Literature, Faith, and the Divided Self." In Gunn 1971, 68-86.

O'Reilley, Mary Rose. 1993. *The Peaceable Classroom.* Portsmouth, NH: Boynton/Cook.

Otto, Rudolf. 1950. *The Idea of the Holy: An Inquiry into the Non-rational Factor in the Idea of the Divine and Its Relation to the Rational.* 2nd ed. New York: Oxford University Press.

O'Toole, Roger. "In Quest of the Hidden Gods in Canadian Literature." In Hewitt 1993, 157-72.

Ozick, Cynthia. 1976. "Notes Towards a Meditation on 'Forgiveness.'" In Simon Wiesenthal, *The Sunflower: With a Symposium,* 184-90. New York: Schocken.

Pacey, Desmond. 1965. "Fiction 1920-1940." In Carl F. Klinck, ed., *A Literary History of Canada: Canadian Literature in English,* esp. 688-93. Toronto: University of Toronto Press.

Palmer, Tim. 1977. "Teslin Experience." *North/Nord* (May-June): 51.

Pascal, Roy. 1960. *Design and Truth in Autobiography.* London: Routledge.

Pecher, Kamil. 1978. *Lonely Voyage: By Kayak to Adventure and Discovery.* Saskatoon: Western Producer Prairie Books.

Pell, Barbara Helen. 1983. "Faith and Fiction: The Novels of Callaghan and Hood." *Journal of Canadian Studies* 18(2): 5-17.

————. 1991. "Faith and Fiction: Hugh MacLennan's *The Watch that Ends the Night.*" *Canadian Literature* no. 128: 39-50.

Phillips, Alan. 1956. "The Tragic Case of the Man Who Played Jesus." A *Maclean's* Flashback. *Maclean's,* 8 December, 22-23, 120-22.

Potter, Robin. 1990. "Moral—In Whose Sense? Joy Kogawa's *Obasan* and Julia Kristeva's *Powers of Horror.*" *Studies in Canadian Literature* 15(1): 117-39.

Pratt, Annis. 1981. "*Surfacing* and the Rebirth Journey." In Davidson and Davidson 1981, 139-57.

Price, Ray. 1976. *The Howling Arctic: The Remarkable People Who Made Canada Sovereign in the Farthest North,* esp. 1-71. Markham, ON: Pocket Books.

Principe, Walter. 1983. "Toward Defining Spirituality." *Studies in Religion / Sciences Religieuses* 12(2): 127-41.

Raffan, James, ed. 1986. *Wild Waters: Canoeing Canada's Wilderness Rivers*. Toronto : Key Porter Books.

———. 1990. *Summer North of Sixty: By Paddle and Portage Across the Barren Lands*. Toronto: Key Porter Books.

———. 1996. *Fire in the Bones: Bill Mason and the Canadian Canoeing Tradition*. Toronto: HarperCollins.

Raffan, James, and Bert Horwood, eds. 1988. *Canexus: The Canoe in Canadian Culture*. Toronto: Betelgeuse Books.

Reader, Ian. 1991. *Religion in Contemporary Japan*. Honolulu: University of Hawaii Press, 1991.

———, Esben Andreasen, and Finn Stéfansson. 1993. *Japanese Religions: Past and Present*. Honolulu: University of Hawaii Press.

Red Cross Society. 1975. *Canoeing: The Adventures of Lester & Linda on Top of the Water World*. N.p.: Red Cross Society.

Redekop, Magdalene. 1989. "The Literary Politics of the Victim." *Canadian Forum* (November): 14-17.

———. 1990. "Interview with Joy Kogawa." In Linda Hutcheon and Marion Richmond, eds., *Other Solitudes: Canadian Multicultural Fictions*, 94-101. Toronto: Oxford University Press.

Redfield, James. 1993. *The Celestine Prophecy: An Adventure*. New York: Warner.

Ricoeur, Paul. 1969. *The Symbolism of Evil*. Boston: Beacon Press.

Robbe-Grillet, Alain. 1965. *For a New Novel: Essays on Fiction*. New York: Grove.

Roof, Wade Clark. 1993. *A Generation of Seekers: The Spiritual Journeys of the Baby Boom Generation*. New York: HarperCollins.

Rose, Marilyn Russell. 1988. "Politics into Art: Kogawa's *Obasan* and the Rhetoric of Fiction." *Mosaic* 21(3): 215-26.

Ross, Val. 1992. "Every Certainty Must Be Surrounded by Doubt." *Globe and Mail*, Saturday, 21 March, C1 and C15.

Ross-Bryant, Lynn. 1980. *Imagination and the Life of the Spirit: An Introduction to the Study of Religion and Literature*. Chico, CA: Scholars Press.

———. 1990. "The Land in American Religious Experience." *Journal of the American Academy of Religion* 58(3): 333-55.

Ruether, Rosemary Radford. 1979. "Motherearth and the Megamachine: A Theology of Liberation in a Feminine, Somatic and Ecological Perspective." In Christ and Plaskow, 1979, 43-52.

Saladin d'Anglure, Bernard. 1984. "Inuit of Quebec." In David Damas, ed., *Handbook of North American Indians*, Vol. 5: *Arctic*, 494-507. Washington: Smithsonian Institution.

Schama, Simon. 1995. *Landscape and Memory*. Toronto: Random House, Vintage Books, 1996.

Scholes, Robert, and Robert Kellogg. 1966. *The Nature of Narrative*. New York: Oxford University Press.

Schrire, T. 1966. *Hebrew Amulets: Their Decipherment and Interpretation*. London: Routledge & Kegan Paul.

Scott, Nathan A., Jr. 1966. *The Broken Center: Studies in the Theological Horizon of Modern Literature*. New Haven: Yale University Press.

————. 1971. *The Wild Prayer of Longing: Poetry and the Sacred*. New Haven and London: Yale University Press.

————. 1983. "The Rediscovery of Story in Recent Theology and the Refusal of Story in Recent Literature." In Robert Detweiler, ed., *Art/Literature/Religion: Life on the Borders. JAAR Thematic Studies* 49(2): 139-55.

Shackleton, Philip, and Kenneth G. Roberts. 1983. *The Canoe: A History of the Craft from Panama to the Pacific*. Toronto: Macmillan.

Shields, Carol. 1993. *The Stone Diaries*. Toronto: Random House, Vintage Books.

Sinclair-Faulkner, Tom. 1977. "A Puckish Reflection on Religion in Canada." In Slater 1977, 383-405.

Slater, Peter, ed. 1977. *Religion and Culture in Canada/ Religion et Culture au Canada*. Waterloo, ON: Canadian Corporation for Studies in Religion.

————. 1978. *The Dynamics of Religion: Meaning and Change in Religious Traditions*. San Francisco: Harper & Row.

————. 1985. "On the Apparent Absence of Civil Religion in Canada." In Henri-Paul Cunningham and F. Temple Kingston, eds., *L'Amitié et le Dialogue entre le Québec et l'Ontario/Friendship and Dialogue between Ontario and Quebec*. Windsor, ON: Canterbury College, University of Windsor.

Smith, A. J. M., ed. 1961. *Masks of Fiction: Canadian Critics on Canadian Prose*. Toronto: McClelland & Stewart.

Smith, Jonathan Z. 1982. *Imagining Religion: From Babylon to Jonestown*. Chicago: University of Chicago Press.

Smith, Mahlon H. 1978. *And Taking Bread . . . : Cerularius and the Azyme Controversy of 1054*. Paris: Éditions Beauchesne.

Smith, Pat. 1977. "The River that Calls to the Bold." *Outdoor Life* (August): 69-74, 94, 96, 98, 104, 107.

Smith, Wilfred Cantwell. 1979. *Faith and Belief*. Princeton: Princeton University Press.

Spettigue, Douglas. 1973. "Beauty and the Beast." In Goetsch 1973, 157-61.

Stackhouse, John G., Jr. 1993. *Canadian Evangelicalism in the Twentieth Century: An Introduction to Its Character.* Toronto: University of Toronto Press.

Staines, David, ed. 1977. *The Canadian Imagination: Dimensions of a Literary Culture.* Cambridge: Harvard University Press.

————. 1981. *The Callaghan Symposium.* Reappraisals: Canadian Writers. Ottawa: University of Ottawa Press.

Stratford, Philip, ed. 1973. *The Portable Graham Greene.* New York: Viking.

Sullivan, Alan. 1944. "When God Came to the Belchers." *Queen's Quarterly* 51: 14-28.

Sutherland, Ronald. 1971. *Second Image: Comparative Studies in Québec/Canadian Literature.* Don Mills, ON: newpress.

Tanner, Adrian. 1979. *Bringing Home Animals: Religious Ideology and Mode of Production of the Mistassini Cree Hunters.* St. John's: Institute of Social and Economic Research, Memorial University of Newfoundland.

Taylor, Charles. 1977. *Six Journeys: A Canadian Pattern.* Toronto: Anansi.

Taylor, Mark C. 1994. "Denegating God." *Critical Inquiry* 20(4): 592-610.

Tennyson, G. B., and Edward E. Ericson, Jr. 1975. *Religion and Modern Literature: Essays in Theory and Criticism.* Grand Rapids, MI: William B. Eerdmans.

Thwaites, Rueben Gold, ed. 1897. *The Jesuit Relations and Allied Documents: Travels and Explorations of the Jesuit Missionaries in New France, 1610-1791.* Vol. 7. Cleveland: Burrows.

Tierney, Frank M., ed. 1994. *Hugh MacLennan.* Reappraisals: Canadian Writers. Ottawa: University of Ottawa Press.

Tillich, Paul. 1957. *The Protestant Era.* Abridged ed. Chicago: University of Chicago Press.

————. 1959. *Theology of Culture.* Edited by Robert C. Kimball. New York: Oxford University Press.

Toyes, William, ed. 1962. *A Book of Canada.* London: Oxford University Press.

Trudeau, Pierre Elliott. 1970. "Exhaustion and Fulfilment: The Ascetic in a Canoe." First published in French in *Jeunesse étudiante catholique* in 1944. In Borden Spears, ed., *Wilderness Canada,* 3-5. Toronto: Clarke, Irwin.

Turner, Lucien M. 1894. *Ethnology of the Ungava District, Hudson Bay Territory: Indians and Eskimos in the Quebec-Labrador Peninsula.* Québec: Presses Coméditex, 1979.

Turner, Margaret. 1992. "Power, Language and Gender: Writing 'History' in *Beloved* and *Obasan*." *Mosaic* 25(4): 81-97.

Turner, Victor. 1977. *The Ritual Process: Structure and Anti-Structure.* Ithaca: Cornell University Press, Cornell Paperbacks.

Twomey, Arthur C. 1982. *Needle to the North.* Edited by William C. James. Ottawa: Oberon.

————, in collaboration with Nigel Herrick. 1942. *Needle to the North: The Story of an Expedition to Ungava and the Belcher Islands.* Boston: Houghton Mifflin.

Ty, Eleanor. 1993. "Struggling with the Powerful (M)Other: Identity and Sexuality in Kogawa's *Obasan* and Kincaid's *Lucy.*" *International Fiction Review* 20(2): 120-26.

Underhill, Ruth. 1965. *Red Man's Religion: Beliefs and Practices of the Indians North of Mexico.* Chicago: University of Chicago Press.

Updike, John. 1963. "Packed Dirt, Churchgoing, A Dying Cat, A Traded Car." In *Pigeon Feathers and Other Stories*, 168-88. New York: Crest.

Utley, Francis Lee, Lynn Z. Bloom, and Arthur F. Kinney, eds. 1971. *Bear, Man, and God: Eight Approaches to William Faulkner's* The Bear. 2nd ed. New York: Random House.

Van Die, Marguerite. 1996. "In Search of an Authentic Spirituality." *Touchstone* 14(1): 7-15.

van Gennep, Arnold. 1960. *The Rites of Passage.* London: Routledge & Kegan Paul.

van Herk, Aritha. 1986. *No Fixed Address: An Amorous Journey.* Toronto: McClelland & Stewart.

VanSpanckeren, Kathryn. 1988. "Shamanism in the Works of Margaret Atwood." In VanSpanckeren and Castro 1988, 183-204.

————, and Jan Garden Castro, eds. 1988. *Margaret Atwood: Vision and Forms.* Carbondale and Edwardsville: Southern Illinois University Press.

Vecsey, Christopher, and Robert W. Venables, eds. 1980. *American Indian Environments: Ecological Issues in Native American History.* Syracuse: Syracuse University Press.

Verduyn, Christl, ed. 1995. *Dear Marian, Dear Hugh: The MacLennan-Engel Correspondence.* Ottawa: University of Ottawa Press.

Vision TV. 1994. *Joy Kogawa.* Arts Express. Director Mark Haslam. Producer Rita Deverall. Broadcast 10 September.

Vogel, Dan. 1974. "A Lexicon Rhetoricae for 'Journey' Literature." *College English* 36: 185-89.

Watt, Frank W. 1959. "Morley Callaghan as Thinker." *Dalhousie Review* 39: 305-13. Reprinted in Smith 1961, 116-27.

Weaver, Robert L. 1962. "A Talk with Morley Callaghan." In *The First Five Years: A Selection from the Tamarack Review*, 116-42. Toronto: University of Toronto Press.

Weisheipl, James A. 1974. *Friar Thomas D'Aquino: His Life, Thought, and Work*. Garden City, NY: Doubleday.

Westfall, William. 1989. *Two Worlds: The Protestant Culture of Nineteenth-Century Ontario*. Montreal and Kingston: McGill-Queen's University Press.

Westfall, William, Louis Rousseau, Fernand Harvey, and John Simpson, eds. 1985. *Religion/Culture: Comparative Canadian Studies/Études canadiennes comparées*. Canadian Issues 7. Ottawa: Association for Canadian Studies.

"Why Pick on Margaret Laurence?" 1980. *United Church Observer* (February): 10-12.

Wiesel, Elie. 1960. *Night*. New York: Avon, Discus Books, 1969.

————. 1990. "The Holocaust as Literary Inspiration." In *Dimensions of the Holocaust: Lectures at Northwestern University*, 4-19. 2nd ed. Evanston, IL: Northwestern University.

Wilder, Amos N. 1969. *The New Voice: Religion, Literature, Hermeneutics*. New York: Herder & Herder.

Willis, Gary. 1987. "Speaking the Silence: Joy Kogawa's *Obasan*." *Studies in Canadian Literature* 12(2): 239-50.

Wilson, Edmund. 1965. *O Canada: An American's Notes on Canadian Culture*. New York: Farrar, Straus, and Giroux.

Winnipeg Art Gallery. 1981. *Belcher Islands/Sanikiluaq*. Exhibition Catalogue. Texts by Bernadette Driscoll, Ed Horn, Patricia Sieber, and Spencer G. Sealy. Winnipeg: Winnipeg Art Gallery.

Wiseman, Adele. 1974. *Crackpot*. Toronto: McClelland & Stewart, New Canadian Library, 1978.

————. 1978. *Old Woman at Play*. Toronto and Vancouver: Clarke, Irwin.

————. 1987. *Memoirs of a Book-Molesting Childhood and Other Essays*. Toronto: Oxford University Press.

Wong, Sau-ling Cynthia. 1993. *Reading Asian American Literature: From Necessity to Extravagance*. Princeton: Princeton University Press.

Woodcock, George. 1976. "Lost Eurydice: The Novels of Callaghan." In *The Canadian Novel in the Twentieth Century: Essays from Canadian Literature*, 72-86. Toronto: McClelland & Stewart.

————. 1977. "Possessing the Land: Notes on Canadian Fiction." In Staines 1977, 69-96.

————, ed. 1983. *A Place to Stand On: Essays by and about Margaret Laurence*. Edmonton: NeWest Press.

Worsley, Peter. 1970. *The Trumpet Shall Sound: A Study of "Cargo" Cults in Melanesia*. London: Paladin.

York, Lorraine M. 1988. *"The Other Side of Dailiness": Photography in the Works of Alice Munro, Timothy Findlay, Michael Ondaatje, and Margaret Laurence*. Toronto: ECW Press.

York, Thomas. 1973. *We, the Wilderness*. Toronto: McGraw-Hill Ryerson.

———. 1976. *Snowman*. Toronto: Doubleday.

———. 1978a. *And Sleep in the Woods: The Story of One Man's Spiritual Quest*. Toronto: Doubleday.

———. 1978b. *The Musk Ox Passion*. Toronto: Doubleday.

———. 1981. *Trapper*. Toronto: Doubleday.

———. 1983. "The Post-Mortem Point of View in Malcolm Lowry's *Under the Volcano*." *Canadian Literature* no. 99: 35-46.

———. 1986. "Liard: Requiem for a River." In Raffan 1986, 136-47.

———. 1988. *Desireless: A Novel of New Orleans*. Markham, ON: Penguin.

Young, Egerton R. 1907. *The Battle of the Bears: Life in the North Land*. Boston and Chicago: Wilde.

Index